This Muslim American Life

This Muslim American Life

DISPATCHES FROM THE WAR ON TERROR

Moustafa Bayoumi

NEW YORK UNIVERSITY PRESS

New York and London

NEW YORK UNIVERSITY PRESS
New York and London
www.nyupress.org

References to Internet websites (URLs) were accurate at the time of writing.
Neither the author nor New York University Press is responsible for URLs that
may have expired or changed since the manuscript was prepared.

ISBN: (hardback) 978-1-4798-3684-0
ISBN: (paperback) 978-1-4798-3564-5

For Library of Congress Cataloging-in-Publication data, please contact the
Library of Congress.

New York University Press books are printed on acid-free paper,
and their binding materials are chosen for strength and durability.
We strive to use environmentally responsible suppliers and materials
to the greatest extent possible in publishing our books.

Manufactured in the United States of America

10 9 8 7 6 5 4 3 2 1

Also available as an ebook

Contents

PART IV. MUSLIMS IN CULTURE

Acknowledgments

This book was written over several years, and I am very grateful to the many people who have patiently listened to me test out my ideas, heard me rant loudly at a television screen, watched me throw a book across a room in disgust, or observed me arch an eyebrow in genuine confusion. I'm even more grateful for their wisdom and generous help in improving my writing and thinking. My parents Hoda and Mohamed Bayoumi, my brother Ahmed, and my sister Imaan have been constant sources of stability, inspiration, and creativity in my life. Eric Zinner and Alicia Nadkarni at NYU Press have been extraordinary to work with. Their patience and professionalism are unmatched, and collaborating with them has been both stimulating and rewarding. My agent Katherine Fausset always has my best interests and best writing at heart, and I thank her for that. Over the span of writing the essays that make up this book, I have also benefited directly from the help of so many people, including Hisham Aidi, Younis Ali, Nezar Andary, Abed Awad, Joel Beinin, Padmini Biswas, Marissa Brostoff, Susan Buck-Morss, Rachel Ida Buff, Roane Carey, Lillian Cho, Rosemary Corbett, James Davis, Ashley Dawson, Ira Dworkin, Emily Field, Anna Liza Gavieres, Zareena Grewal, Jonathan Guyer, Juliane Hammer, Salah Hassan, Sally Howell, Richard Kim, Robert Ji-Song Ku, Amitava Kumar, Cynthia Ai-Fen Lee, Ben Lerner, Neil J. Levi, Alex Lubin, Timothy Marr, Sophia McClennen, Patrick McGreevy, Scott McLeod, Scott Michaelson, Vanessa Mobley, Rob Nixon, John Oakes, Sana' Odeh, Gary Okihiro, Amitabh Pal, Christian Parenti, Vijay Prashad, Lizzy Ratner, Betsy Reed, Shara Richter, Corey Robin, Colin Robinson, Andrew Ross, Matthew Rothschild,

Hussein Saddique, Zohra Saed, Liliana Segura, Andrew Shryock, Paul Silverstein, Nikhil Pal Singh, Neil Smith, Michael Sorkin, Jean Stein, Jean Tamarin, John Kuo Wei Tchen, Chris Toensig, Ellen Tremper, Katrina Vanden Heuvel, Sudhir Venkatesh, Carl Weinberg, Naomi Zeveloff, and Sharon Zukin. My profound thanks to all of you.

Introduction

My Muslim American Life

In August 2011, almost exactly ten years after the terrorist attacks of 2001, the Associated Press published an article titled "With CIA Help, NYPD Moves Covertly in Muslim Areas." The article's authors, Matt Apuzzo and Adam Goldman, described how the New York Police Department was working with officials "on loan" from the CIA to develop a massive and covert surveillance program that directly targeted the entire Muslim community in and around New York City.[1] Initially, the NYPD flatly denied the reporters' findings. "Someone has a great imagination," NYPD spokesman Paul Browne said.[2] The AP then posted on their website a trove of leaked internal documents from the police department that proved not only the existence of the program but also that the department felt free to lie outright to its public about its actions. Veteran police reporter Len Levitt also gained access to internal documents, and on September 5 published an article (reprinted two days later by the *Huffington Post*) on the scope of the surveillance.[3] Levitt noted that the NYPD had placed confidential informants in seven Muslim student associations (MSAs) at local colleges and that Brooklyn College, where I teach, and Baruch College had been listed as MSAs "of concern." Levitt wrote about one confidential police report that listed "42 top tier 'persons of interest,'" which included "a lecturer at Brooklyn College." For weeks, people assumed that this lecturer must be me.

Frankly, I wondered the same while also thinking that it would be absurd for the police to waste their resources on me. The Associated Press called me to ask me if I thought I was being surveilled, and a *New York Times* columnist also interviewed me about the report. Later, someone I know and trust who was shown the file told me that it had identified someone else. Of course, just because I was not the person named in the report does not mean that the NYPD has not spied on me. It just means I don't know for sure.

Others have learned something different. Mohammad Elshinawy is a young Egyptian American from Brooklyn with a popular following among New York's devout Muslims. I know Mohammad, who was once my student, and he and I also spent some time together when I was writing my book about Brooklyn's Arab Muslim youth. I could tell even then that he was a rising star with religious conservatives. Always dressed in a galabeyya with a kufi on his head, a fist-length beard on his chin, and sneakers on his feet, Mohammad commanded the respect of Brooklyn's young Muslims with his eloquence, intelligence, scholarly knowledge, and mastery of Qur'anic Arabic. It wasn't just the young people who were attracted to Mohammad. He has also been the subject of fastidious NYPD surveillance. According to Apuzzo and Goldman, Mohammad's popularity had initially attracted the interest of the FBI, which became concerned that he might have been recruiting young men to fight overseas. That investigation was concluded with no charges filed. Yet the NYPD decided to pursue the matter—and Mohammad—further.[4]

I wondered what it's like to know you've been surveilled by the police, so I contacted Mohammad to ask him. He invited me to one of the regular classes he offers on the Qur'an at Masjid Al-Ansar, a simple storefront mosque in Bensonhurst, Brooklyn, that, as reports indicate, has also been under NYPD surveillance. After the class, we went to a quiet room in the mosque's basement to talk. Boxes of canned foods, ready to distribute to the needy, surrounded us as we sat on the carpeted floor. I asked Mohammad what he felt after learning about the surveillance on him and its extent.

"Apprehension," he said, after thinking a while. "To what degree is this going to affect me?" He shared that he carefully considered his actions and that he would "try to take a stand and get past this hump." Mohammad was referring to being a plaintiff in a lawsuit filed by the ACLU (still pending as of this writing, in January 2015) against the police department. "There's no reason why we should consider ourselves second-class citizens," he said, speaking about Muslim Americans generally. "I'm born in this country like anybody else," he said.

From the documents leaked to the AP, we know the character of the surveillance practiced on Mohammad and the NYPD's views on the young man. Labeling his race as "ME," that is, Middle Eastern, the police files describe Mohammad's views as "hardcore Salafi ones."[5] (*Salafis* are scriptural conservatives who seek a belief system based on their understanding of the early days of Islam, and the police department operates under the assumption that they are particularly prone to violence.) One report states that the "TIU [Terrorism Interdiction Unit] believes that [Mohammad] is a threat due to the fact that he is so highly regarded by so many young and impressionable individuals,"[6] as if charm were a weapon. In the same report and under the heading "Surveillance Objective" is written, "Target moves on a daily basis to many different spots. Every day of the week is beneficial. . . . [Most beneficial would be] after 1500 (after target gets off of work),"[7] revealing essentially that Mohammad is a hardworking young man. The spying even invaded his love life and followed him around the city. The report continues, "Surveillance has revealed many things re: this target. His change of auto, the fact that he was going to get married b/c surv[eillance] observed him shopping for diamond rings w/ a female in the diamond district."[8] I asked him about this detail. "I took my fiancée to go buy her a diamond ring, and even then I'm being tailgated," he told me. "Many times we knew we were being tailgated," he explained, "it's just like, what are you going to do? Call the cops on the cops?" He laughed. "It's quite a predicament!"

◆ ◆ ◆

Looking closely at the NYPD surveillance program, we can get a larger sense of its dangerous presumptions and misguided activities. The program began in 2002, when Police Commissioner Ray Kelly hired David Cohen, a former deputy director for operations at the CIA, as his deputy commissioner of intelligence. Cohen succeeded in getting a judge to relax provisions of the Handschu Agreement, a 1985 consent decree developed in response to a lawsuit against the NYPD for spying on the constitutionally protected activity of political groups in the 1960s and 1970s. The Handschu Agreement previously allowed police surveillance only when officers had specific information a crime would be committed or was being planned. Under the new rules adopted in 2003, police no longer needed evidence to begin an investigation, just the *possibility* of criminal activity.

Cohen established four units in his Intelligence Division—the Demographics Unit, the Intelligence Analysis Unit, the Cyber Intelligence Unit, and the Terrorism Interdiction Unit—and hired Lawrence Sanchez, a CIA analyst, to oversee intelligence. Using data from the 2000 US census, the intelligence division proceeded to chart where the Muslims in New York lived.[9]

This mapping has precedents. It recalls a 1919 map of ethnic New York drafted by the NYPD and New York State Police that identified certain ethnic neighborhoods in an effort to root out socialists, communists, and anarchists.[10] It's reminiscent of when the Census Bureau provided the government with information on where Japanese Americans lived to assist the War Relocation Authority in interning them during World War II.[11] And it bears a resemblance to specially tabulated statistics on Arab American populations, indicating zip-code-level breakdowns of Arab Americans by country of origin, which the Census Bureau produced for Homeland Security from August 2002 to December 2003.[12]

The NYPD did more than exploit publicly available data, however. They also sent out "rakers," plainclothes officers who could blend in to the community, and "mosque crawlers," informants working for the police. (Rakers were so dubbed because Cohen described their actions as akin to "raking an extinguished fire pit.")[13] The Intelligence Division viewed everything about ordinary Muslim life as suspicious and catalogued it all. They established sports leagues as a way to spy on Muslim youth.[14] They recorded license plate numbers from the cars of mosque visitors. They noted where Muslims got haircuts and they eavesdropped on conversations in cafés.[15] They considered it suspicious when café televisions were tuned to Al Jazeera and when they were not. (The "Egyptian Locations of Interest Report" states that in one café "the Al Jazeera news channel is prohibited inside this location because the owner feels it brings extra scrutiny from law enforcement.")[16] They made more than seventy-five visits to thirty-four "targeted" travel agencies in South Asian communities around New York to discover that there were four principal airlines to Pakistan: Pakistan International Airlines, Emirates Airlines, Kuwait Airways, and Gulf Air.[17] They also often got facts wrong, identifying Sephardic Jews and Lebanese Christians as Syrian Muslims, Coptic Egyptians as more numerous than Muslim Egyptians in New York, and Sunni Muslims as Shi'i Muslims.[18]

More troubling still, the NYPD designated selected mosques as "Terrorism Enterprises," meaning any visitor to these Muslim houses of worship could be investigated and that speech, including sermons, would be monitored and recorded.[19] "It was an unprecedented moment in the history of American law enforcement," Apuzzo and Goldman write in *Enemies Within*, their book about the surveillance program. "The NYPD regarded houses of worship—and everyone who prayed there—as possible criminal organizations."[20]

All of this netted, the NYPD was later forced to admit, not a single lead on suspected terrorist activity.[21] After the facts of the program were no longer deniable and due in large part to the mobilizing efforts of New York's Muslim communities and their allies, the department announced in April 2014 that they would disband the Demographics Unit. They did not however announce a halt to other aspects of their Muslim community surveillance, including designating mosques as "Terrorism Enterprises."[22]

Nor has the NYPD announced an end to using informants to monitor Muslim communities without any probable cause. We now know the inner workings of informant life. One informant, Shamiur Rahman, who was a regular attendee of Mohammad's lectures, emerged from the shadows in October 2012, revealing on his Facebook page that he had been sent by the NYPD to observe Muslims and "bait" them into saying inciting things, particularly statements containing "jihad" and "revolution."[23] For this he was paid as much as a thousand dollars a month and given leniency on misdemeanor marijuana possession charges.[24] According to a *New York Times* report from May 2014, such practices are continuing.[25] The end of the Demographics Unit does not mean the end of bias-based policing of New York's Muslims, who can still count on being treated by the NYPD as harbingers of terrorism just by going about their everyday affairs.

◆ ◆ ◆

Why would the NYPD expend such massive resources—the counterterrorism and intelligence units are staffed by nearly a thousand employees and operate with a combined budget of over a hundred million dollars (2010 figures)—to spy on the mundane and the ordinary? The reasoning behind their actions must be their belief that Muslims will almost necessarily become, if they aren't already, terrorists or supporters of terrorism. Testifying before the Senate Committee on Homeland Security and Governmental Affairs in 2007, Lawrence Sanchez, the CIA official who worked with the NYPD, explained how the NYPD aims to crawl not just into the mosques but into the souls of Muslims to reveal their true essence, even before they know themselves. "Rather than just protecting New York City citizens from terrorists," Sanchez said, "the New York Police Department believes that part of *its mission is to protect New York City citizens from turning into terrorists*."[26] From there, he explained how it was proper to trample on the constitutional rights of ordinary Muslims. Testifying that the NYPD now scrutinizes "what most people would say would be non-criminal, would be innocuous, behaviors that could easily be argued in a Western democracy, especially in the United States, [are] protected by First and Fourth Amendment rights," Sanchez said, "[we don't] look at them in a vacuum, but . . . look across to them as potential precursors to terrorism."[27]

The same prejudicial assumptions of the inevitably violent Muslim have been found in training documents used by both the FBI, which also hired a former CIA official, Philip Mudd, to run its counterterrorism operations, and the US military.[28] (The manner in which domestic law enforcement generally has been integrated with the country's intelligence services during the War on Terror also begs serious study.)

Nor is this assumption limited to the United States. In Guantánamo Bay, scores of prisoners have been cleared for release since 2010 by the US government's own Guantánamo Review Task Force, and yet dozens of these men remain behind bars and bereft of hope, most having been incarcerated without charge or trial for more than twelve years. Why? Because Congress and the Pentagon have dragged their feet on releasing the men, arguing that they should not be freed due to the future possibility that they will return to their home countries only to take up hostilities against the United States. In this case, a past of abuse by the United States might make that argument more tenable, but even here a New American Foundation study found that 8.8 percent of returned captives have undertaken "militant activity," significantly below the Pentagon's official estimate of 14 percent.[29]

Then there are the drones. In 2012, the *New York Times* described President Obama's vastly expanded program of drone warfare during the War on Terror and reported that when it authorizes a strike, the White House "in effect counts all military-age males in a strike zone as combatants . . . unless there is explicit intelligence posthumously proving them innocent."[30] This partly reflects a shell game used by the White House to show how they are minimizing civilian casualties, and former CIA officials have expressed dismay at the concept. One called it "guilt by association" that has led to "deceptive" estimates of civilian casualties. "It bothers me when they say there were seven guys, so they must all be militants," a CIA official told the *New York Times*, adding, "they count the corpses and they're not really sure who they are."[31] A year after this revelation, President Obama stated that "the high threshold that we've set for taking lethal action applies to all potential terrorist targets, regardless of whether or not they are American citizens."[32] But what qualifies as a "potential terrorist" has never been delineated. And while the official line is that the US military does not target males in Afghanistan and other declared or undeclared war zones solely because they are of military age, the *Nation* has shown that the practice not only continues but is even recorded in internal reports that mention MAMs (military-aged males),[33] as if all males of that age are reducible (and thus justifiably killed due) to their potential for terrorism.

◆ ◆ ◆

This idea that you are seen not as a complex human being but only as a purveyor of possible future violence illustrates the extraordinary predicament of the heart of contemporary Muslim American life. To be a Muslim American today is to be full of potential, and not in the sweet way that grandmothers and elementary school teachers use the word. The state has enveloped itself in a near religious task, to sneak and peek into the conscience of one set of its citizens and residents and their coreligionists abroad. In this *Minority Report* world, the police aim to patrol the minds of Muslims for what they believe they will think and not for their actions.

Nor is this point of view limited to government. That Muslims will ultimately reveal themselves as usurpers and organizers of future chaos and terror exists in American society at large, where constructing a mosque is often viewed not innocently but as part of a larger plan for the future takeover of the country, despite how ridiculous that sounds and impossible that would be. This notion reached its media apex with massive demonstrations in 2010 against the planned construction of a Muslim cultural center in the vicinity of Ground Zero (see Chapter 8), but Muslim communities around the country have faced uphill battles to establish Islamic centers and mosques for years. In 2012, the Pew Forum on Religion and Public Life published a study using media sources that catalogued fifty-three examples of community resistance to new mosques in twenty-one states.[34] Similarly, at least thirty-two state legislatures have drafted bills barring judges from considering foreign law including sharia (Islamic legal principles) in their decisions. The guiding force behind these linked agitations is the notion of "creeping sharia," that is to say, in their ordinary expressions of life, Muslims are both untrustworthy and conquest-minded, and soon the American Constitution will be superseded by Islamic law. In late August 2013 North Carolina became the seventh state to sign such a bill into law, and in November 2014 voters in Alabama overwhelmingly approved an anti-sharia ballot initiative. Behind both anti-sharia bills and anti-mosque agitation is the suspicion less of what Muslims are doing and more of what they will do with the law and their property in the future. In the grammar of Islamophobia, the future is tense.

The scary, duplicitous, and secret life of Muslims is perhaps most shamelessly displayed in Showtime's blockbuster series *Homeland*. Nick Brody is a returning Marine who had been captured in Iraq and held for eight years by the terrorist Abu Nazir. Brody is essentially reprogrammed during his captivity while caring for Abu Nazir's son—who is subsequently killed in a drone strike—into adopting Islam, and when he returns to the United States, he seeks to avenge the boy's death and fight for his new faith. Brody leads a double life, a public one where he is an American hero who becomes a congressman and is eventually tapped as a vice presidential running mate, and a private one where he is not only a secret Muslim but also a secret terrorist. *Homeland*'s whole suspense and momentum derive not from what Brody is but what he might become, an American hero or a Muslim terrorist. The show feeds off the same presumption of future malfeasance that is the essence of today's anti-Muslim prejudice.

◆ ◆ ◆

"I am in the strenuous and far from dull position of having news to deliver to the Western world," James Baldwin wrote in 1979, and his news is simple and straightforward, "*black* is not a synonym for *slave*."[35] The situation is disturbingly similar today. "Muslim" is not a synonym for "terrorist." And yet the automatic association of Muslim Americans with terrorism has become completely institutionalized and thoroughly commonsensical, even though it flies in the face of the evidence. In fact, terrorist acts or attempts thereof by Muslim Americans over the past dozen years have been extremely rare, far fewer than the number of attacks carried out by right-wing extremists. According to the Triangle Center on

Terrorism and Homeland Security, terrorist acts perpetrated by Muslim Americans in the United States since 9/11 have killed thirty-seven people, and the majority of those deaths are attributed to two attacks: one by Major Nidal Hasan, who killed thirteen fellow soldiers in Fort Hood, Texas, and the other the series of shootings by the "Beltway snipers" who, unconnected to the War on Terror (and mainline Islam), killed eleven people. The Boston Marathon bombers were responsible for another four deaths in 2013. By contrast, 133 people were killed by non-Muslims in mass shootings in 2013 alone.[36] Another report, published by West Point's Combating Terrorism Center in 2012, found that between 1990 and 2012, non-Muslim far-right extremists have committed 4,420 violent acts in the United States that have killed 670 people and injured 3,053 more, and the number of attacks has risen precipitously since 2000 and especially since 2007.[37] Polling data also indicate that Muslim Americans are in fact the least likely major religious group in the country to support military attacks on civilians.[38] And according to the investigative journalist Trevor Aaronson, the vast majority of those Muslim Americans who have been arrested on terrorism or terrorism-related charges over the past dozen years have been vulnerable losers nabbed in sting operations that come perilously close to entrapment, small-time offenders with distant links to radicals overseas, or immigrants caught lying to federal officials. According to Aaronson, independent plots that have risen to credible threats number just five—rather amateurish—cases.[39]

Terrorism is a serious issue, and five attempts are clearly five too many. All those who have been victims of terrorism should be mourned and justice must be served. And yet some sense of perspective and proportionality surely ought to be maintained. Instead, however, the national security apparatus routinely invokes the fear of terrorism, implicitly or explicitly by Muslims, to assume ever-expanding powers over American lives and to justify military intervention overseas. The image that the country is under siege by these Muslim terrorists and their sympathizers is regularly reinforced, and the minuscule amount of violence that can be associated with Muslim Americans is magnified and decontextualized, seen as a true expression of Islamic belief rather than occurring within the context of global warfare. In important ways, the constant promotion and creation of the Muslim American threat displaces the violence of the War on Terror overseas back on the image of the violent Muslim terrorists who must live among us.[40] Don't worry about facts. The image of the Muslim terrorist is a very useful one.

◆ ◆ ◆

Such images and notions matter because, taken together, they create a kind of War on Terror culture that is continuously reflected and reinforced across American society. It's important to understand not only what War on Terror culture is but also the costs it has had on Muslim Americans specifically and on social and political life in the United States generally. War on Terror culture assumes that Muslims collectively are responsible for and sympathetic to all acts of violence by individual Muslims everywhere, unless and until they explicitly say otherwise. But even then, their words are often doubted since Muslims are seen as doctrinally prone to lying and violence. If any Muslim commits a horrible act of violence, the action is automatically assumed to be a heinous political feat. With non-Muslim Americans, the situation is different, as Conor Friedersdorf explains. "When mass killers are native-born whites," he writes, "their motivations are treated like a mystery to [be] unraveled rather than a foregone conclusion."[41] And there's more. A *Washington Post* columnist recently discovered that major news media won't even consider an act of violence as terrorism unless the government names it as such first, giving the government, apropos of War on Terror culture, tremendous power over labels and abdicating the media's own independence.[42]

War on Terror culture also means that Muslim American history is forgotten, as if Muslims existed in the United States only after September 2001. War on Terror culture represents Muslims always and only through the War on Terror lens and never on their own terms. War on Terror culture means that Muslim job applicants, according to a 2014 study by researchers at the University of Connecticut, receive "32 percent fewer emails and 48 percent fewer phone calls than applicants from the control group, far outweighing measurable bias against the other faith groups."[43] War on Terror culture promotes the seductive synergy of militarism and entertainment (remember when Michelle Obama, flanked by soldiers in dress uniforms in the White House, announced the Best Picture Oscar for *Argo*?) while rationalizing or ignoring the massive civilian death toll of the War on Terror. War on Terror culture means that the 9/11 Memorial, supposedly dedicated to ending intolerance and ignorance, offers pamphlets in nine languages but bizarrely not in Arabic, and the 9/11 Museum tour concludes with a film considered by many to be inflammatory toward Islam.[44] War on Terror culture is essentially the deep institutionalization of George W. Bush's simplistic proclamation that "either you are with us, or you are with the terrorists,"[45] as if there can be no other options, as if one can't oppose the horrors that the War on Terror delivers and the murderous nihilism of terrorism simultaneously.

◆ ◆ ◆

Because War on Terror culture ascribes a programmed and malevolent future to Muslims, it marks almost anything Muslims say about themselves as immediately suspect, part of a larger plot of apologetics at best or propaganda at worst. In this way, it not only denies the rich history of Islam in America but also sees Islam as always and forever a foreign and a foreigner's faith to the United States. The good news, however, is that War on Terror culture is not the only game in town. Resistance to its simplistic worldview has motivated a small but growing War on Terror counterculture, a large part of which is reflected in cultural production by and about Muslim Americans and probing scholarship on Muslim Americans in recent years. The audiences for this kind of work have also expanded and deepened.

Resistance to the dictates of War on Terror culture can be found in novels such as Mohja Kahf's *The Girl in the Tangerine Scarf*, Randa Jarrar's *A Map of Home*, Mohsin Hamid's *The Reluctant Fundamentalist*, and Amy Waldman's *The Submission*, all serious attempts to ponder the complexities of contemporary Muslim life. Documentary films such as *The New Muslim Cool* and *The Muslims Are Coming!* challenge conventional ways of thinking about Muslims in the United States. Major cultural institutions such as New York's Poetry House and the National Endowment for the Humanities have developed programs to educate the broader public about the lives and traditions of Muslims, here and abroad. *The Daily Show* and *The Colbert Report* have frequently lampooned manifestations of Islamophobia through their invaluable satire. And universities, high schools, and houses of worship across the country have hosted countless speakers and held innumerable seminars with Muslim Americans in attempts to gain greater understanding of Muslim American lives.[46]

Scholarly inquiry into Muslim American history, life, and realities has produced other probing work, including Hisham Aidi's *Rebel Music: Race, Empire, and the New Muslim Youth Culture*, Evelyn Alsultany's *Arabs and Muslims in the Media*, Louise Cainkar's *Homeland Insecurity*, Sohail Daulatzai's *Black Star, Crescent Moon: The Muslim International and Black Freedom beyond America*, Kambiz Ghaneabassiri's *A History of Islam in America*, Zareena Grewal's *Islam Is a Foreign Country*, Deepa Kumar's *Islamophobia and the Politics of Empire*, Sunaina Maira's *Missing*, Timothy Marr's *The Cultural Roots of American Islamicism*, Junaid Rana's *Terrify-*

ing Muslims, Steven Salaita's *Anti-Arab Racism*, Denise Spellberg's *Thomas Jefferson's Qur'an*, and many more.[47] This War on Terror counterculture reflects the desire to investigate Muslim American life beyond the clichés of law enforcement and popular culture, however overwhelming those may be, and represents a point of optimism in a general period of political pessimism. Much more, however, is needed.

This book reflects my attempts since 2001 to respond to War on Terror culture and its repercussions on Muslim American life. Some chapters are drawn directly from my own experiences. Over the past few years, I have been an extra in an Orientalist film about American women shopping in Abu Dhabi, a terrorist suspect (or at least my namesake "Mustafa Bayoumi" was) in a detective novel set in Pittsburgh, the subject of a trumped-up controversy over a book I had written, and a participant in a somewhat strange conversation with an officer of the US Citizenship bureau. Many Muslim Americans have similar stories. To be a Muslim American today often means to exist in that slightly absurd space between exotic and dangerous and between victim and villain simply because of people's assumptions about you.

This Muslim American Life is arranged in four sections: Muslims in History, Muslims in Theory, Muslims in Politics, and Muslims in Culture. In the first section, I investigate the lesser-known but no less significant aspects of American history that involve Arab and Muslim Americans. These include the early community of Arab sojourners who established "Little Syria" in Lower Manhattan (almost exactly at Ground Zero), the spiritual and musical connections between Muslim Americans and African Americans, and the legal history and present of Muslims through the prism of immigration law and enforcement. It is barely recognized, for example, that the legal precedents for contemporary immigration policies directly targeting Muslims in the United States have their roots in the Chinese Exclusion Acts of an earlier era.

"Muslims in Theory" considers not Muslims and their adherence or nonadherence to a belief system but rather how Orientalism today both replicates and differs from the classical Orientalism that preceded it, as identified by Edward Said in his influential book. The chapters here delve into the consequences of the production of knowledge about Muslims from ideological positions created and promoted by the War on Terror. Today, Orientalism is alive and well and is often promoted by Muslims themselves, but these latest practitioners are hardly the eccentric polymaths of Orientalism's past. They are often deeply imbricated in the American power structure, where they usually reinforce old Orientalist tropes by assuming the role of the multicultural translator between societies. Understanding contemporary Orientalism is crucial to comprehending the relationship between difference and power in a pluralistic society.

Part III (Muslims in Politics) analyzes the political consequences of the War on Terror on Muslim Americans. The chapters here underscore how repressive policies of the national security apparatus and populist opposition have produced a complicated landscape that Muslim Americans have had to navigate over the years. Both civil society and the state have created simplistic and essentially racialized caricatures of Muslim Americans that inhibit their entry into the mainstream and often even seek to muzzle their voices. Islamophobia has not only permeated law enforcement but also, as polling data indicate, mixed with a white anxiety about losing a privileged place in society, a sentiment shared by many older white Americans.

Part IV (Muslims in Culture) examines how Muslims have been represented in contemporary American culture and how American culture has been used against them, even as a weapon of war. (Chapter 13, for example, reveals the US military's use of music as torture against War on Terror detainees.) I consider the multicultural politics of contemporary films, where African American lead characters supposedly understand Arabs and Muslims better than their white counterparts, and examine the rise of a (putatively) highly competent CIA in film and television shows, where the police procedural replaces the action movie as the genre of choice for the War on Terror. Understanding the dynamics of War on Terror culture and its relationship to the racialization of Muslim Americans is necessary if we wish to grasp the complex interplay among culture, power, and race.

Culture, law, politics, and theory are not discrete and separate entities unto themselves. Each significantly informs the other, and this is perhaps especially true in the War on Terror, where the specter of Muslim malfeasance has had far-reaching consequences in all of these domains. Using a variety of approaches, the chapters in this book intervene in these various realms and point to the ways they are connected. The larger idea behind the book is a general program of interference in the representational and political logic that prevails regarding Muslims and Muslim Americans, and to that end these chapters are written in a variety of registers in the hope of expanding the counterculture of resistance to War on Terror logic.

◆ ◆ ◆

The facts of Muslim American life are important for all Americans, and not just Muslims, to understand. Because Muslim Americans are now routinely treated differently from other Americans, how American society deals with its Muslims has become a question at the heart of the democratic project itself. War on Terror culture rationalizes the differential treatment of one group of citizens, and this treatment has been generally supported by the public. Even in liberal New York City, the NYPD program of surveillance polled at a 58 percent approval rate in 2012.[48] Even more worrisome is how the surveillance of Muslim American life today is replicated on a much larger scale by the federal government, again and always in the name of fighting terrorism. Edward Snowden's revelations into the gargantuan program of surveillance by the National Security Agency have shown that the government feels emancipated from constitutional principles of preserving privacy while at the same time requiring overwhelming secrecy for its actions, just as the NYPD has done with New York's Muslims. Even if you care little about Muslim American rights, you ought to be concerned about the government's mission creep more than any trumped up Muslim American sharia creep. The excessive secrecy of the government together with the demands of full transparency of the citizenry threatens the fundamental arrangement between those who govern and the governed. Americans of all types are expected to acquiesce to intrusions into their private lives, supposedly for greater security, while any objection is interpreted as "having something to hide."

But having something to hide—or having the right to hold an inner life and to be free to determine how much of yourself you show to others—is not only a guarantee of our democracy but also a necessary part of being human. Losing that right is troubling and dangerous for the same reason that Elaine Scarry identifies as the dark innovation of the Patriot Act. "The Patriot Act inverts the constitutional requirement that people's lives be private and the work of government officials be public; it instead crafts a set of conditions in which our inner lives become transparent and the workings of the government become opaque. Either one of these outcomes would imperil democracy; together they not only injure the country but also cut off the avenues of repair," explains Scarry.[49] A related notion is often expressed this way: democracy means that the government should be afraid of its people, not the converse. What is clear is that the metastasizing growth of the national security state specifically and War on Terror culture generally jeopardizes this fundamental arrangement between citizen and state.

This Muslim American Life examines some of the complexities of Muslim American life and highlights some of the most basic questions about how US political and cultural life is organized today. A recurring concern here is that we do not yet understand or appreciate the profound ways that the War on Terror has created a political ecology of its own, one that relies on excessive secrecy, differential rights, innovative forms of racism, expanded executive power, and permanent war, while also threatening to undermine our bedrock principles of equality and privacy, so enthralled have we become with fighting terrorism and expanding militarism. Perhaps the real issue to address is not what will become of Muslim Americans in the future, but what is becoming of us Americans.

PART I

Muslims in History

1

Letter to a G-Man

Let me ask you something. Have you heard the story of the vizier's son? His father, the minister, had offended the ruler, and so he and his family were imprisoned for a very long time, so long in fact that the son knew only prison life. He reached the age of reason shortly after his release and, one night at dinner, asked his father about the meat he had been eating. "It's lamb," said the father. The son then asked the father, "What is lamb?" The father described the animal to the son, to which the son replied, "Do you mean it is like a rat?" "No!" said the father. "What have lambs to do with rats?" And the same continued then with cows and camels for, you see, the son had seen only rats in prison. He knew no other animal.

You may be wondering why I begin this brief correspondence with such a story, but I beg your indulgence. There will be time for all things. Suffice to say, as the son shows us, confinement defeats the imagination. Call it arrested development if you will, but if you are forced to stay put, how can you discover the delicacy of lamb, sprinkled generously with garlic and massaged with allspice, roasting over an open flame? Perhaps you can almost taste it now. Yes, the mind wanders, and the wanderer's mind, well, expands, you could say. But without knowledge or history or experience, the son could learn of these things only once it was too late. I hope it is not too late for you—and for me.

You see, I fear that you have become like the son. You believe only what you already know, see only what you want to see, but you must ask yourself how you understand those things.

I have been told that you have arrested hundreds of us and seek to question thousands more. I imagine you are looking for me. You are concerned, naturally, after the eleventh of September, as we all are. I too watched the towers fall, as did everyone I know, with a tear in my eye and the air stuck hard in my lungs. Who could have imagined such malefaction! I prayed for the people lost in those towers, just as I have since prayed for the innocents everywhere, my benedictions sounding like Walt Whitman's brassy cornet and drums, which, as he said, play marches for conquer'd and slain persons. Didn't we all suffer on that terrible day, the families of the dead most of all?

The city itself was in mourning, with its gaping wound right there on the skin of Lower Manhattan. And here I am going to tell you something I presume you do not know. This is almost the exact spot where, just over a century ago, the first of our extended Arab family came to this country. Have you ever wondered how Cedar Street got its name? I cannot tell you precisely, but I like to think it was because on Cedar Street, the Lebanese merchants from Zahle would sell you milk as sweet as honey and honey as rich as cream. We came first for the 1876 World's Fair then began arriving in larger numbers, until in the 1890s we lived busily between Greenwich, Morris, Rector, and Washington Streets. By the early part of the twentieth century, our community expanded, reaching from Cedar Street on the north to Battery Place on the south. The western border was no less than West Street, and to the east, Trinity Place. But the center of our world was always Washington Street, a lane now blocked by emergency vehicles and ten-foot fences. To us, Washington Street was never just a street. It was our *Amrika*! After passing through Ellis Island, we would trudge up Manhattan Island with our weathered bags, looking for a friendly face in all the frenetic energy of New York, until we could hear a little Arabic and smell the food from home, knowing that on a street named for an American we had found Little Syria.

We came, like so many others, simply to make a better life for ourselves and our families. You could shovel gold on Washington

Street, we were told, and so we trekked across the Atlantic, endured the verminous hostelries of Marseilles, and arrived with our satchels stuffed with hope. City life was new to most of us, since we had lived typically in villages and hamlets, and it was exciting. I remember what Abraham Rihbany wrote, back in 1914.

> New York is three cities on top of one another. The one city is in the air—in the elevated railway trains, which roar overhead like thunder, and in the amazingly lofty buildings, the windows of whose upper stories look to one on the ground only a little bigger than human eyes. I cannot think of those living so far away from the ground as being human beings; they seem to me more like the *jinnee*. The second city is on the ground where huge armies of men and women live and move and work. The third city is underground, where I find stores, dwellings, machine shops, and railroad trains. The inside of the earth here is alive with human beings; I hope they will go upward when they die.[1]

His words never seemed so tragically real to me.

We came as sojourners, and after establishing ourselves in New York, we launched out, men and women both, around the country as pack peddlers. Loading up on goods from the stores on Washington Street, we carried what felt like the world on our backs. Our shops were fables to you. Never had you seen our soft rugs for sale, or a gossamer web of silken lace with Arabic letters hugging its border. Boxes rested on boxes in our tiny dark shops, full of carved olivewood trinkets or luxurious satins or silver wire as thin as a spider's web. As the *New York Daily Tribune* put it in 1892, "In the midst of all this riot of the beautiful and odd stands the dealer, the natural gravity of his features relaxed into a smile of satisfaction at the wonder and delight expressed by his American visitor. But the vision ends, and with many parting 'salaams' one goes back to the dust and dirt, the noise and bustle" of Washington Street.[2]

We found no magic in our stores, however, just opportunity. We carefully folded the crocheted tablecloths of linen and stiff silk dress collars and loaded them with the spicy perfumes and soft talcum powders into our packs. The scrubbing soaps and gentle creams came next, and on top the rosaries, crosses, and carved icons that the people across this country so loved to buy from us, the Holy Land vendors. These are the things we carried. Jewelry and notions, we used to call them, and if you stopped to talk to us along our route, you might, as someone once said, buy a story with your bargain.

From the beginning then, our lives here have been about being on the move, carting goods and people across borders to make life a little bit better, a little bit easier, just a little more comfortable. We were the ones who brought the city to the country. We were Internet shopping before eBay, the catalogue before Sears. We went places others would not, namely into the warm hearths of African American homes that ringed the cities we visited. There, the food was heavier and the laughter heartier, and we would be treated to a hospitality we recognized like home. Detroit, Chicago, Fargo, Kansas City, Minneapolis, Fort Wayne, we knew the vein-like crisscrosses of this country before Jack Kerouac spoke his first French word. And we walked, mostly, and then we ached to come back to Washington Street, where we could replace our worn soles and enjoy a little backgammon before heading out again.

But that was a long time ago, and, well, nothing gold can stay. Maybe it is true that nostalgia makes time simple by the loss of detail, but today, things seem so different. Since those early days, we have become doctors and lawyers, writers and engineers, but we are still shopkeepers and taxi drivers, and we continue to move lives around this country. And yet, these days many of us sit stationary in our homes, unsure of what will happen to us if we step beyond the threshold of our doors. But I will come to that, all in good time, my good man.

We came from Mount Lebanon, from Syria and Palestine, but you called us all Syrians or, less accurately, Turks. We were mostly Melkite and Maronite, but there were a few Muslims, Druze, and Jews among us. By the 1920s, we had grown as a community into Brooklyn as well as Manhattan, on Joralemon Street, State Street, and Boerum Place, close to Atlantic Avenue, where you find many of our shops today. We continued to trade, and we worked in dusty factories, mostly sewing clothes and fine lace.

But in fact everything started to change in the 1920s. I talk not only about how, in the years leading up to that troubled decade, the immigration authorities became increasingly frustrated by our dusky looks, questioning whether we were "free white people" or "Asiatics." This racial ping-pong game used a strange chromatic logic that mostly bewildered us, and after the 1924 Johnson-Reed Act and the harsh depression of the 1930s, the numbers of our newcomers dwindled. Rather, I refer also to our daring to dream of self-determination back home.

After the door closed on the Sublime Porte, the dissolution of the Ottoman Empire was supposed to mean that we would have the right to determine our own fates. You visited us under the auspices of the King-Crane Commission, and we welcomed and admired you, believing you would support us in the pioneer spirit of independence from foreign rule. But what we were left with were mandates and protectorates, leading to fracture and complaint in a moment when we felt unified and needed each other. The Europeans did not rule lightly, something I was sure you would have understood, but you have consistently lived up to underestimation, I dare say. It was the catastrophe of 1948, however, that broke our hearts. Tell me, what did the Palestinians do to warrant having their homes seized from them, their worlds disrupted, their lives bulldozed now for over sixty years? Because another people wanted the land the Palestinians had always lived on, they—the Palestinians—must be dispossessed into misery and squalor? Indeed the genocidal horror inflicted on the Jewish community in Europe was evil unmasked, but what had this to do with the Palestinians, except to turn them into the victims of another policy of extermination and cultural supremacy? It seems I am asking so many questions, but why you continue to deny the rights of the Palestinians just confounds me. It seems that their "crime" is simply to be born Palestinian, and in this scheme, a Palestinian life counts less than another. Yet there is no greater wrong in the world, for whoever degrades another degrades me and you and all of us.

Your ears prick up now that I am talking about the Palestinians. I think that when you hear this word, all you hear is terrorism. To us, we hear the echo of dispossession and the call for justice, but these days especially it appears to us that you are criminalizing all references to us and our Palestinian family, and it is affecting how we live here. For over sixty years we have been speaking to you about this tragedy, but the actions of a handful of lunatics, madmen who have never until recently and only when convenient spoken about Palestine, have given you the motivation to shut us up and shut us down. You are infiltrating our mosques and gathering places, tapping our phones, detaining us by the hundreds, and seizing our charity. At airports you search us, and if you find Allah on a leaf of paper, you accuse us of sedition. We are beginning to wonder what you think you are protecting from your cars and radios, the people of this country or policies abroad that continue an injustice and lead to slaughter. But never mind that for now. There will be time. First, before you continue to cast us as perpetual foreigners, let me tell you why Muslim New York is our modern Granada.

For over half a century, we crossed the Atlantic to land on its avenue in Brooklyn. No doubt, you know of this constellation of stores, restaurants, butchers, and bookshops, their wares piled high like the old places on Washington Street. But does it surprise you to hear that our first recorded community organized around a mosque, back in 1907, stood not on this thoroughfare but in Williamsburg, Brooklyn, and was founded by a group of Polish, Lithuanian, and Russian Muslims? By 1931, this American Mohammedan Society purchased three buildings on Powers Street for worship and community affairs. But Islam on this land surely precedes these intrepid travelers, for the first of us Muslims to arrive in this country dates back far before the birth of the republic. (You are confused because I had written we arrived in the late nineteenth century, and so you think I contradict myself. But I am large. I contain multitudes.)

Islam in this country is about as old as Virginia, and the first Muslims were brothers and sisters of our faith who were captured on the African continent and brought here solely for their labor. Have you read the slave statutes, like this early one, from 1670, which states that "negroes, moores, mollatoes and others borne of and in heathenish, idollatrous, pagan and mahometan parentage and country . . . may be purchased, procured, or otherwise obteigned as slaves"?[3] We labored and suffered, and yet we continued to pray, fast, and recite the word of Allah whenever we could.

Take Ibrahim Abdur Rahman, for example. A son of royalty from Futa Jallon in West Africa, he was captured and made into a slave, landing in Natchez, Mississippi, in 1788. Over the next forty years, he was known to steal away to the riverbank when he could. There he would sit alone and scratch out Arabic words in the dirt and remember home. Later, the public learned about brother Ibrahim and his talents, and with his newfound notoriety, he sought to return to his people. Thus began a nationwide tour for Ibrahim. Paraded around the country by the American Colonization Society as an African curiosity, he raised money for his and his family's release from bondage and travel back to the African continent. This tour took Ibrahim not only to our New York but also to the White House, where he met John Quincy Adams. It seems the always polite Ibrahim had a sly, winking view of the politics of this country.

He described his visit simply. "I found the President the best piece of furniture in the house," he states in a letter.[4]

We are lucky to have Brother Ibrahim's story preserved. Most of our sisters and brothers who were enslaved have sadly fallen through history's sieve. We do have enough evidence, though, to know that Muslim slaves dot the forcefully tilled landscape of this country throughout its history and across its geography, from Natchez to New York and beyond.

In addition to this part of our family there are the Muslim mariners, many of whom arrived in the ports of Brooklyn, ruddy faced, out of breath, and eager for a place to bow their heads in remembrance of God. They surely came in the seventeenth, eighteenth, and nineteenth centuries. But we know that from 1939, after they landed, they made their way to State Street, in the heart of the Arab community, where Sheikh Daoud Ahmed Faisal and his wife Khadija had their mosque, the Islamic Mission of America. (It is still there, but you must know that already.) In the cramped quarters of the brownstone mosque, sailor prayed with seamstress, African American shoulder to shoulder with Arab. It is said that the Sheikh, by day employed by the railroad (again, on the road!), and his wife were individually responsible for spreading the faith to sixty thousand souls.

In fact, what we have always loved about this city is that we were never lost in it. By discovering each other, we found ourselves here. The Indian Muslims found the Albanians, the Malays prostrated beside the Africans, and all in front of Allah only. We didn't need mosques, only a clean place to lay our foreheads gently on the ground. The sun gave us all the direction we needed. In those early years, like today, we converted brownstones and storefronts into prayer halls and mosques. And it continues. Did you know, for example, that for the thousands of Muslims who worked in the area around the World Trade Center there was a cavernous room used for Friday prayer? From the beginning, we have lived here in a kind of plurality that reminds me of Cordoba, or Haroun el-Rashid's Baghdad, and seems rivaled only by Mecca during Hajj.

But then after September 11, our halls and mosques had targets painted on them, sometimes quite literally. What was for us a geography of freedom and opportunity transformed overnight into a frightening topography of rage. In the Bronx, our taxis were set on fire; in Manhattan, two drivers were beaten; in Bensonhurst, nine livery cars and taxis were vandalized. Don't move, these thugs seemed to be telling us, because we are coming for you. Death threats, physical assaults, verbal harassment, and a handful of murders across the country are what we (and our brother Sikhs) endured. We were shocked and angry on September 11 too, and then we were afraid. When Timothy McVeigh bombed the building in Oklahoma, was it right to seek retribution on any face that reminded you of him? (Instead, then too, we were blamed, and we suffered.) Vengeance is a strong emotion, but as Cleopatra tells her attendant Charmian, "innocents 'scape not the thunderbolt" (II.v.77).

By the smoke of my breath, we survived this terrible time, with great thanks to the grace of our neighbors. They deserve a thousand blessings and one more, these decent, good-hearted people who wanted to help, understand, and accompany us around our cities and neighborhoods. They helped restore the streets as sites of circulation for us. But while all this was happening, I dare say, now we have you to contend with. Do you realize how you are chipping away at this sense of security we were just beginning to feel again? I think you do.

There are many stories to tell, like our Afghan brother (shall we call him Yousef K?) who was visiting his immigration lawyer's office in Lower Manhattan and was stopped by the police. They inquired into his religion, and after he responded Muslim, he was put into detention. Or then there is the story of Brother Butt. Someone must have been telling lies about Mohammed Rafiq Butt, for without having done anything wrong he was arrested one fine morning. It was September 19, and the FBI was following lead 1,556, a telephone tip from someone in South Ozone Park, Queens. The caller was concerned that two vans had stopped outside Mr. Butt's apartment building and six "Middle Eastern–looking men" exited from each vehicle (no matter that Mr. Butt lived there with three other Pakistani men). After they arrested him, the FBI took a day to determine that this harmless fifty-five-year-old man was innocent even to the temptations of the world ("He no smoke, he no drink, he don't go nowhere," is how his nephew put it).[5] On October 23, after being detained for almost five weeks at the Hudson County Jail, Mohammed Rafiq Butt took his last breath and died that Tuesday morning, apparently of a heart attack. May God have mercy on his soul.

You see, my good man, we have lost our faith in your activities. You are turning what was for us an open geography into some kind of penal colony. Hundreds of us now languish in your prisons, not even sure why. You have admitted to the press that we have nothing to do with terrorism, and that we have committed no crime, but still we cannot walk away, even if a judge has ordered us free. Instead, you invoke an emergency, bond is laid aside, and we sit alone for twenty-three hours a day, the lights blazing the whole time so that night has lost its identity to day. Then you won't tell us whom you have arrested. We have a difficult time finding out where our friends are as you fly them around the country with shackled legs and hands in midnight planes. You claim everyone has an attorney, but we have heard differently. You come in the middle of the night and take away our brothers and fathers and sons and tell us nothing. Then you require us to "volunteer" for interviews, your reason for choosing us simply the kink of our hair, the caramel of our skin, the country name stamped on our passport. We have felt the freedom of the road in this country for a long time, and so you will understand if we are bewildered that this could happen here.

The other day, I heard a professor say that this was a time when we as a society should be thinking about what the balance between liberty and security should be, but the problem is that most of the country is willing to trade someone else's liberty—namely ours—for their own sense of security. He is a smart man, this professor, and he makes me wonder if this is the deal you have entered us into. While waiting for you, I have been reading James Madison. (Surprised? Didn't I tell you I have been here for over a century?) Since September, haven't we become vulnerable to the passions of the majority? I was under the impression that this required your greater vigilance for our safety, since, as Madison writes, "In a society under the forms of which the stronger faction can readily unite and oppress the weaker, anarchy may as truly be said to reign, as in a state of nature where the weaker individual is not secured against the violence of the stronger."[6] You mouth the words of protection, but then why do we feel your violence lashing our backs?

Everywhere you say you are looking for rats, but I think you are finding lambs and unwilling to admit this. So many of us came here to escape terrible restrictions on our lives, not to rediscover them. But all around the world—in Chile, Iran, Iraq, Nicaragua, the Congo, Indonesia, Panama, South Africa—hasn't the problem historically been not that you can't tell the difference between the rats and the lambs, but that you have preferred the rats?

Perhaps you would feel safer if I came to your office? Save you a trip? Under normal circumstances I would, but right now I would prefer not to. Like Bartleby, I have become a wanderer who refuses to budge. So send me off to the Tombs, if you wish. What will I discover there but the Egyptian masonry and forlorn history that lonely souls have scratched onto the stone in their spare time, for time is all they have in the Tombs.

In the meantime, they tell me that you are failing to fetch me, but keep encouraged. You may be missing me from one place, and so you search another. But I am here, my good man, under your boot soles. I am at home. I have stopped here, waiting for you. If I go anywhere these days, it is only to my roof, to hear the call to prayer from the mosque on Atlantic Avenue or the Sunday church bells on Pacific, and I sing along in what must sound like the yelp of a Barbary pirate to some. But, to me, these tunes are the sign of democracy. Don't you think so, too?

So come, ask me your questions. I will listen to them with devoted concentration, my head angled like a mendicant. But I won't answer them right away, for you must first have a sip of my syrupy coffee, a bite of crumbly sweet halawa, and a taste of our hospitality. There will be time for all things, believe me. And though you hardly know who I am or what I mean, I will be good to you nonetheless. We have much to discuss, you and I, and a long night ahead of us. Yalla, my good man, hurry and arrive. I've been expecting you.

East of the Sun (West of the Moon)

Islam, the Ahmadis, and African America

Sepia Tones

Traveling somewhere between living in a racialized state and stating the life of a race lies the story of African American Islam. Found in narratives of struggle and spirit, of edification and propagation, of incarceration, incarnation, and ideology, and of blacks, Asians, and Middle Easterners, this is a tale seldom told and even less often heard. When it does get some play, the way is in a single key. Separation is sounded brassily as the dominant chord, modulating being minor into a major ideology. The dissonances of dissidence. From Moorish Science to Garveyism, from Elijah's honor to Malcolm's rage, Islam is understood as a tool of politics, pliant to complaint and made to speak a language of plain truth against the tricknology of white folk. The soul almost disappears, replaced with an iconography of militarized Islam, boots and bowties battling white supremacy, dividing One Nation Under God with the Nation of Islam.

The fate of Malcolm concludes this narrative by necessity. Epiphanies of a universal spirit clash with narrow-minded parochialisms in a death match of blood and assassination. Malcolm is lionized and history, tragically, marches on. But did this battle between the particular and the universal, between Islam as a unique expression of African American political aspirations for separation and Islam as a universal religion of belonging first find its articulation with Malcolm's rupture with Elijah Muhammad, or has the customary story we have up until now been unable to comprehend the complexity of Islam in the African American experience? Is the divide between the universal and the particular so easily drawn as a picture in black and white, or are there sepia tones of black, brown, and beige that call out to be seen? What follows is an examination of the browns and beiges, a look at the notes and tones of the Muslim experience as it was lived before September 11, 2001.

Three tableaus compose this triptych. The first involves an Asian immigrant, the second looks at Brother Malcolm, and the third is a study in sound. All three are signifying the idea of Islam in the United States as a faith finding a context in which to belong along with a place from which to disagree.

The Mufti

Islam in African America has a history as long as memory, when Muslim slaves from Africa wrapped their faith tightly around them as invisible armor against daily degradation. But the practice does not seem to continue. Religious revivalists in the early part of the twentieth century, mostly in the North where large numbers of new migrants sought the strength of a community, found populations willing to listen and eager to believe. In 1913, Timothy Drew donned a fez and claimed Moroccan heritage for his people in the Moorish Science Temple. For all its imaginative reconstruction, the Moorish Science Temple has little under the surface to connect it to worldwide Islam. But its spirit of displacing the term "Negro" from blacks, of thinking of darker-skinned peoples as Asiatics and Moroccans, of allying Drew Ali with "Jesus, Mohamed, Buddha, and Confucius"[1] is part of the productive tension between separatism and universalism that will follow all African American Islam throughout the rest of the century. But it would be in the next decade, with the growth of the Ahmadiyya community, that the Asian connection forges ahead.

One night in January 1920, a gentle and bespectacled Muslim by the name of Mufti Muhammad Sadiq left London for New York to become one of the first "Pioneers in the spiritual Colonization of the Western world."[2] This phrase, conveyed by the then leader of the Ahmadiyya movement in India, Mirza Mahmud Ahmad, to the Mufti's work, interestingly linked Ahmadiyya missionary activity with British rule and with its own missionary activity, along with the pioneer mythology of the New World. The Ahmadis had objected to the manner in which British missionaries were defaming Islam by reviling the Prophet Muhammad, and set out not just to correct this error but also to illustrate how Jesus was a prophet of Islam. They had observed how missionaries in the East had succeeded in misrepresenting Islam and felt that a proactive agenda of missionizing was needed to counteract this damage. Recent Hindu-only movements in India also fueled the drive to survive in a world of plural faiths. "Reason itself revolts against this exclusiveness," wrote Ahmadi founder Ghulam Ahmed.[3]

The Ahmadiyya community began in late nineteenth-century India with the figure of Mirza Ghulam Ahmad, a charismatic reformer who believed he had received divine revelations, starting in 1876, requiring him to promote the unity of all religions as manifest through Islam, whose chief object is "to establish the unity and majesty of God on earth, to extirpate idolatry and to weld all nations into one by collecting all of them around one faith."[4] It is a *particular* universalism. In seeking this unity, Ahmad would call himself "the Mahdi of Islam . . . the Promised Messiah of Christianity and Islam, and an avatar of Krishna for the Hindus,"[5] a claim that would ultimately oust him and his movement from the mainstream Muslim establishment. We should note how Ahmad's ideas are an attempt to confront communal feelings in India of his day, and how this relationship between faith and nation would resonate in the American Ahmadiyya movement.

Also of note are the links between the putative universalism of colonialism, which saw the spread of Western values as a mission manifest in direct and indirect colonial rule (*la mission civilisatrice*), to the missionary activities of the Ahmadis. Ahmadi missionizing, particularly in its enterprising New World aspects, thus borrows heavily from the script of European expansion and accepts modernity's commonplace division between the spiritual and secular worlds ("the spiritual colonization") where the East is spiritual and the West material. A significant difference, however, divides the methodologies of Western expansionism and Ahmadi missionary activity, for the Ahmadis were addressing the rest of the world as a colonized people and the religious foundation of their work is thus by definition a minority religion, unencumbered by state apparatuses or ideology. Its universalism percolates from below rather than being dusted from above, thus achieving a kind of dissident political flavor separate from the tastes of dominant rule.

In 1920, the movement, fresh from its missionary successes around the world (including England and West Africa) and full of the optimism that the New World is supposed to hold, sent its first missionary to the United States. Mufti Muhammad Sadiq boarded his ship in London and, each day, entertained his fellow passengers with his erudition. "Say, if you love Allah, follow me; then will Allah love you," he is reported to have intoned. Before the end of the trip, Sadiq is said to have "converted four Chinese men, one American, one Syrian, and one Yugoslavian to Islam."[6]

The American authorities were hardly as sanguine with Sadiq's sagacity. They seized him before he could leave the ship, accusing him of coming to the United States to practice polygamy, and placed him in a Philadelphia detention house. So began a dark hour for the gentle Sadiq. Seven weeks later, he was eventually released, but not before making nineteen other converts in jail, from Jamaica, British Guyana, the Azores, Poland, Russia, Germany, Belgium, Portugal, Italy, and France.

What Sadiq found when he reached the welcoming shores of the United States was a history of institutional racism and Asian exclusion laws for which he was unprepared. White nationalism would already be working against the Mufti's message. Later he would write that

> if Jesus Christ comes to America and applies for admission to the United States under the immigration laws, [he] would not be allowed to enter this country because: 1. He comes from a land which is out of the permitted zone. 2. He has no money with him. 3. He is not decently dressed. 4. His hands have holes in the palms. 5. He remains bare-footed, which is a disorderly act. 6. He is against fighting for the country. 7. He believes in making wine when he thinks necessary. 8. He has no credential to show that he is an authorized preacher. 9. He believes in practicing the Law of Moses [polygamy].[7]

Originally conceiving of his work as broad-based, ecumenical, multiracial missionary activity, Sadiq soon realized that whites were bitter and fearful of his message and African Americans interested and open. Early reports indicate that several Garveyites attended his lectures and were among his first converts, and the white press seemed generally baffled and lost in its own prejudices when considering the movement. One account tells us that "all the audience has adopted Arabic names. . . . There is the very dark Mr. Augustus, who used to belong to St. Marks church in this city [Chicago], but who now sings a pretty Arabic prayer and acts rather sphinx-like. Half a dozen Garvey cohorts are counted, one in his resplendent uniform. There is one pretty yellow girl and another not so pretty."[8]

The fact is that the Ahmadiyya movement attracted women and men. It formed a community of black, brown, and white people in a scattering of cities across the eastern half of the country (and St. Louis). But it mostly attracted African Americans, who were also given early leadership roles.[9] Participating in Islam vitally meant discovering the history of black contributions to Islam, a topic generating some interest broadly in the black press at the time. In these years, articles appeared in the *Crisis* (1913), the *Messenger* (1927), and *Opportunity* (1930) about Islam, notably about Bilal, the Abyssinian slave freed by Prophet Muhammad and Islam's first *muezzin*, illustrating Islam's historic connection with Africa.[10] It is important to underline that Islam within the Ahmadiyya community was not considered a religion just for blacks but a religion in which blacks had an *alternative* universal history to which to pledge allegiance. Christianity and narrow nationalisms allowed no such thing, as the *Moslem Sunrise*, the Ahmadi journal, argued. In 1923, it printed a half-page exhortation on "the real solution of the Negro Question" calling on African Americans to see that "Christian profiteers brought you out of your native lands of Africa and in Christianizing you made you forget the religion and language of your forefathers—which were Islam and Arabic. You have experienced Christianity for so many years and it has proved to be no good. It is a failure. Christianity cannot bring real brotherhood to the nations. So, now leave it alone. And join Islam, the real faith of Universal Brotherhood."[11]

Universal brotherhood, of course, sounds similar to Universal Negro, as in the Improvement Organization, and links should be made between the philosophy of Garveyism and the Ahmadis, but again not simply through the lens of separatism but a reconfigured universalism. Considering the racial and religious divisions in the world, the Ahmadis reinterpreted the Islamic concept of *tawheed*, the oneness of God, as unifying the world, people, and faith around Islam (as Ghulam Ahmad wanted for India). In the American context, then, Ahmadi thought opened a critical space for race in the realm of the sacred. In this way, African Americans could metaphorically travel beyond the confines of national identities. They could become "Asiatics" and remain black, could be proud of their

African heritage *and* feel a sense of belonging to and participation with Asia. Being plural in this scheme meant not having to feel the psychic tear of double consciousness, but a way of living wholly in the holy. This ecumenicalism could be very powerful, both spiritually and politically. By being open-palmed about life when the secular world is clenching fists at you meant that your pluralist unity viewed the divisions of the world as contemptibly parochial.

By 1940, the movement could claim around ten thousand converts. Its impact would be wider still, and in his early years it would reach the ears of Malcolm X.

Brother Malcolm

Malcolm X, the eloquent minister of information for Elijah Muhammad, is commonly seen as speaking the fire of separatism and black pride until his transformative Hajj in 1964 tamed his message, as he discovered the true universal spirit of Islam. Conventional as this story is, with its Augustinian turns of the will, it fails when confronted with history. The rise and development of Malcolm's message is a story of the conflict between the particular universalism of Ahmadi-type Islam against the more narrow confines of Nation of Islam creed.[12] When we understand this, we can view the intellectual development of Malcolm as a way of thinking through the role of faith in determining consciousness, and that that activity itself for Malcolm was hardly a settled issue.

Consider, for example, the fact that early in his life and while considering the value of Islam while in prison, Malcolm was visited by an Ahmadi, Abdul Hameed, who was on his outreach to local populations. Abdul Hameed even sent Malcolm a book of Arabic Muslim prayers, which Malcolm memorized phonetically.[13] This contact may help to explain why, after being released from Charlestown prison on parole, Malcolm too identifies himself at least once as an "Asiatic," which I have been arguing is not false consciousness of African American history or self-hatred, but a strategic belief in the particular universal of Islam. The incident was as follows.

In 1953, Malcolm, who was now a fully fledged Muslim and member of Elijah Muhammad's flock, was pulled aside one day at his work at the Gar Wood factory in Wayne, Michigan, by the FBI. He had failed to register for the Korean War draft, the agent needled him, and was thereby jeopardizing his parole. Malcolm heeded the warning and registered, but how he registered is noteworthy. Under the section on citizenship, which read, "I am a citizen of . . . ," Malcolm inscribed "Asia." On his form proclaiming his conscientious objector status, he stated his belief that "Allah is God, not of one particular people or race, but of All the Worlds, thus forming All Peoples into One Universal Brotherhood." Asked to identify his religious guide, Malcolm wrote, "Allah the Divine Supreme Being, who resides at the Holy City of Mecca, in Arabia."[14]

Unlike orthodox Nation of Islam creed, which would connect Allah with W. D. Fard and the religious guide as Elijah Muhammad, Malcolm identifies Allah with the God of Islam and, like the Ahmadis, stresses the universal character of God. We could perhaps cynically see this move as a means to defeat the draft by identifying with a more orthodox religion than the Nation, but to do so is to miss the manner in which Malcolm would later repeatedly seek to integrate the Nation into the fold of worldwide Islam. In 1960, after the scholar C. Eric Lincoln coined the term "Black Muslims" for Nation followers, Malcolm objected vehemently. "I tried for at least two years to kill off that '*Black* Muslims,'" he said. "Every newspaper and magazine writer and microphone I got close to [I would say] '*No!* We are black *people* here in America. Our *religion* is Islam. We are properly called "Muslims"!' But that 'Black Muslims' name never got dislodged."[15]

Following his break with Elijah Muhammad, Malcolm would separate his religious and the political organizing through the creation of the Muslim Mosque, Incorporated and the Organization of

Afro-American Unity, respectively, and he would become involved in actively connecting Arab and African political movements to the African American struggle. During his 1964 pilgrimage to Mecca, for example, he made several stops in Africa and the Middle East to address local audiences. He participated in the Cairo conference of the Organization of African Unity, where he delivered a speech to the delegates on July 17, and he participated in the founding moment of the Palestine Liberation Organization during the same trip.[16]

This tension, between the Ahmadi vision of a particular universal vision of Islam and the Nation's notion of an Islam for black people, underscores the conflict between two very different roles for religion in the political sphere. Admittedly, the Ahmadi spirit is less confrontational, less public, less typical of the struggle we have come to recognize as identity politics, and yet it is still revolutionary in its own way by providing a radical ontology of self. To reorient one's body toward the Orient means a refusal to engage with the first principles of white America's definitions of blackness, but instead to cut to the heart of an old American principle, the freedom of worship. Yet unlike the primary demand placed upon American religion, that religion be relegated solely to the private sphere, Islamic faith is seen as enveloping and thereby surpassing national belonging.

Reverberating through the African American community, this notion that a reconfigured universal faith can free your mind and body gained ground. While the Nation used the media (and the media used the Nation) to promote its belief, this other vision of Islam was quietly seeping into the pores of African American communities around the country, giving them a spiritual place to repudiate the nation of America not with the Nation of Islam but with a new universalism. Genealogically, this idea should be seen as descending from the Ahmadiyya movement, and musically it had a soundtrack that large segments of the American public were listening to. Many of the major figures of midcentury jazz were themselves directly influenced by the Ahmadiyya movement, and the yearning for a universal and spiritual sound was in large part a result of Ahmadiyya labor.

A Love Supreme

In 1953, *Ebony* magazine felt the rise of Islam among the jazz musicians of the era was sufficiently important to publish its article on "Moslem Musicians." "Ancient Religion Attracts Moderns" spoke its headline, and it centered on the importance of jazz among musicians. Drummer Art Blakey, we are told, "started looking for a new philosophy after having been beaten almost to death in a police station in Albany Ga., because he had not addressed a white policeman as 'sir.'"[17] Talib Dawood, a former jazz player and Ahmadi, introduced Blakey to Islam. Blakey's house was a known center for Islamic learning, and in an important engagement at Small's Paradise in Harlem, he organized a seventeen-member band, all Muslim, as the Messengers. Later, the band's personnel would change, as would the name (to the Jazz Messengers), but the Islamic influence in jazz would continue.[18]

Other important figures of the period also converted to Islam. Yusef Lateef, Sahib Shihab, Ahmed Jamal, and McCoy Tyner would all convert, and Dizzy Gillespie, Miles Davis, and John Coltrane would all be significantly influenced by its spirit. It is with John Coltrane that I want to conclude this chapter, since his influence has been so remarkable in the jazz sound and because his debt to other Eastern philosophies is relatively well known. But his relationship to Islam has not, to my knowledge, been sufficiently acknowledged despite the fact that it can be heard in his most famous work.

To have a soundtrack to a movement does not mean to play an anthem. Rather than indicating a representational scheme of signifying a specific community, I am interested in listening for the ways in which the yearning for a new kind of community, one based on a new universalism that has a (but not by necessity the only) base in Islam, can be heard in the ways in which the music is pushing itself. Coltrane's search for a tone that could extend the saxophone is well known, as is the critics' initial bewilderment to his pitch. He himself talked about his desire to incorporate the fullness of expression in his music. "I want to cover as many forms of music that I can put into a jazz context and play on my instruments," he wrote in his notebooks. "I like Eastern music; Yusef Lateef has been using this in his playing for some time. And Ornette Coleman sometimes plays music with a Spanish content."[19] In an unreleased session from his Village Vanguard recordings, Coltrane is also playing with Ahmed Abdul Malik, a Sudanese bass and oud player who was part of Monk's band, a regular partner to Randy Weston, and an innovator in incorporating Middle Eastern modal organization in jazz improvisation. Coltrane's sidemen regularly included Muslim musicians from Philadelphia, and he himself, married to Naima (a Muslim) and, after 1957, increasingly interested in all things spiritual, regularly engaged his friend, piano player Hassan Abdullah, in discussions about Islam.

Space prevents me from etching in detail the milieu in which Coltrane repeatedly encountered and considered Islam. Instead I want to move toward a conclusion in a musical note by considering the ecumenical sound of Islam found in Coltrane's most commercially successful recording, *A Love Supreme*. Significantly, Coltrane was often portrayed by the media of his day as blowing the sounds of black rage. The Angry Young Tenor was the musical equivalent of the angry Malcolm X. But Coltrane never saw his music this way. Responding to his critics, he said, "If [my music] is interpreted as angry, it is taken wrong. The only one I'm angry at is myself when I don't make what I'm trying to play."[20] Later he would be quoted as saying this about the philosophy of his music: "I think the main thing a musician would like to do is to give a picture to the listener of the many wonderful things he knows of and senses in the universe. That's what music is to me—it's just another way of saying this is a big, beautiful universe we live in, that's been given to us, and here's an example of just how magnificent and encompassing it is."[21] If there is a tendency to view this wisdom as apolitical, liberal claptrap, it is I think misplaced. Searching for the universal in a minor key is less about escape, or about colonizing the spiritual experiences of the dark world to rejuvenate an exhausted Western sensibility, in the mode of Richard Burton through George Harrison. Coltrane's universal is a search for a big philosophy of sound, which repudiates the thin, reedy existence of American racial politics, and it does so, often, by an invocation of Islam.

"During the year of 1957, I experienced, by the grace of God, a spiritual awakening which was to lead me to a richer, fuller, more productive life." So wrote Coltrane in the famous liner notes for *A Love Supreme*. The notes continue in this tenor, and anyone with an ear attuned to Islamic language will hear its echoes. "NO MATTER WHAT . . . IT IS WITH GOD. HE IS GRACIOUS AND MERCIFUL. HIS WAY IS IN LOVE, THROUGH WHICH WE ALL ARE. IT IS TRULY—A LOVE SUPREME—."[22]Al-rahman, al-raheem. The Gracious, the Merciful. The two qualities that follow God everywhere in the Muslim tradition are invoked by Coltrane, who ends his text with "ALL PRAISE TO GOD." Al-hamd'ulillah. Consider the first track, "Acknowledgement." Built around a simple, four-note structure, this piece is an attempt to unify and capture the rapture of the divine. Listen how, two-thirds of the way through, Coltrane meanders around the simple theme in every key, as if to suggest the manner in which God's greatness truly is found everywhere, and then the ways in which the band begins to sing the phrase "A Love Supreme," like a roving band of sufi mendicants singing their *dhikr*. The words could change. As the love is extolled, the phrase begins to include the sounds of "Allah Supreme," another Arabic expression, Allahu Akbar. Coltrane makes the connection from "A Love Supreme" to Allah Supreme for his entire listening audience, forever delivering a sound of Islam to the world of American music.

To appreciate the depth of mutual involvement between blacks and Asians means not just acknowledging how histories of faith exist to be excavated, which illustrates a level of shared struggle toward an acceptable ontology for living in the racialized United States, but also investing the sacred with the possibilities for radical thought, even if its effects are less visible to us than the legacy of political activism through ideologies of separatism. Ahmadi Islam was the space where this place was opened up for many African Americans. It defines a certain aesthetics of living, where the text to life is in a language white America cannot read and the sounds of existence flutter beyond white America's ears. This isn't about being omni-American, to use a phrase associated with Albert Murray, but it is about assimilating into the omnipresence of a just universal order. It is where blacks become Asians and Asians black, under color of divine law.

Racing Religion

The Jew is one whom other men consider a Jew: that is
the simple truth from which we must start.
—Jean-Paul Sartre, *Anti-Semite and Jew*

But what exactly is a black? First of all, what's his color?
—Jean Genet, *The Blacks: A Clown Show*

Late in 1942, as World War II raged overseas, a Yemeni Muslim
immigrant named Ahmed Hassan quietly appeared one day in
front of a US district court judge. The Michigan resident had come
to court for a hearing regarding his petition for naturalization,
and while we don't know what he wore that day, it was probably
something carefully chosen to downplay his "extremely dark complexion," as described in the judge's decision.[1] Hassan, after all, was
making his official appearance in front of the court to prove that he
was a white person and, therefore, eligible for citizenship.

Although Hassan was one of the first Arab Muslims to petition for American naturalization, his case was far from unique.
Beginning in 1790 and until 1952, the Naturalization Act had limited citizenship to "free white persons" but without exactly defining what makes a person white.[2] Thus, many people, primarily of
Asian descent, had appeared in front of the courts before Hassan
to argue that they were "white by law," to borrow a phrase from
Ian Haney Lopez's book of the same name.[3] The immigration laws
had changed over the years. In 1870, for example, the Naturalization Act was amended to include "aliens of African nativity and to
persons of African descent,"[4] and in 1940 language was added to

include "races indigenous to the Western Hemisphere."[5] Nonetheless, certain Asians, beginning with the Chinese, had been excluded from American citizenship since 1878.[6] In 1882, Congress passed the first Chinese Exclusion Act, and in 1917, most immigration from Asia was further curtailed with the establishment of what Congress called the "Asiatic Barred Zone."[7] The reasoning here was that the country should not admit people who had no chance of naturalization. Despite all these changes, it was still far from clear just what race Hassan was, especially with Yemen sitting squarely on the Arabian Peninsula in Asia.

Hassan certainly knew he had a fight ahead of him and was aware that the battle would be about his group membership and not his individual qualifications. He understood that the court would want to know if Arabs were white or yellow, European or Asian, Western or Eastern. He probably knew that the court would wonder if Arabs, as a people, could assimilate into the white Christian culture of the United States or if they were, by nature, unsuited to adapt to the republic where they now lived. After all, in previous "racial-prerequisite cases," as they are called, such political and cultural questions were commonly asked, although they traditionally narrowed in simply on the color of one's skin. Even then, as Haney Lopez tells us, the courts adopted shifting standards of whiteness, first using scientific knowledge (now largely discredited) or congressional intent and then adopting the test of "common understanding."[8]

We know that Hassan was aware of the impending questions and the legal history of immigration by the fact that he came to court that day armed with affidavits stating that his coloring "is typical of the majority of the Arabians from the region from which he comes, which [in] fact is attributed to the intense heat and the blazing sun of that area."[9] Under his arm were other affidavits, claims by unnamed ethnologists declaring that "the Arabs are remote descendants of and therefore members of the Caucasian or white race, and that [Hassan] is therefore eligible for citizenship."[10] He had done his homework. He had hope.

Whatever optimism he may have had, however, was soon dashed. Hassan's petition was denied. In his three-page decision dated December 14, 1942, Judge Arthur J. Tuttle straightforwardly stated that "Arabs are not white persons within the meaning of the [Nationality] Act."[11] Interestingly, Tuttle based his determination of Hassan's whiteness not principally on the color of his skin but primarily on the fact that he was an Arab and Islam is the dominant religion among the Arabs. "Apart from the dark skin of the Arabs," explained the judge, "it is well known that they are a part of the Mohammedan world and that a wide gulf separates their culture from that of the predominately Christian peoples of Europe. It cannot be expected that as a class they would readily intermarry with our population and be assimilated into our civilization."[12]

Religion determines race. At least in 1942 it did, and so Arabs were not considered white people by statute because they were (unassimilable) Muslims. But by 1944, a mere seventeen months later, things changed radically. At that time, another Arab Muslim would petition the government for citizenship. His name was Mohamed Mohriez, and he was "an Arab born in Sanhy, Badan, Arabia," who came to the United States on January 15, 1921. Unlike Hassan, however, Mohriez would succeed in his petition. District Judge Charles E. Wyzanski, who ruled in Mohriez's favor, made a point of explaining in his brief decision (delivered on April 13, 1944) that the global political leadership of the United States requires its adherence to the principles of equality that it espouses. After citing *Hassan* and stating his position ("the Arab passes muster as a white person"), the judge ended his decision by admitting that the "vital interest [of the United States] as a world power" required granting Mohriez's petition.[13] Why? Wyzanski explained that his decision was necessary "to promote friendlier relations between the United States and other nations and so as to fulfill the promise that we shall treat all men as created equal."[14] If in *Hassan* religion produces race, then in *Mohriez*, politics directly sways legal racial determination.

The last of the Asian exclusion laws was repealed in 1952 in favor of a restricting quota system of immigration. In 1965, the law changed again, abandoning the quota system entirely and making the racial prerequisite cases, with their now antiquated racial language, look like history. But half a century after the *Hassan* decision, and following the terrorist attacks of September 11, Arabs and Muslims have again been repeatedly forced to undergo state scrutiny and official state definition simply because of their group membership and not because of their individual qualifications. Reminiscent of the earlier racial prerequisite cases, today's post–September 11 state policies also teeter uncomfortably on race, religion, and contemporary politics, and the result has been mass exclusions and deportations of Arab and Muslim men from the United States in a strategy that, I argue, can properly be described as deliberate and racist.

Specifically, I am talking about the policy known as "special registration," a program of the Bush administration's War on Terror that drew on the history of the racial prerequisite cases for its authority and its practice. When it was first announced, special registration provoked some critical commentary from journalists and legal scholars, but it has hardly been investigated in depth. It bears looking into, however, for an inquiry into its mechanism should reveal at least two things: the insufficiency of past critiques of legal racial formation (like Haney Lopez's) to address how political expediency affects state definitions of race and the fact that through special registration the government, in effect, turned a religion, namely Islam, into a race. The rest of this chapter elaborates these points, but since the details of special registration are not well known, it is worth reviewing the program in detail before continuing.

What's So Special about Special Registration?

On September 11, 2002, the one-year anniversary of the terrorist attacks on the United States, the Bush administration established the National Security Entry-Exit Registration System (NSEERS) as part of its strategy in the War on Terror.[15] The program was formally ended by the Obama administration on April 28, 2011.[16] NSEERS, commonly known as "special registration," was a controversial and poorly executed program, and it was particularly reviled in the American Muslim community, where the brunt of its enforcement was felt.

What exactly was special registration? It was a government-mandated system of recording and surveillance that required all nonimmigrant males in the United States over the age of sixteen who were citizens and nationals from select countries to be interviewed under oath, fingerprinted, and photographed by a Department of Justice official.[17] These procedures applied to non-immigrant visitors as they crossed the border and entered the United States. Until December 2, 2003, this also applied to those already in the country (what the Department of Justice termed "call-in" registration). All those who were required to register had to provide proof of their legal status to remain in the United States, proof of study or employment (in the form of school enrollment forms or employment pay stubs), and proof of residential address (such as a lease or utility bill).[18] Some also had to supply any and all of their credit card numbers and the names and addresses of two US citizens who could authenticate their identity, and had to answer questions regarding their political and religious beliefs.[19] Before the program was modified, registrants also had to reregister within forty days with a Department of Justice official if they remained in the country for more than thirty days, and then again annually. In addition, special registrants could enter and exit from the country only from specific ports of entry. Each and every time he entered and left the country, the nonimmigrant male had to go through the byzantine and arduous registration process again.

It goes almost without saying that special registration was heavily burdensome on the registrant, and those who underwent it complained that they were treated as if they were guilty of a crime and had to prove their innocence, thus flipping an avowed tradition of American jurisprudence (innocent until proven guilty) on its head. The execution of the program also came under fire. When the deadline for the first call-in registration passed in December 2002, mayhem ensued, particularly in Southern California, where, according to the *Washington Post*, hundreds of men (almost twelve hundred nationwide) were incarcerated in mass arrests on alleged immigration violations.[20] Ramona Ripston, executive director of the American Civil Liberties Union (ACLU), compared special registration to World War II measures against Japanese Americans. "I think it is shocking what is happening. It is reminiscent of what happened in the past with the internment of Japanese Americans," she told Reuters.[21] Many of the men arrested had been in the country for over a decade and had families in the United States (with US citizen children), and many more complained that their status was, in fact, legal but that their paperwork was incomplete due to Immigration and Naturalization Service (INS) backlogs.[22] Tens of thousands of lives were disrupted by the special registration program, many more if we consider the collateral effect on families. After implementation began in October 2002, NSEERS had registered at least 83,519 men and boys domestically (and over 93,740 at points of entry).[23] Out of this number, 13,799 were served with "Notice to Appear" subpoenas, meaning that deportation proceedings had begun in their cases.[24] Not a single charge of terrorism was levied as a result of special registration.[25]

Just what was going on here? If special registration was meant to be a program to net terrorists, as the government claims, then it was clearly a colossal and expensive failure. The Department of

Justice stated that "in light of the attacks against the United States on September 11, 2001, and subsequent events, and based on information available to the Attorney General, the Attorney General has determined that certain nonimmigrant aliens require closer monitoring when national security or law enforcement interests are raised."[26] But the criterion for "closer monitoring" of certain people was based almost exclusively on a single fact: national origin. Kris Kobach, an architect of the program, is unapologetic about such broad-based selection. "We had to just use the very blunt instrument of nationality [for special registration]," he explains.[27] But the dull thud of this blunt program was its own stupidity since it was unlikely to result in the capture of a terrorist, who, if he or she were in the country already, would logically not bother to register before carrying out any nefarious activity. Since the mechanism (i.e., the profile) of the program was known, it was also highly unlikely to catch an incoming terrorist, who would again logically search for ways to circumvent special registration's categories.

Initially focused on citizens and nationals from five states (Iran, Iraq, Libya, Sudan, and Syria), the list of targeted nations requiring registration ballooned to twenty-five countries, some in North and East Africa (Egypt, Tunisia, Algeria, Morocco, Somalia, Eritrea), others in West Asia (Yemen, Kuwait, Saudi Arabia, United Arab Emirates, Qatar, Oman, Bahrain, Lebanon, Jordan), South Asia (Pakistan, Bangladesh, Afghanistan), Southeast Asia (Indonesia), and East Asia (North Korea). Six of these countries are listed by the State Department among the seven state sponsors of terrorism (the initial five, plus North Korea; Cuba is the seventh, and its absence is telling). Two of these countries (Iraq and Afghanistan) have recently been invaded by the United States, and the vast majority of the rest are allies of the United States. This fact alone—that the overwhelming number of men who were subject to special registration came from friendly countries—is significant, for it proves that something else other than enemy nationality was operative here.[28]

That special registration was a discriminatory program is incontrovertible. Ostensibly, it discriminated by gender, age, national origin, and citizenship status. The discrimination was, in all likelihood, entirely legal under the plenary power doctrine, a century-old Supreme Court decision that holds that Congress and the executive branch have sovereign authority to regulate immigration without judicial review.[29] That decision dates from 1898, upheld Chinese exclusion from the United States, and is still considered good law. Furthermore, according to legal scholar Gabriel Chin, the plenary power doctrine approves discrimination based not only on national origin but also on race:

> In immigration law alone, racial classifications are still routinely permitted. In recent decades, courts in the District of Columbia and the First, Second, Fifth, Seventh, Eighth, Ninth, Tenth, and Eleventh Circuits have said not only that aliens may be excluded or deported on the basis of race without strict scrutiny, but also that such racial classifications are lawful per se. Apparently no court has even hinted to the contrary. These circuits merely honor an unbroken line of Supreme Court decisions holding that "Congress may exclude aliens of a particular race from the United States" and, more broadly, that an alien seeking admission "has no constitutional rights regarding his application."[30]

It ought to be noted that in the publication of its rule in the *Federal Register*,[31] the Department of Justice cited key plenary power decisions to give special registration its legal legs on which to stand.[32] Since the Chinese exclusion cases provided the foundation for the plenary power doctrine, special registration thus has its own direct connection to Chinese exclusion.

One should also note that little unites the disparate group of special registration countries but that they are all Muslim majority nations.[33] To argue, as the Department of Justice did, that what unifies the list is not Islam but the "heightened risk of involvement in terrorist" activity (presumably al-Qaeda membership) just does not hold.[34] By the government's own admission, al-Qaeda activity had already been discovered in France, the Philippines, Spain, Germany, and Britain, but no visitors from these countries were required to undergo special registration. Indeed, the case of Richard Reid, the so-called shoe bomber, who converted to Islam (and thus is not a "citizen or national" of a Muslim country), underscores the limitations—or falsity—of such an argument.

Special registration accomplished several things, nonetheless. It reinscribed, through a legal mechanism, the cultural assumption that a terrorist is foreign-born, an alien in the United States, and a Muslim, and that all Muslim men who fit this profile are potentially terrorists. But special registration also did more than this. Special registration made legal and executive sense to the government because it participated in a long bureaucratic tradition found in American law of racial formation. Through its legal procedures, special registration was a political and bureaucratic policy that created a race out of a religion.

Racing Religion

How does special registration "race" Islam? To begin answering this question, we need to investigate the relationship between religious and racial difference in American politics and to understand how both racial and religious difference can be exploited in ways that are racist by definition. Racism is, of course, a complex social phenomenon that is difficult to sum up in just a few words. George Fredrickson, however, offers a useful definition in his book-length essay on the topic. According to Fredrickson, racism "exists when one ethnic group or historical collectivity dominates, excludes, or seeks to eliminate another on the basis of differences that it believes to be hereditary and unalterable."[35] While racism may at times appear similar to religious clashes, Fredrickson sees them as, in fact, quite distinct for the important reason that in religiously based systems or conflicts, the opportunities for conversion have always been present as a way to defeat one's own marginal status. In a religious conflict, it is not who you are but what you believe that is important. Under a racist regime, there is no escape from who you are (or are perceived to be by those in power). Thus, Fredrickson correctly finds racial and not religious division as driving the Spanish Inquisition's purity of blood laws. "Anti-Judaism became anti-Semitism," he explains, "whenever it turned into a consuming hatred that made getting rid of Jews seem preferable to trying to convert them, and anti-Semitism became racism when the belief took hold that Jews were intrinsically and organically evil rather than merely having false beliefs and wrong dispositions."[36] Jews and Muslims in medieval Spain were both collectively marked as dangerous and excludable because of a belief in their innate and hereditary natures. Exclusion was preferable to conversion.[37]

How one's religion or culture is apprehended, for example, can also assume a racist character. During the Spanish Inquisition, certain cultural (not necessarily religious) practices labeled one as a Jew or a Muslim. Changing one's sheets on Friday could make one Jewish in the eyes of the Christian community,[38] just as sitting on the ground (as opposed to in a chair) proved one was Muslim.[39] As the explanatory power of scientific theories of race has declined in our contemporary world, culture has again assumed a prominent role in determining and describing racial difference. As Etienne Balibar puts it, "Culture can also function like nature, and it can in particular function as a way of locking individuals and groups a priori into a genealogy, into a determination that is immutable and intangible in origin."[40]

Racism, however, should not be seen as something that is necessarily irrational or is a "consuming hatred," as Fredrickson describes it. While these certainly are historic realities, racism must also be understood as a careful ideology that is, unfortunately, politically useful, particularly in circumstances where one is called upon to define oneself against another. It determines the other, and it does so through various institutions, the law being a primary one among them. It also has historically led to three different categories of material consequences: exploitation, extermination, and exclusion.[41] All three, unfortunately, have their precedents in American history, as Michael Omi and Howard Winant point out in *Racial Formation in the United States*:

> From the very inception of the Republic to the present moment, race has been a profound determinant of one's political rights, one's location in the labor market, and indeed one's sense of "identity." The hallmark of this history has been racism, not the abstract ethos of equality, and while racial minority groups have been treated differently, all can bear witness to the tragic consequences of racial oppression. The examples are familiar: Native Americans faced genocide, blacks were subjected to racial slavery, Mexicans were invaded and colonized, and Asians faced exclusion.[42]

Here is a short history of racism in the United States, from extermination (of Native Americans) to exploitation (slavery and colonization) to exclusion (of Asians). It is in the last of these, exclusion, where special registration operates.

With its broad-brush focus on national origin, special registration juridically excluded thousands of Muslims by category and created a barrier that repelled even more. Special registration created a vast, new legal geography of suspicion for the US government, a geography that in some way mirrored the "Asiatic barred zone" of the 1917 Immigration Act. It may not have prevented visitors from entering, but it made it onerous to penetrate the border. Perhaps it would be more correct to say that special registration, rather than barring entry, drew a burdensome zone around Muslim-majority countries.

But special registration again did more. In requiring that citizens and nationals of those countries suffer through its burdens, special registration collapsed citizenship, ethnicity, and religion into race. Under the special registration guidelines, immigration officers were charged with the authority to register whomever they had reason to believe should be specially registered. This procedure extended to nonimmigrant aliens whom the inspecting officer had "reason to believe are nationals or citizens of a country designation by the Attorney General."[43] In a memo to regional directors and patrol agents, the INS clarified that this included cases such as "a nonimmigrant alien who is a dual national and is applying for admission as a national of a country that is not subject to special registration, but the alien's other nationality *would* subject him or her to special registration."[44] Numerous reports since special registration began indicated that birthplace was used as the trigger to determine the "reason to believe" one should be registered.

In fact, soon after special registration began, registering dual nationals became commonplace and sparked a minor international incident. Canada issued a rare travel advisory for its citizens visiting the United States, since the United States was discriminating between types of Canadian citizenship. The United States offered Canada assurances that dual citizenship would not automatically trigger special registration, and Canada withdrew its advisory. Canadian citizens who are nationals from the listed countries, however, continued to complain that birthplace triggered registration automatically.[45]

The implications of every national being required to register are that if you happen to hold dual citizenship with, say, Sweden and Morocco, or if you were born in Morocco but are not its citizen, or if you were born out of Morocco but to parents who are Moroccan, then you qualify. Swedish citizenship, even if it is your only citizenship, is no protection from special registration if you were born or your parents were born in one of the listed countries. The reason why this in particular is troubling is that, considering the broad geography of special registration, it makes descent or inheritability of Islam (and gender) the defining criterion. And that inheritability has nothing to do with enemy nationality since most of the listed nations are considered allies of the United States. Nor has it anything to do with belief or political affiliation since it says nothing about each individual's worldview. Rather, it is only about one's blood relationship to Islam. Through that blood relationship, legal barriers have been established to exclude as many Muslims as possible, and that fact consequently turns Islam into a racial category.

The Arabian Gulf of Racial Difference

Troubling as all this is, the relationship of Islam to racial definition in the United States is not new with special registration, and it is important to review this past to understand the history that special registration has to US political and racial logic. In fact, the combination of Islam and immigration has its own legal history in the United States, and we can discover that by surveying some of the key racial prerequisite cases from 1909 to 1944, particularly cases like *Hassan* and *Mohriez* in which the petitioners are Muslim or come from countries with Muslim majorities. While we may be accustomed to thinking of racial definition as being determined by the color of one's skin, what we observe here is that religion in general, and Islam in particular, plays a role in adjudicating the race of immigrants seeking naturalization in the United States. The various immigration acts that constitute the body of racial exclusion laws did not explicitly place religion inside a logic of race, but the courts did repeatedly note the religion of an applicant, and that in itself was often a deciding (if not the deciding) factor in determining the race of the petitioner. Although the physical attributes of the applicants were often discussed, the main question surrounding many of these cases, as in the *Hassan* decision cited earlier, was actually about the ability to assimilate to the dominant, Christian culture.

The cases are worth a look. An initial review reveals, as one might expect, that many did rely simply on ocular proof to determine race. Race, it would appear, was the color of one's skin, no more and no less. This seems to be the case with the Syrian Costa George Najour, who in 1909 went before the district judge to petition for citizenship. The judge was impressed that Najour "is not particularly dark, and has none of the characteristics or appearances of the Mongolian race, but, so far as I can see and judge, has the appearance and characteristics of the Caucasian race."[46] Najour's petition was granted.

Similarly, skin tone is called into question when, in 1909, four Armenians petitioned for naturalization. "I find that all were white persons in appearance, not darker in complexion than some persons of north European descent traceable for generations," writes the district judge in that case.[47] Likewise, in *U.S. v. Dolla* (1910), the Circuit Court of Appeals makes the determination that in this case it lacks jurisdiction, but not without first noting the facts of the case, with a novelist's detail.[48] The court states that Dolla, an Afghan who lived in Calcutta before coming to the United States, has a "complexion that is dark, eyes dark, features regular and rather delicate, hair very black, wavy and very fine and soft." It continues,

> On being called on to pull up the sleeves of his coat and shirt, the skin of his arm where it had been protected from the sun and weather by his clothing was found to be several shades lighter than that of his face and hands, and was sufficiently transparent for the

blue color of the veins to show very clearly. He was about medium or a little below medium in physical size, and his bones and limbs appeared to be rather small and delicate. Before determining that the applicant was entitled to naturalization the presiding judge closely scrutinized his appearance.[49]

His race was written on his body, just above his tan line.

In the case of the Syrian Tom Ellis (1910), the judge notes that "ethnologically, [Ellis] is of Semitic stock, a markedly white type of race," although the judge does concede that "the words 'white person' . . . taken in a strictly literal sense, constitute a very indefinite description of a class of persons, where none can be said to be literally white, and those called white may be found of every shade from the lightest blonde to the most swarthy brunette."[50] Ellis, too, was admitted.

In Ex parte *Shahid* (1913), the petitioner was, once again, a Syrian, yet this time "in color, he is about that of walnut, or somewhat darker than is the usual mulatto or one-half mixed blood between the white and the Negro races."[51] *Shahid* is most interesting because the judge acknowledges the limitations of phenotypical race. "One Syrian may be of pure or almost pure Jewish, Turkish, or Greek blood, and another the pure-blooded descendant of an Egyptian, an Abyssinian, or a Sudanese. How is the court to decide? It would be most unfortunate if the matter were to be left to the conclusions of a judge based on ocular inspection."[52] Taking up the argument that "free white persons" meant "Europeans," the judge goes on to acknowledge that that definition, too, is problematic since that "would exclude persons coming from the very cradle of the Jewish and Christian religions."[53] Although he seems bothered by such a line of thought ("such arguments are of the emotional ad captandum order that have no place in the judicial interpretation of a statute"), the judge relies on the strict application of the separation of powers to devolve himself of any greater comment on the matter.

Shahid will be excluded, he explains, not because of his race but simply on his "own personal disqualitifications [*sic*]."[54]

The first time a Syrian is denied naturalization because of his race occurs with Ex parte *Dow*, in 1914.[55] Again, the court finds it necessary to write the skin of the applicant. "In color he is darker than the usual person of white European descent, and of that tinged or sallow appearance which usually accompanies persons of descent other than purely European."[56] Dow is first denied naturalization because, "following the reasoning set out in Ex parte *Shahid*," the court here construed "free white person" to mean "inhabitants of Europe and their descendants."[57] The district judge laments this, for Dow, he argues, is a capable man, but making law is beyond the power of the court. To prove his point, the judge mixes nation, religion, and race in an exasperated (and racist) appeal. "No race in modern times has shown a higher mentality than the Japanese. To refuse naturalization to an educated Japanese Christian clergy-man and accord it to a veneered savage of African descent from the banks of the Congo would appear as illogical as possible, yet the courts of United States have held the former inadmissible and the statute accords admission to the latter."[58]

Dow is appealed, and at first affirmed, as geography takes precedence over skin color. ("There is no known ocular, microscopic, philological, ethnological, physiological, or historical test that can settle the question of the race of the modern Syrian; but the applicant and his associates are certainly Asiatics in the sense that they are of Asian nativity and descent and are not Europeans.")[59] On further appeal to the Fourth Circuit Court of Appeals (*Dow v. United States*, 1915), the decision is reversed, and Dow is finally admitted citizenship.[60] In fact, the Syrian community mobilized every resource it had for the Dow case, as described by Alixa Naff.[61]

All these cases take place before *U.S. v. Thind* (1923),[62] the Supreme Court case that Haney Lopez cites as shifting the reasoning of the courts. Prior to *Thind*, the courts depended largely on so-called scientific knowledge to determine whiteness. After *Thind*, the notion of common understanding of what whiteness is held sway. It would seem, then, that in the bulk of the cases I have thus far discussed, race is understood primarily as the color of one's skin and secondarily as geographically determined. Skin color influences the decisions in *Najour*, *Halladjian*, *Dolla*, *Ellis*, *Shahid*, *Dow*, and others. In discussions of race, this is to be expected. Geography, too, plays a role in these cases, but what about religion?

All of the Syrians to come before the court during the racial exclusion era were Christian, and the court often found it important to underline this fact in every instance it could. In *Ellis*, the court reiterated the fact twice in the first paragraph of its decision. "The applicant is a Syrian, a native of the province of Palestine, and a Maronite. . . . It may be said, further, that he was reared a Catholic, and is still of that faith."[63] In *Halladjian*, the court not only draws attention to the confessional traditions of the Armenians but uses their Christianity as proof of their eligibility for naturalization. "Race . . . is not an easy working test of 'white' color," averred the court,[64] which then moved to discuss eligibility in terms of "ideals, standards, and aspirations." "In the warfare which has raged since the beginning of history about the eastern Mediterranean between Europeans and Asiatics, the Armenians have generally, though not always, been found on the European side. They resisted both Persians and Romans, the latter somewhat less strenuously. By reason of their Christianity, they generally ranged themselves against the Persian fire-worshippers, and against the Mohammedans, both Saracens and Turks."[65] The decision goes so far as to explain why Armenians are part of the Eastern Church and to excuse them for it. "Present war and their remoteness are said to have prevented the Armenian bishops from attending the Council of Chalcedon in the fifth century. Thus, they say that they were misled as to the pronouncement of that Council, and so a schism arose without heresy on their part."[66] Whereas Catholicism was a liability for a long time for Italians and Irish in the United States, it was considered favorably with regard to the Armenians, illustrating the shifting boundary of acceptability. "During the Crusades and afterwards many Armenians came into the obedience of the Roman Catholic Church, while retaining distinctive rites and customs."[67] Religion becomes the ultimate arbiter of admissibility, though, the court argues, without prejudice. "These facts are stated, without reproach to the followers of Mohammed or Zoroaster, because history has shown Christianity in the near East has generally manifested a sympathy with Europe rather than with Asia as a whole."[68] Christianity turns Armenians white.

In *Shahid*, too, the religion of the petitioner is proclaimed in the beginning. "According to his statement he is now 59 years of age, was born at Zahle, in Asia Minor, in Syria, and came to this country about 11 years ago, and is a Christian."[69] Dow, we are told, "is a Maronite—a Christian."[70]

After *Thind*, who is referred to not as an Indian but as a "high caste Hindu," the decisions adopt more explicit language regarding religion (as science is discarded and replaced with culture). Another case involving the right of Armenians to naturalize comes before the court in 1925. The case of *U.S. v. Cartozian* (1925) references both *Ozawa v. United States* (another Supreme Court decision from 1922 disallowing Japanese to naturalize) and *Thind* in its decision. It argues that "it is now judicially determined that mere color of the skin of the applicant does not afford a practical test as to whether he [the petitioner] is eligible to American citizenship."[71] Thus, the court feels emancipated from judging hue and tone and relies largely on religion (and assimilation) in its determination. "Although the Armenian province is within the confines of the Turkish empire, being in Asia Minor, the people thereof have always held themselves aloof from the Turks, the Kurds, and allied peoples, principally, it might be said, on account of their religion, though color may have had something to do with it."[72] In *Wadia v. United States* (1939), the court substitutes "ethnicity" for "race," calling Wadia "of the Parsee race," and feels compelled to disclose facts that must be important to its deliberations, including that "he was a follower of Zoroaster."[73]

By the 1940s, we have the two notable petitions of *Hassan* and *Mohriez*. Unlike the petitioners mentioned directly above, Hassan and Mohriez are both Muslim (at least by name). What makes their cases noteworthy is not just their faith community but the short span of time between when an Arab Muslim is considered nonwhite (Hassan) and when an Arab Muslim is officially considered white (Mohriez).[74] It is this abrupt shift, mirrored in the sudden creation of a Muslim race by special registration, that should concern us, for it illustrates not just the capricious nature of racial formation but also the depth to which contemporary American politics creates race, rather than race always creating politics.

But the legal scholars generally don't view *Hassan* and *Mohriez* through this perspective. Consider law professor John Tehranian's article "Performing Whiteness: Naturalization Litigation and the Construction of Racial Identity in America."[75] Here, Tehranian correctly states that the "racial-determination games [of the courts] often produce judicial opinions riddled with internal contradictions and dadaistic logic that find Arabs to qualify as white in some situations and nonwhite in others."[76] He argues that "the potential for immigrants to assimilate within mainstream Anglo-American culture was put on trial"[77] by these cases (and he explicitly discusses *Hassan* and *Mohriez*, among others, in the article). Tehranian labels the assimilation potential of petitioners as "the performance of whiteness." "Successful litigants," in Tehranian's view, "demonstrated evidence of whiteness in their character, religious practices and beliefs, class orientation, language, ability to intermarry, and a host of other traits that had nothing to do with intrinsic racial grouping."[78]

While Tehranian's discussion is valuable for the way it accounts for religion as a racial determining category, its organizing principle of "performance" confuses the fact that the judge performs "whiteness" through his adjudication, not the litigant through testimony. Tehranian, to paraphrase W. B. Yeats, confuses the dancer for the dance. Hassan surely came to court ready to act the part of a white person, but the judge would not admit the act, since his own performance of whiteness requires denying Hassan's petition. More important, however, the judge could not admit Hassan because the political culture of the time would not allow for it. The inertia of America's racial tradition kept the categories consistent. By the time we get to Mohriez, the political situation has changed, with the United States shedding its isolationist past for global dominance as the war nears its conclusion. With that transformation (manifest in the judge's explicitly political reasoning in his decision), the racial logic of the United States has been sent into flux.

Regrettably, Haney Lopez in his otherwise fine book also fails to account adequately for the role of politics in racial formation. He reaches the conclusion that "the incremental retreat from a 'Whites only' conception of citizenship made the arbitrariness of U.S. naturalization law obvious."[79] But there is nothing arbitrary about the racial shift from *Hassan* to *Mohriez*, or the creation of Islam as a post–September 11 racial category. These are clearly political decisions that have calculated consequences. While he does provide some historical context throughout his book for the reasons for racial flux, Haney Lopez seems unwilling to discuss politics in depth. In fact, the idea sometimes just drops out of the discussion. Consider this sentence from *White by Law*, where the idea simply disappears. "One might argue that [a judge's] views turned on cultural or political, rather than racial, prejudice. However, these forms of prejudice blur together, each fading into the other. Indeed the concept of race incorporates, and arguably partially arose out of, cultural prejudice."[80] Instead of a sustained investigation into the politics of whiteness and the whiteness of politics, what we get from Haney Lopez is an appeal for whites to "relinquish the privilege of Whiteness,"[81] thus making it clear that, for him, race making in the law is less a system of rational domination by the state than a problem of individual white identity (which he explicitly labels "white race consciousness").

But politics matters a great deal, and it always has, as Yale historian Rogers Smith understands. Smith has exhaustively examined thousands of citizenship cases in the United States and has come to the conclusion that inclusion in the United States has not been determined by an overarching theory of liberalism or by republican notions of citizenship. Rather, "American citizenship laws have always emerged as none too coherent compromises among the distinct mixes of civic conceptions advanced by the more powerful actors in different eras."[82] The point is to recognize how labor or civil unrest or, especially for our purposes, war aids in producing citizenship and inclusion, which in the history of the United States functions through political power and along the definitional axis of race.

One of the most painful examples of race in flux during American history must be Japanese internment during World War II. The signing of Executive Order 9066 resulted not only in the internment of over 110,000 people of Japanese ancestry, but also in the removal of the protections of citizenship, at the stroke of a pen, for over 70,000 of them.[83] Race trumped nationality. If you were born in the United States to Japanese parents prior to February 18, 1942, for example, you were an American citizen. But on February 19, you were born an enemy alien.[84]

There are other cases as well, situations that resolved into inclusion rather than exclusion. In 1943, for example, following US entry into the war, Congress repealed the Chinese Exclusion Acts (but set a paltry quota of one hundred Chinese immigrants a year, following the Immigration Act of 1924, which established a minimum quota of one hundred immigrants per year per country). President Roosevelt described the measure "as important in the cause of winning the war and of establishing a secure peace,"[85] and told Congress that Chinese exclusion had been a "historic mistake."[86] Whereas Asians had been since 1917 an undifferentiated mass of people living in a barred zone of immigration, Chinese were now politically and ontologically distinct (especially from Japanese) and had achieved a type of honorary white status as evidenced by their (limited) ability to immigrate and naturalize. In his decision on Mohriez's petition, Judge Wyzanski shows he is aware of this fact. The end of the Mohriez decision reads, "And finally it may not be out of place to say that, as is shown by our recent changes in the laws respecting persons of Chinese nationality and of the yellow race, we as a country have learned that policies of rigid exclusion are not only false to our professions of democratic liberalism *but repugnant to our vital interests as a world power.*"[87] Sometimes politics, and not just personal or cultural prejudice, produces race.

The Armenian State of Exception

The point that I have been making in this chapter is not only the one that Haney Lopez discusses in his book, namely that the law produces race, but also that we need to examine racial formation through law and policy as a rational system of administration and domination rather than as an example of individual prejudice or capriciousness to understand its full impact. Only then can we possibly imagine new political formations that will not be dependent on race as a principle of political domination. Moreover, what special registration proves is that any group can be racialized through America's traditions and then be sent into administrative hell through the bureaucracy of the state (what Hannah Arendt calls "rule by Nobody").[88] Racialization operates through a legal past and enables a legal machinery to provide differential rights, partic-ularly to immigrants, who are the most vulnerable owing, in part, to the plenary power doctrine.[89]

In the case of special registration, we can also witness the bizarre memory of a bureaucracy. American history has long operated through a kind of racial logic that has its own inertia (call it tradi-tion) as well as its own adaptability (call it political expediency), and at times both sides of American race policy will career right into each other. Under special registration, this is precisely what happened. As the cases of *Halladjian* and *Cartozian* illustrated, Ar-menians—as a Christian people who live in the Middle East—were a particular conundrum for the courts. In fact, in *Hassan*, the judge cites the *Cartozian* case in his decision. Judge Tuttle writes, "The court there [in *Cartozian*] found, however, that the Armenians are a Christian people living in an area close to the European border, who have intermingled and intermarried with Europeans over a period of centuries. Evidence was also presented in that case of a considerable amount of intermarriage of Armenian immigrants to the United States with other racial strains in our population. These facts serve to distinguish the case of the Armenians from that of the Arabians."[90] And yet, in a twist that can reveal only the strange pull of history on a bureaucracy, the Justice Department published the list of the third "call-in" group for registration on December 16, 2002. Designating Pakistan and Saudi Arabia as countries whose male citizens would be subject to special registration, the depart-ment also included Armenia on its list. Without comment, Arme-nia was dropped the next day.[91]

Race, Terror, and Bureaucracy

Special registration is not necessarily a nefarious plot to racialize Islam, but it is a bureaucratic and cultural response to political turmoil. This is not to say that religious bigotry no longer exists.

If we consider the words of deputy undersecretary for defense, Lieutenant General William Boykin, who claims that "my God [is] a real God," and a Muslim's God is "an idol," and that the United States must attack radical Islamists "in the name of Jesus,"[92] we find that his statements participate not in racializing Islam but in older traditions of religious prejudice that, sadly, are still with us. Moreover, we should not exonerate special registration from the charge of being a legal method of racial formation, even if it does not subject all Muslims to its procedures and despite the fact that not every Muslim majority country is included on its list. In fact, what special registration accomplishes is the production of a typology of Muslim for the War on Terror, and by defining one type, it colors the whole population. What it produces is a kind of racial anxiety among Muslims, non-Muslims from Muslim countries, and those who are perceived to be Muslim. Every immigrant male in these groups must disidentify from the Muslim-as-terrorist figure, sometimes officially (as with special registration) or unofficially, as political policy and cultural attitudes bleed into each other. Suspicion is coded into law through race.

In fact, like Operation TIPS (Terrorist Information and Prevention System) (which asked us to spy on our neighbors), special registration is best understood as a form of political theater. It allows a new bureaucracy (homeland security) to parade itself as being hard at work. The public is both the cast and the audience in this play. While it is acted out, we are propelled into living in an increasingly militarized and surveyed society. And when government actions impact Muslim populations so visibly, the public understands what is politically acceptable (even if criminally prosecutable) behavior. Meanwhile, the government bureaucracy can mobilize statistics and bodies to prove that it is cleansing the country of a terrorist threat, all at the expense of Muslims in the United States.

What was particularly disheartening, however, was the academic silence around special registration while it proceeded apace.

Without outspoken critique, special registration continued to race Muslims and to bind whiteness in the United States with political exigency and with notions of culture and Christianity. However, as Arendt says, "Neither violence nor power is a natural phenomenon . . . they belong to the political realm of human affairs whose essentially human quality is guaranteed by man's faculty of action, the ability to begin something new."[93] From the beginning of its inception, special registration, in its continuation of this country's past of racial formation and rule through racial ways of thinking, was in fact begging us to begin something new.

PART II

Muslims in Theory

4

Sects and the City

I had almost forgotten I'd sent in an application when the email message appeared, like Mr. Big, out of nowhere and landed in my Inbox. "Hi Moustafa," it began, as if we were old friends. "Thank you for emailing us regarding your interest in working on *Sex and the City 2*."

No way. In August 2009, I half-jokingly answered an email message posted on a listserv requesting "lots of Middle Eastern men and women" as extras for the second *Sex and the City* movie. Although I must have been one of the very few in the Tri-State Area to possess all the talents requested in the email (legal to work, Middle Eastern, and between eighteen and seventy years old), I still never thought I would be selected. Two months later, I got the call.

"The scene we want you to be in shoots next week," read the email message. "The 4 main girls will be in the scene & there will be about 150 Background Performers." Fantastic! Like many men, I pretend to know nothing about *Sex and the City*. (Is it *Sex* in *the City* or *Sex* and *the City*? I've been known to ask, disingenuously.) But who didn't think that Carrie and Mr. Big should have just gotten over it and gotten on with it? Who didn't tear up over Samantha's breast cancer, who didn't pity Miranda for having to move all the way out to Brooklyn, and who hadn't held onto a secret TV crush on Charlotte for years? Really. Who?

The shoot would take two days of ten to twelve hours each, and be full of "all super hot, fashionable, VIP types." The setting was "a Hot Hookah Club/Lounge in the Middle East. Think Dubai, 100+ degrees. Very chic & wealthy International crowd. Socialites, International Businessmen, Professional Athletes, Models, & Diplomats."

The men were to dress "in suits (lightweight, summer fabrics), or shirt/slacks, dress shoes. NO SNEAKERS!" The women "should be in fabulous dresses, skirts/blouse, dressy shorts, sexy tops. Elegant, chic & fashionable. High end designer brands—Gucci, Chloe, Louis Vuitton, Chanel, Balenciaga, DVF, etc (or whatever you own that can pass for designer). Definitely heels (pumps, wedges, open toe, ankle booties). NO FLATS, NO BOOTS!"

I didn't know what Balenciaga was, but I did know that this was all superhot, superfashionable, and superintimidating. I'm a professor. I have a professor's wardrobe. Twelve-year-olds on the subway have more fashion intelligence than I do. What was I going to wear?

While combing through my closet, I rationalized my participation. I was curious to see how *Sex and the City* represent us Arabs. It's not as if this intelligent series usually had much to say about international affairs, Carrie's relationship with Aleksandr Petrovsky notwithstanding. I had a hard time believing that sleeping around was about to turn into *Sleeper Cell* with better footwear. For once maybe Arabs would be portrayed as more than just sinister terrorists or hyperpatriotic Americans, and I was set to be a part of this. But honestly, it was the glamour that drew me in.

When I arrived, I saw that everyone really was beautiful. And the extras weren't all Arabs. There were Russian women with bee-stung lips and push-up bras, and rail-thin Africans with closely cropped hair. One woman wore an outfit that was a huge playing card, while another, an Egyptian woman from New Jersey, was given a dress with a low-cut back and told to wear it backward, giving her this incredibly plunging neckline. Men went into wardrobe wearing business attire but came out in leather outfits and tracksuits. I was sporting my best beige linen suit from, well, H&M. Two people from wardrobe took one long look at me, one cocking his head to the side. "He's fine, I guess. Ex-pat table." That didn't sound good. It sounded off-camera.

The bus to the studio was late, so on this wintry October morning, two hundred extras, primped for the hottest nightclub in the desert, walked three industrial blocks in our stilettos and pointy shoes to the film set in Greenpoint, Brooklyn. We were put into position and told to look as if we were having fun, but not to make a sound or drink our drinks. ("It's called acting!" one of the assistant directors lectured us.) And then the belly dancers were called in.

I know. How can a movie be set in the Middle East without belly dancers? It would be like Bond without the gadgets, or *Gossip Girl* without all the black people (oh, wait). There were also waiters crisscrossing the room in Aladdin-like costumes, an Arab dude doing really bad karaoke, and a group of swarthy men leering lasciviously at the four main characters before sending them drinks. We were directed to cheer loudly (but without making any sound) when the MCs of the nightclub cajoled the *American* girls to perform their own musical number, presumably because the whole world wants to cheer on American girls. And cheer I did, every time, hour after hour, as Carrie, Samantha, Miranda, and Charlotte kept running past me and on stage, one take after another.

The scene was all gyrating midriffs, funny ethnics, and lecherous Mediterraneans. I suppose I was more disappointed than surprised. By one o'clock in the morning, the assistant director called "check the gate," which means that shooting a particular scene has finished and we were done for the night, but to me the words suggested the way the entertainment industry lets some things in and keeps others out. Perhaps I'd reinforced the very stereotypes I hoped I might help diminish.

I got home well after two o'clock, realizing that maybe I was an English professor and not a movie actor after all. The only line going through my head was Conrad's, from *Heart of Darkness*: "The glamour's off!"[1]

It could have been worse. I could've been a Middle Eastern extra on *24*.

5

A Bloody Stupid War

When a war breaks out people say, "It's too stupid; it can't last long." But though a war may well be "too stupid," that doesn't prevent its lasting. Stupidity has a knack of getting its way; as we should see if we were not always so much wrapped up in ourselves.
—Albert Camus, *The Plague*

Early in 1945, a community analyst for the War Relocation Authority, the US government agency responsible for Japanese internment during World War II, published a rather opportunistic, if bizarrely sensitive article in the *Journal of American Folklore* on the poetry of the Tule Lake internment camp. Life in the camps was never normal, and at Tule Lake it was among the most difficult. Hemmed in by "tall, man-proof fences," watched over by armed guards and floodlight towers, fingerprinted and interrogated again and again, camp residents endured a mixture of monotony and terror over their fate. One must imagine that the residents—inmates, really—felt as if they existed somehow outside of both time and space, that they had been jettisoned from history and geography as they waited in their makeshift desert barracks. The article tells us that all the residents except the children were "embittered and disaffected."[1]

Among the many activities of adult camp residents were the poetry clubs, and the authors of the article catalogue the products of the Tule Lake Senryu circle. Senryu is a traditional poetic form similar to haiku and, according to the article, is composed by two people in turn. One of the Tule Lake Senryu poems lamented:

Changeless
In the place of exile
Is the temperature[2]

Today, this sad and lapidary verse reminds us of a regrettable chapter in American history. But it is striking that one can imagine the exact same lines being written today to describe life in another camp, lost somewhere in a land of scorching heat, seemingly outside of both time and place. This camp began operation in January 2002, was built by a subsidiary of the notorious Halliburton Corporation for $9.7 million, and has housed a total of 780 residents, according to analysis by the *New York Times* and National Public Radio, with 122 people remaining in the camp as of January 19, 2015.[3] The captors boast of the fact, as US officials did during Japanese internment, that the residents are permitted to observe their cultural practices. Interrogations are frequent here, and suicide attempts, a grave sin in Islam, are not uncommon. Ocean surrounds the camp, which in turn is encircled by green mesh so that the inmates cannot see the water. Early reports from when the detention facility opened in this incarnation of the War on Terror indicate that cooperation with interrogators was rewarded with handfuls of dates or McDonald's Happy Meals or ice cream sandwiches. At first, most detainees were caged in cells measuring eight by seven feet and let out only twice a week for showers and exercise. Spray-painted on the floor in each cell was an arrow with the information, "MAKKAH 12793 km," indicating the direction of Muslim prayer and constantly reminding the detainees of their exile from their world. Since then, the facility has expanded into a series of smaller prisons and is run at a total annual cost of more than four hundred million dollars.[4] This facility's name is Camp Delta, and it is on the island of Cuba, but it might as well be on Mars.

Indefinitely

Camp Delta, one of several locations where the United States has held those it labeled as "unlawful enemy combatants" in its self-described War on Terror, exemplifies the strange new geographies of empire in the twenty-first century. Although the phrase "enemy combatant" has now entered the journalistic lexicon, it has no precedent in US or international law. Whoever is designated an "enemy combatant" by the executive branch sits in a legal netherworld, the threat of indefinite detention swinging overhead like a sword of Damocles. In fact, a senior Defense Department official stated back in 2004 that the Pentagon was planning on holding a large portion of the detainees at Camp Delta for many years, perhaps indefinitely—a logically consistent position, since the War on Terror, almost by definition, has no foreseeable end.[5]

The camp's Cuban location is significant, not only because of its reverberations with American imperial history, but also because the US government argued that captives housed outside of US territory are not entitled to constitutional protections. In 2004, the Ninth Circuit Court of Appeals disagreed with this position, pointing out that the US exercises "complete jurisdiction and control" over the base at Guantánamo Bay, where the detention facilities were built.[6] If it is not Cuban (they own it but do not run it) and not American (they run it but do not own it), then where in the world is Guantánamo Bay?

The Supreme Court heard arguments about the jurisdictional address of the Camp Delta prisoners in April 2004, and ruled in June 2004 that detainees had the right to petition US courts over their detention. Congress then passed the Detainee Treatment Act in 2005, limiting habeas corpus for detainees. By 2008, the Supreme Court had again ruled that detainees should have the right to challenge their detentions in US courts. A task force in President Obama's Justice Department next issued a report in 2010 saying that around fifty people should be detained indefinitely and without trial (as of January 2015, the number of so-called forever detainees stands at thirty-five). By 2012 the Supreme Court seemed to retreat from its position by refusing to hear appeals in seven habeas petitions filed by prisoners challenging their detentions. The ping-pong game continues. Meanwhile, dozens of detainees linger, day by day and year by year, in their changeless place of exile.

Press reports also indicate that the US government has routinely threatened captives on other battlefronts, as well as suspected "enemy combatants," with indefinite detention (or, sometimes, transfer to Guantánamo Bay) if they did not cooperate sufficiently with American authorities. Coercion and torture have taken place in Iraq, where at one point the United States was holding some thirteen thousand people in the now infamous Abu Ghraib prison without legal recourse. Torture has also been reported at the Bagram Airfield in Afghanistan, where hundreds of others were held. In various terrorism-related prosecutions in the United States, such as in the case known as the Lackawanna Six, the government also threatened indefinite detention.[7] Two US citizens, José Padilla and Yasser Hamdi, also experienced the strange geography of the War on Terror as they sat in a Navy Brig, their legal counsel circumscribed, awaiting verdicts of the Supreme Court. As when the *Hirabayashi*, *Yasui*, and *Korematsu* cases challenged the constitutionality of Japanese internment, the judiciary will continue to delineate the legal boundaries of the prosecution of war, but in this circumstance, as the war drags on for much longer than World War II and Japanese internment, even the Supreme Court doesn't seem up to the task to mark the boundaries between the acceptable and the unacceptable, the permissible and the unthinkable, the smart course of principle and the folly of politics.

The Scale

What is the connection between the painful history of Japanese internment and the machinations of the contemporary War on Terror? The similarities are legion, yet when one considers the examples above, the differences are also very apparent. If, as Edward Said has written, "the task of criticism is to make distinctions, to produce differences, where at present there are none,"[8] then the critic's other obligation must surely be to connect disparate moments through their affinities in order to understand the historically constituted nature of power.

Japanese internment affected close to 120,000 people, over 70,000 of them American-born citizens. (Those who were not American-born were not eligible for citizenship, owing to the naturalization laws of the time, which excluded Asians.) Of course, the scale of liberties lost to internment during the War on Terror is much lower. Internment of Japanese and Japanese Americans sent an entire civilian population to prison, though they were innocent of any crime. The bald truth of the contemporary confinements is that, without competent systems of adjudication, we have no way of knowing how many innocent civilians are being held captive. Anecdotal evidence, however, suggests from the beginning that many of the Guantánamo detainees were hardly the "most dangerous, best trained, vicious killers on the face of the earth," as Defense Secretary Donald Rumsfeld described them.[9] In February 2004, the United States repatriated three Camp Delta residents who ranged from thirteen to fifteen years of age. In fact, there have been fifteen minors held at Guantánamo since the War on Terror began. Earlier repatriations have included a 78-year-old deaf man who couldn't understand his interrogation, a taciturn 105-year-old man, several kidnapped taxi drivers, confused farmers, and a man with so serious a head wound he was known to his captors as Half-

Head Bob. Of the 780 men held, fewer than 4 percent have faced or will face some kind of formal charge.[10]

Other comparisons between Japanese internment and the contemporary war find more common ground, but not true symmetry. Hundreds of thousands of lives were disrupted by Japanese internment, due to not only the loss of liberty, but also bank seizures, lost homes, assailed dignity, and other costs that are difficult to measure. Outside US borders, such disruption is almost impossible to quantify. But in the domestic sphere, the Council on American Islamic Relations has stated already in 2002 that US government actions against Muslims had affected the lives of over sixty thousand people.[11] Dozens of Muslim charities have had their assets seized or are under investigation, and money transfers from the United States to the Middle East and Africa have become extraordinarily burdensome. Muslims in the United States have threatened to sue Western Union for discriminatory practices; in several documented instances, the company refused to wire money for people with Muslim-sounding names, reportedly out of fear of prosecution under the Patriot Act. According to the New York magazine *City Limits*, American Express had been arbitrarily canceling the accounts of American Muslims for the same reason.[12]

By far the biggest difference between Japanese internment and the contemporary War on Terror is that, out of racist fears and vengeance, Japanese internment uprooted and denied due process to people who were US citizens. As historian Peter Irons has shown, the War Department promoted the fears even when it knew them to be groundless.[13] Irons documents the astonishing deception and suppression of evidence practiced by the War Department and the Justice Department, and illustrates the degree to which the Supreme Court itself deliberately misconstrued the arguments before it in order to render a judgment on internment in favor of the executive branch. "The war power of the national government is 'the power to wage war successfully,'" reads the *Hirabayashi* decision (quoting Charles Evan Hughes, a justice during the interwar period).[14] According to Irons, Chief Justice Harlan Fiske Stone was intent on achieving this outcome, regardless of the cost to Japanese Americans or the Constitution or the idea of citizenship itself.[15] The Court even argued, through twisted logic of its own, that people of Japanese descent could reasonably be thought to be disloyal since they had suffered so much discrimination throughout American history, which had only "intensified their solidarity and . . . prevented their assimilation as an integral part of the white population."[16] Intern them we must, the Court was saying, because historically they are our victims.

Neither questions of loyalty nor intimations of internment are absent from contemporary discussions surrounding the War on Terror. In February 2004, after hearing Muslims criticize the imbalance in US foreign policy, New York Congressman Peter King claimed that "85 percent of the mosques have extremist leadership in this country," and that "most Muslims, the overwhelming majority of Muslims, are loyal Americans, but they seem unwilling to come forward [to cooperate with law enforcement]."[17] Similarly, less than a year after the September 11, 2001, attacks, Peter Kirsanow, a civil rights commissioner appointed by George W. Bush, inflamed opinion in a community he had been contracted to defend when he stated that "if there's another terrorist attack and if it's from a certain ethnic community or certain ethnicities that the terrorists are from, you can forget about civil rights in this country." Kirsanow added that such an attack could lead to internment camps, quipping, "Not too many people will be crying in their beer if there are more detentions, more stops, more profiling. There will be a groundswell of public opinion to banish civil rights."[18] The quasi-official provenance of such ideas, and the frequency with which they circulate, is troubling indeed. As the Israeli historian

Tom Segev wrote of talk of "transfer" of Palestinians, "There are ideas that should have black flags over them."[19]

More than a dozen years into the War on Terror, only a handful of American citizens have lost their liberty and been denied the right to defend themselves. A replica of the recognized error of World War II internment is difficult—though not impossible—to imagine. Yet this is not to say that citizenship rights have been bravely respected. If, during the years of Japanese internment, the government abandoned defense of the rights of American citizens, today the United States feels empowered to abandon the rights of everyone else.

Collapsing Citizenship

Consider the immigrant population. After the September 11 attacks, more than five thousand immigrants were rounded up by early law enforcement sweeps in a systematic effort of selective prosecution. One man, Benemar Benatta, was held for a total of 1,780 days.[20] Although the charges against these people were minor civil violations, they were often brutalized in detention—beaten frequently, deprived of sleep and medical care, forced to eat pork—to the point that even the Justice Department's internal auditor published a two-hundred-page report criticizing the inhumane treatment.[21]

Next came special registration, a Justice Department initiative that juridically turned Islam into a racial category. (See Chapter 3 for a discussion on special registration.) Special registration required all visa-holding men from twenty-five Muslim countries (and North Korea) to undergo an onerous ordeal of fingerprinting, interviewing, and photographing upon entry and exit. Complying with the program meant that over 13,800 men with visa problems faced perhaps the largest mass deportation in American history, even though large numbers of them had lived in the country for years, had applied lawfully for adjustment of status, and have

American-born children. Their lives and their families' lives were ripped asunder by the fallout of September 11. The sweeps and programs of the government effected a removal of Muslim men from the United States based on the sole fact that they came, at some point in their lives, from Muslim countries.[22]

Soon after special registration began, registration of dual nationals became commonplace, and it sparked a minor international incident. Canada issued a rare travel advisory for its citizens visiting the United States, since the US government was discriminating between types of Canadian nationality.[23] The United States offered Canada assurances that dual citizenship would not "automatically" trigger special registration and Canada withdrew its advisory. Canadian citizens who are nationals from the listed countries, however, continued to complain that birthplace was triggering registration automatically.[24] One case, the traumatic story of Maher Arar, is particularly noteworthy. This Canadian citizen landed in the United States in transit on his way home to Canada, whereupon the US government detained him and shipped him to Syria, his birthplace, where he endured months of torture, presumably at the request of US officials.[25] Canadians were livid over the Arar case, which proved to them that, US assurances notwithstanding, citizenship does not matter. Only descent counts.

Nowhere from Anywhere

One must look closely at the aggregate effects of these programs, combined with the geographic spaces where they occur, in order to discern what is going on. We should consider special registration through the emptiness of the airport interrogation room, see the weightlessness of the Navy Brig holding Hamdi and Padilla, examine the bureaucratic moonscape of the Bagram Airfield in Afghanistan, and peer through the chain-link cages at the occupied tip of an embargoed Caribbean island. None of these places exist in any meaningful sense of the word. They are empty spaces, because they have become administrative dumping grounds for superfluous bodies in the government's prosecution of its war. Outside of time and space, yet regulated like a prison, these are not the ends of the earth but more like floating penal colonies for the uncondemned (for even the condemned get a hearing where they are condemned). In these places, there is no means of challenging one's fate. Rights have evaporated like a kettle whistling itself dry.

Japanese internment and the War on Terror teach us that citizenship and place are inextricably linked, and when the place is nowhere, the person has been expelled not just from a nation but in a sense from humanity itself. We are perhaps accustomed to thinking about citizenship largely as a marker of identity, as proof of belonging that manifests itself in demands for inclusion in the narrative of history, say, or in the literary canon. There is no doubt of the importance of such enterprises, but something is lost if we consider citizenship as an entry permit into the nation. Citizenship is not just an identity marker. It is a legal condition—and not just any legal condition. Citizenship, in Hannah Arendt's memorable phrase, is the "right to have rights." For better or worse, our human rights are premised on us having a nation, a territory, a place to make laws and lives, and citizenship is the mechanism by which we can claim being grounded in the world.

Yet again and again, the government declares that citizenship is essentially worthless. In the case of Japanese internment, the consequence was a loss of home and geography. The desert locations of internment, nowhere from anywhere, were not chosen capriciously but were dictated by the logic of a policy of expulsion. The camp is the necessary consequence of the loss of citizenship and the nation because displacement is a necessary consequence of the loss of citizenship. Similarly, Palestinians are a people without rights because they are a people without land, for occupied land too is displaced land, displaced from the functioning of law and the concept of human rights.

When one considers the Japanese internment camps of World War II or Camp Delta on Guantánamo Bay, one cannot escape the disastrous fact that the US government has derogated the guarantees of citizenship with unabashed contempt, and it has effected this policy through a removal of geography from the human world. No one understood this better than Arendt, who in *The Origins of Totalitarianism* connected the idea of human rights, land, and citizenship with extraordinary acumen:

> The fundamental deprivation of human rights is manifested first and above all in the deprivation of a place in the world. . . . We became aware of the existence of a right to have rights (and that means to live in a framework where one is judged by one's actions and opinion) and a right to belong to some kind of organized community, only when millions of people emerged who had lost and could not regain these rights because of the new global political situation. The trouble is that this calamity arose not from any lack of civilization, backwardness or mere tyranny, but on the contrary, that it could not be repaired, because there was no longer any "uncivilized" spot on earth, because whether we like it or not we have really started to live in One World. Only with a completely organized humanity could the loss of home and political status become identical with expulsion from humanity altogether.[26]

Point of Indistinction

If the location of Camp Delta tells us something about the new geography of the US empire, its purpose reveals something about the empire's production of knowledge. Under the Bush administration, the stated rationale for housing inmates at Guantánamo was twofold: security and intelligence gathering. Facing the April

2004 Supreme Court date, the administration began advertising the merits of its penal colony by underlining its intelligence value in particular. A March 21 article in the *New York Times*, titled "Guantánamo Detainees Deliver Intelligence Gains," was oriented expressly around this idea. Steve Rodriguez, the overseer of Guantánamo interrogations, is quoted explaining how, even if the detainees were flown to Cuba in 2002, authorities can still extract valuable information from them. "I thought that when I first came here, there would be little to gain," says Rodriguez. "But when they talk about what happens in certain operational theaters, the locations of certain pathways, that information doesn't perish."[27]

One ought to pause on this remarkable little phrase—information doesn't perish. This is the kind of phrase that one can venerate, that renders an attitude, and here the orientation revealed is nothing less than the ability of power to force itself to life at the expense of the living. Victory in a potentially never-ending war assumes a relationship of power to the production of knowledge where wisdom has fallen into intelligence and knowledge has lapsed into information. With this phrase, something more than the lives of the detainees is being slowly destroyed.

"The most radical and only secure form of possession is destruction, for only what we have destroyed is safely and forever ours," writes Arendt in *The Origins of Totalitarianism*.[28] Although this insight may seem counterintuitive, one can easily make sense of it by considering how, in the War on Terror, people may die but "information doesn't perish." What is being possessed through destruction today is not Iraq or Afghanistan but the whole international order. In other words, the stakes are not the blatant violation of the Geneva Conventions, but the ability of the all-powerful to claim sovereign exception to the rules, and, thereby, possess the right to determine the rules. The United States takes possession of the law by destroying it.

Guantánamo Bay may be cut off from the world, but it is hardly shrouded in secrecy. In fact, there is ample evidence that while Camp Delta houses those captives the US government considers least worthwhile, the higher "intelligence value" subjects have often been stashed away in more remote climes such as the island of Diego Garcia, the military base in Kandahar, or various undisclosed locations across the globe.[29] Guantánamo may have been a ruse of sorts, diverting attention from the even more heinous detentions and interrogations being carried out elsewhere and in hidden sections of Guantánamo, a point confirmed by the Senate Select Committee on Intelligence's report on the CIA's detention and interrogation program.[30] But what does it mean when the ruse itself is nothing short of a gross exception to customary and agreed upon standards of behavior among nations and peoples? Such imperious behavior on the part of the United States betrays a logic of sovereignty where the sovereign, as Giorgio Agamben argues, "is the point of indistinction between violence and the law, the threshold on which violence passes over into law and law passes into violence."[31]

Here is a kind of creative destruction not captured by Joseph Schumpeter's pioneering use of the phrase as an inexorable condition of dynamic capitalism. By destroying the international system of laws and nations, and placing itself as the true sovereign outside of the order because of its power to force its exceptional quality, the United States has rendered brute power into the most important meaning-producing activity in the world. This fact alone has implications for the empire and the production of knowledge.

Regimes of Truth

Ever since Edward Said's groundbreaking study *Orientalism*, we have become accustomed to considering the relationship between conquest and knowledge through a Foucauldian lens of power.

The production of knowledge, Said argues, is never an innocent or timeless enterprise but is always located somewhere in the world and carries with it worldly consequences. "The nexus of knowledge and power creating the 'Oriental,'" Said writes about Orientalism, "in a sense obliterated him as a human being." Orientalism, as a discourse, "is produced and exists in an uneven exchange with various kinds of power."[32]

One can argue over whether Said totalizes the entire enterprise of knowledge of the other, or if he correctly identifies the coercive tendency of knowledge in power to treat its subject as a "commodity" and not an "interlocutor."[33] Yet despite one's inclination, the pivot upon which the argument turns is a Foucauldian formulation of knowledge and power that we have thoroughly assimilated into notions about the production of knowledge. "We should admit," writes Foucault, "that power produces knowledge (and not simply by encouraging it because it serves power or by applying it because it is useful); that power and knowledge directly imply one another; that there is no power relation without the correlative constitution of a field of knowledge, nor any knowledge that does not presuppose and constitute at the same time power relations."[34] Said's use of Foucault's model has served as a critique for area studies for a generation. But during the current War on Terror, perhaps there is an entirely different "regime of truth" operating. The knowledge produced out of Orientalism, according to Said, was partisan and racist, it was produced from a position of superiority and facilitated conquest, but it was still driven by a certain will to knowledge, regardless. Thus, Said can elaborate upon the high-handed and colonial assumptions behind the work of earlier Orientalists, people like H.A.R. Gibb and Louis Massignon, while still pointing to their "erudition" and "extraordinary achievements."[35] In Said's narrative, American study of the Arab Middle East has historically been far less impressive than its European counterpart. However, the contemporary "regime of truth," begun and directly promoted by the

Bush administration, must be seen as sinking even lower than the field characterized by Said in 1978. This decline is not accidental or de-evolutionary. Rather, it is constitutive of the contemporary configuration of power's relationship to knowledge, for what we are currently living is likely the overcoming of (or attempts to overcome) Foucault's power/knowledge paradigm. Until now, a will to knowledge enabled power and that power produced more opportunities for knowledge. Currently, we are witnessing the birth of a pure and simple will to power, without the burden of knowledge, and where more knowledge just creates more complications.

Regime of Stupidity

In other words, perhaps it is time to admit that the War on Terror is not just a stupid war. It is a war designed to make us stupid. How much real inquiry into our present condition, for example, has been stymied by the mesmerizing quality of the word "terrorism"? As international law expert John Whitbeck has argued, the whole world has become "ensnared by a word"—a word that, in Bush's language certainly, but not his alone, "explain[s] and justifie[s] everything, past, present and future."[36] There have been numbly ideological elements within every administration and behind the prosecution of any war, and anti-intellectualism has a long history in the United States, but at no point in history has global political rhetoric been entirely oriented around a single word that has been so emptied of content, its only substance being a shadow on the wall in the figure of a bearded Muslim man with eyes of burning rage. Such stupidity, furthermore, extends beyond the obvious locations of the White House and the media sphere.

Consider how the Coalition Provisional Authority (CPA), the early civilian wing of the American occupation in Iraq, had only sixteen Arabic speakers among the sixteen hundred Americans on its payroll as of June 2003.[37] Such facts are not just mistakes or oversights; they should be seen within a structure of meaning where the remaking of the Middle East has nothing to do with the history or aspirations of the region's peoples, and everything to do with the region's political and economic domination by the United States. Similarly, one could examine the vaunted Iraqi "interim constitution" signed on March 8, 2004, not at the level of its political arrangements, but simply for its rhetorical imagination. Arabic lends itself well to grandiloquence, but the Transitional Administrative Law, in its lumbering and pedestrian prose, seems immediately foreign, bureaucratic, and imposed.

If the Global War on Terror is in fact designed to make us stupid, then the stupidity is fueled by abandonment of the belief that knowledge is power and power produces knowledge. Instead, the current regime of truth, propelled by its own world historical mission, seems to believe in the brutishly simple idea that power is knowledge. Power, when sufficiently supreme, can impose its own realities. So Arabic speakers become almost unnecessary, except for intelligence gathering. With its unrivaled ability to refashion and create, the United States needs only to legislate by decree, and the only specialists required are the experts not of the colonized but of the colonizer, those who study the arrangements of royal power. Napoleon's savants accompanying him on the conquest of the new Egypt are not Denon and his ilk but specialists in American law, brigades of computer aces for complex military hardware, and an army corps of public relations engineers. After all, in a world where "information doesn't perish," history becomes useless.

Out of Sync

Other initiatives launched during the War on Terror stress the uncomfortable fact of the purposeful stupidity in the War on Terror. The International Studies in Higher Education Act of 2003, which was passed by the House of Representatives in October but not by the Senate, sought to reauthorize five years of funding for international area studies centers (known as Title VI centers). But the funds came with strings attached. The bill required international studies programs in US universities to undergo political monitoring by a committee appointed by Congress and demanded, among others things, that Title VI centers provide government recruiters (including intelligence agencies) with full access to their students, and that the secretary of education initiate a study to scrutinize "foreign language heritage communities" in the United States in the interest of national security. The bill, at bottom, sought to dumb down scholarship by policing it for adequate patriotism. Meanwhile, it promoted the conversion of as much Title VI–produced knowledge as possible directly into intelligence.[38]

Behind this act were right-wing pundits, namely Stanley Kurtz, Daniel Pipes, Martin Kramer, and David Horowitz, who energetically seek to silence views on Israel that oppose their own. As with the precedent of the McCarthy hearings prompting anticommunist purges at universities, scholarship about the Middle East is put under the direct gaze of lawmakers. More than intimidation, however, the mechanisms behind this attack lower the level of political analysis to a Manichean simplicity of either you are with "us" or you are with the "terrorists." Partisan knowledge that props up the United States and Israel lies on one side of the divide. Everything else is rubbish. The International Studies in Higher Education Act attempted not only to legislate away dissent, but to induce scholars of the Middle East to internalize this particular regime of stupidity.

Similarly, in 2004 the Ford and Rockefeller Foundations added to their grant agreements "antiterrorism clauses" so imprecise that universities could have lost foundation support simply for sponsoring a lecture on the life of Nelson Mandela or showing a film about the Weathermen. Ford's grant agreements stated that the foundation would withdraw funding if university expenditures promoted "violence, terrorism, bigotry or the destruction of any state," while the Rockefeller Foundation demanded that grantees not "directly or indirectly engage in, promote or support other organizations or individuals who engage in or promote terrorist activity." Predictably, objections over foundation support for Palestinian organizations precipitated the Ford Foundation's rewrite of its grant agreements. Nine elite universities—including Harvard, Yale, Princeton, and Columbia—protested the clauses by writing letters of objection to the foundations, claiming the new language would "run up against the basic principles of protected speech on our campuses."[39] Sadly, even our legendary foundations don't seem immune to the manufactured stupidity of the War on Terror.

Nor is the stupidity limited to educational institutions. The Bush administration began in February 2004 to promote a vague Greater Middle Eastern Initiative (GMEI), which was supposed to exhibit a newfound US commitment to the political and social development of the region.[40] But from the beginning, the GMEI ran into a wall. Like the State Department's Middle Eastern Partnership Initiative (MEPI), the GMEI seemed to be based primarily on two documents published by the United Nations, the Arab Human Development Reports of 2002 and 2003. Whatever their merits, these documents were compromised since their conclusions could not venture into two realms: criticism of individual Arab states and criticism of Israel. GMEI is organized around the pillars of democracy, knowledge, and women's empowerment. (MEPI is organized around four issues: democracy, education, women, and economics.) No one would argue that advances in all three areas are not needed in the region, but the GMEI suffered from its own stubborn insistence on ignoring the fundamental place that the Palestinian issue holds in the Arab world. The initiative called on countries in its regional purview—the Arab states, Turkey, Pakistan and Afghanistan—to adopt major economic and political reforms. In exchange, the states would receive greater cooperation from the West in terms of increased aid, security arrangements, and access to the

World Trade Organization.[41] As the *Village Voice* put it, the initiative "was conceived as a security document, not a developmental road map"; its blindness to the Palestinian issue was regarded in the Arab world as "demeaning and insulting."[42]

Even Zbigniew Brzezinski, President Jimmy Carter's national security advisor, seemed at wit's end over this initiative, calling it "out of sync with regional realities."[43] Brzezinski quoted Dick Cheney as saying that the spread of democracy was "the precondition for peace and stability," and then described how Cheney's position "appeared to many to be a rationalization for postponing any effort to resolve the Israeli-Palestinian conflict. Moreover, it ignored the historical reality that democracy can flourish only in an atmosphere of political dignity. As long as the Palestinians live under Israeli control and are humiliated daily, they will not be attracted by the virtues of democracy. The same is largely true of the Iraqis under the American occupation." The GMEI was viewed by many Arabs as prescribing a willful forgetting of their Palestinian brethren—in exchange for a promised massage by the hands of imperial power. None of these objections mattered to the Bush administration. They mattered even less to the Israeli government, which continued to impose its will on the Palestinians regardless of their livelihoods, future, or historical claims. The US administration's language was muted and gentler, but the GMEI illustrated how the Bush administration shared with the Sharon government the inability to entertain opposing views, the notion of absolute power usurping the need for (even colonial) knowledge of the other, and the belief that turning the world stupid will cement the success of their designs. What should be apparent now is the urgent need for a lasting resolution to the Palestinian question that is driven by recognizing their dispossession and by righting it justly. Such a resolution would obviously have had an immeasurably greater regional impact than the Bush administration's chosen tack of forcibly producing a compliant Iraqi nation.

Surely, imagination—and not stupidity—can be marshaled to guarantee rights for two peoples, Jewish and Palestinian Arab, whose histories and futures are fully intertwined. Separation, by barriers or borders, is not a dream, but an unworkable nightmare. In 1968, everyone involved in the conflict knew that the solution to the Palestinian question was an independent Palestinian state because the facts on the ground supported it. Today, considering the deep penetration of Jewish settlement in the West Bank, the persistent cantonment of the Palestinians and the continual dispossession of Palestinian Arabs, including those inside Israel, from land and livelihoods, perhaps the best human answer for the conflict lies in the creation of a binational state organized around equality in citizenship with protections of communal and confessional rights. Arab life in general cannot improve without justice for the Palestinians. With justice for the Palestinians, Jewish culture—a great and largely unrecognized loss for Arab and Muslim civilization—could be reintegrated into the region. But such arguments can scarcely be made in most American venues, out of a willful disavowal of wisdom. Dependency on Israeli and US visions for the region has turned us stupid.

Midair Suspension

Despite the madness of floating geographies and blind knowledge, there is cause for optimism, if only for the simple fact that we can refuse to be made stupid. There is a standing imperative for all those who can to expose the inanity of waging war on nouns and the cupidity of pauperizing one of the potentially richest nations on earth. Now, so completely out of the earshot of power, ideas and conscience have the opportunity to emancipate themselves from the status quo. Ideas and conscience must become more directly oppositional and political, not only out of respect for wisdom or a moral obligation, but because the imperial projects of the twenty-first century simply will not work. It is time for US and Israeli governments to recognize that, regardless of descent or faith, all peoples harbor within them that persistent itch to determine their own destiny. The flowers and candy American soldiers were told to expect on the streets of Iraq became improvised explosive devices and rocket propelled grenades. The US imperial hand is stretched beyond its reach, and world missions based on the belief that brute power "is" and everything else "is not" do not merely offend our notions of knowledge. They injure our sense of being human.

Goha, the inveterate fool and trickster of Arab folklore, has an instructive tale about stupidity. One day, Goha was arrested for a minor crime. Paraded in front of the judges, he sat and waited for them to determine his fate. The judges, in all their wisdom, decided that the poor man was simply too stupid to live, and they sentenced him to death by hanging. Goha was taken to the death chamber where he met his executioner, while the judges took their seats in the gallery. The rope was slung around Goha's neck and the executioner pulled the trapdoor lever. But instead of dying, Goha began to flail about as if he had something important to say. The executioner looked to the judges, who nodded to the executioner, and he slowly lowered Goha from midair suspension. As soon as his feet touched the ground, Goha screamed at the executioner. "You idiot!" he yelled. "I almost died up there!"

Today, the judges have charged themselves with a world historical mission. For it to succeed, they must enforce a global regime of stupidity. More than ever before, we cannot afford to be left hanging.

6

The God That Failed

The Neo-Orientalism of Today's Muslim Commentators

Thirty years ago, Edward Said published *Orientalism*, the highly influential study challenging the authority of Western representations of the "Orient" through the twin prisms of knowledge and power. Said identified Orientalism as a type of discourse which possesses "a will or intention to understand" what was non-European, and "in some cases to control and manipulate what was manifestly different."[1] The study of the Orient, moreover, did not operate as an innocent intellectual pursuit but functioned as a handmaiden to empire. The Orientalist always spoke for the Orient and in so doing developed a style for "dominating, restructuring, and having authority" over both an object of study and a region of the world.[2]

The Orientalist, according to Said, was a sort of translator—often literally so—of the Orient to the Occident but was always translating one culture for another from the detached perspective of a learned Westerner. This distance endowed the Orientalist with his or her "flexible positional superiority,"[3] so that "the relation between the Orientalist and Orient was essentially hermeneutical: standing before a distant, barely intelligible civilization or cultural monument, the Orientalist scholar reduced the obscurity by translating, sympathetically portraying, inwardly grasping the hard-to-reach object. Yet the Orientalist remained outside the Orient, which, however much it was made to appear intelligible, remained beyond the Occident."[4] It is this distance—in part physical, but more fundamentally ontological—that preserved the essential framework of an "us" and a "them." As we shall see, distance becomes more difficult to maintain in a globalizing age.

Said also shows us how, in the Orientalist canon, "Islam" accounts for the sum total of any Muslim's experience. From Islam comes everything and to Islam goes everything, and Orientalism's aim is to drive this point home with a repeated and relentless monotony. "It is evident that anything is possible to the Oriental," writes British Orientalist Duncan Macdonald, because the "supernatural is so near that it may touch him at any moment."[5] Thus, a recurring theme in Orientalist work is that "Islam" is the regulator of life and "from top to bottom,"[6] a motif Said characterizes as not just intellectually lazy but a model of intellectual production that would be inapplicable to the serious study of Western culture. There the humanities and social science engage in "complex theories, enormously variegated analyses of social structures, histories, cultural foundations, and sophisticated languages of investigation,"[7] but none of that is found in the Orientalist world of "Islam." In short, it is not politics that produces (varieties of) Islam in history. Instead, "Islam" produces politics.

It is almost facile to point out that Orientalism, like imperialism, never seems to go out of style. In fact, in the age of terror, it has reemerged with a vengeance. *New York Times* correspondents such as Robert Worth prepare themselves for war reporting in Iraq by reading the old Orientalist Bernard Lewis,[8] who himself has had virtually unparalleled access to the corridors of power in the Bush era. The old trope of "Islamic imperialism" is resuscitated in Efraim Karsh's book by the same name. *The Arab Mind*, trash scholarship from a generation ago, is dusted off, reissued, and sent into wide circulation in the US military; it was cited in a September 2, 2007, report in the *New York Times* as a reference book in the library of a counterinsurgency colonel in Iraq.[9]

But there is a (somewhat) new twist on an old doctrine, and it is worth paying it some attention. Today, contemporary multiculturalism melds with old-style Orientalism in the writings of Ayaan Hirsi Ali, Irshad Manji, and Reza Aslan, three commentators who self-describe either as Muslim (Aslan), ex-Muslim (Hirsi), or barely Muslim (Manji). Each also claims to reveal the true nature of Islam to Western audiences, promising an insider message of telling it to you like it is! (Hint: everything Muslims do *is* motivated by Islam.) The fact that these explainers are themselves Western Muslims in some sense collapses the Orientalist distance between East and West; in other senses it does not, for there would be no need for explainers if there were no wide differences between peoples.

Ayan Hirsi Ali was born in war-torn Somalia, which she fled as a child, eventually winning asylum in the Netherlands, where she later rose to prominence as a legislator known for her anti-immigrant views. She is the author of several works, including the screenplay for *Submission*, a short film about the treatment of women in Islam by Theo van Gogh (for which she provided the voiceover narration and for which van Gogh would later be assassinated by Mohammed Bouyeri). She has written several books, including a collection of essays called *The Caged Virgin: An Emancipation Proclamation for Women and Islam*, and an autobiography titled *Infidel*. After questions arose regarding the truthfulness of her statements regarding her own immigration petition, Hirsi Ali left the Netherlands and relocated to the United States. She quickly received permanent residency, which was announced by the US government through a press release (hardly a common practice, to say the least), and she began working at the American Enterprise Institute, a conservative think tank. Irshad Manji was born in Uganda under Idi Amin's tyrannical rule. She and her family fled the East African dictatorship when she was four years old, settling in Vancouver, Canada, where she was raised. Manji is the author of *The Trouble with Islam: A Muslim's Call for Reform in Her Faith*, repackaged as *The Trouble with Islam Today* for the paperback version. Reza Aslan was born in Iran in 1972. He and his family left Iran after the revolution in 1979, when he was about seven years old, settling in the United States. Aslan is the author of *No god but God: The Origins, Evolution, and Future of Islam.*

The very existence of these explainers indicates the substantial presence of Muslims in the West, and each of their books either implicitly or explicitly raises the specter of misguided or dangerous Muslims living in our midst. The force of their message in other words is a mission: "Islam" can (or will naturally) be converted from its current treachery into a benign and more palatable force for the Western world. I offer that this is simply a ridiculous message, and that to focus on "Islam" is to entertain a distraction that takes us away from attending to the many serious political issues of our time.

Scholars may have little use for the autobiographical musings of Hirsi Ali or the puerile polemics of Manji. Nevertheless, the fact remains that Manji, Hirsi Ali, and Aslan have become some of today's most prominent explainers of "Islam." According to a search on BookScan (performed on October 5, 2007), Hirsi Ali's book *Infidel* has sold more than 120,000 copies in hardcover. Manji has sold more than 60,000 total copies of *The Trouble with Islam*, and Aslan's *No god but God* comes in at over 70,000 sales. Moreover, each author is accorded significant media exposure and is credentialed by various institutions and think tanks of higher learning and the power elite, from Yale University (where Manji was a fellow) to the conservative American Enterprise Institute (where Hirsi Ali is a fellow) to CBS News (where Aslan was a consultant). There should be no question that their influence is significant. Their offerings about "Islam," however, raise doubts, for these are the kind of explanations that demand explanation.

The idea of Orientals talking to Western audiences in a Western medium has its predecessors; Fouad Ajami, the Lebanese American historian, chronicler of Arab failures, and close confidant of several members of the Bush administration, immediately comes to mind. According to Adam Shatz, a contributing editor at the *London Review of Books*, "Ajami's unique role in American political life has been to unpack the unfathomable mysteries of the Arab and Muslim world and to help sell America's wars in the region."[10] But, in the cases of Hirsi Ali and Manji, who compose narratives centered on their own religious experiences, one could page back to the conversion narratives found in early editions of the *Muslim World*, a journal that began publishing in 1911, for precursors. There we find such narratives by Muslims as "How Christ Won My Heart," written by "an Indian Convert" in Lahore. We can read "A Mohammedan Imam's Discovery of Christ," published in 1916, or "The Story of My Conversion," written by one J. A. Bakhsh in 1926. These brief stories narrate the struggle to proclaim one's belief in Christ in the face of Muslim obscurantism in the Muslim world, and they come with all the good news that the Gospel is spreading in Muslim territory. Comparing these essays with Hirsi Ali's and Manji's texts holds insofar as both sets of narratives describe the fundamentally closed world of Islam, but the similarity basically ends there. For one thing, the distance between the Muslim and Christian worlds is still fundamentally alive in the old narratives, as one or two converts along the missionary way may bode well for the power of the Gospel, but do not reveal a fully formed social movement. Moreover, the early narratives are essentially about the righteousness of Christianity in the world. Today's Muslim commentators speak from their authority as Muslims to talk not about the glories of Christianity but about the failings of Islam.

And the failures are many. Hirsi Ali, Manji, and Aslan all point to a clearly articulated set of problems that can be summarized as follows: "Islam" is or has become a totalizing system that lags behind the wheel of progress, defies individuality, and blindly oppresses its followers. What differs among them is how this happened, when it happened, and if there is any opportunity to emancipate Islam from itself.

Manji and Aslan take on the old cliché of "the closing of the gates of ijtihad." Ijtihad, of course, refers to the Islamic juridical principle of independent reasoning within religious law. Ijtihad has a long history within Islam and Islamic jurisprudence, and many commentators (Manji and Aslan among them) have argued that the practice of ijtihad was essentially snuffed out in the ninth or tenth century CE. This idea is commonly referred to as "the closing of the gates of ijtihad" in favor of irrational obedience to religious authority, and this closed door, in Manji and Aslan's hands, explains the current intellectual, moral, and political stultification of "Islam." Aslan, for example, writes that "the Traditionalist Ulama, who at that time dominated nearly all the major schools of law, outlawed [ijtihad] as a legitimate tool of exegesis . . . signal[ing] the beginning of the end for those who held that religious truth . . . could be discovered through human reason."[11] Manji, too, notes that "Baghdad oversaw the closing of the . . . gates of ijtihad and therefore the tradition of independent thought," which led to a "freez[ing] of debate within Islam" so that "we in the twenty-first century live with the consequences of this thousand-year-old strategy to keep the [Islamic] empire from imploding."[12]

Furthermore, all three commentators—Manji, Aslan, and Hirsi Ali—point to the problems of hadith transmission (the system by which the sayings of the Prophet Muhammad are passed down through the ages) to argue that Islam has been forever beset by human fallibility, and the Ulama have been able to manipulate their believers into what modern science can now reveal as blind systems of oppression.

The problem with drawing attention to the inherent limitations of hadith transmission and the closure of the gates of ijtihad, two common preoccupations among many Orientalist schools, is that they are both nonissues. In 1984, Wael B. Hallaq asked "Was the gate of ijtihad closed?" in an important article with that query as its title, answering that "a systematic and chronological study of the original legal sources reveals that these views on the history of ijtihad after the second/eighth century are entirely baseless and inaccurate."[13] (Many others who read inside the tradition, from Albert Hourani to Said Ramadan, reach the same conclusions.) Hallaq composed another retort to the perennial issue of hadith transmission in another essay, "The Authenticity of Prophetic *Hâdith*: A Pseudo-Problem." In brief, Hallaq here argues that since the science of hadith, a pursuit within Islamic jurisprudence, contains within it the means to adjudicate "strong" from "weak" *ahadith*, the Western discovery of hadith forgery is largely, in his word "pointless."

We can make a point, however, by noticing the reliance of these contemporary travelers in Islam on such explanations. Manji's and Aslan's texts go to considerable lengths to pinpoint a period of Islamic glory (for Aslan, it is the period of the Prophet; for Manji it is al-Andalus—Islamic Spain) in counterpoint to today's distress. Hirsi Ali, on the other hand, ultimately finds nothing redeemable in Islam but argues that Muslims "don't have to take six hundred years to go through a reformation" and need to "examine [their faith] critically, and to think about the degree to which that faith is itself at the root of oppression."[14] All three are invested, in other words, in drawing a singular narrative account of Islam, where the faith is both a singular system and a singular force in the world, and they rely on the production of a Grand Narrative to achieve their goals. But if poststructuralism has taught us anything it should be skepticism of all Grand Narratives, since Grand Narratives by design are propelled by such singular causes and effects that move their story forward in world historical time.

In fact, many Salafi literalists—those who reject the major schools of Islamic law and instead argue for a direct reading of the Qur'an and sunnah (the sayings and actions of the Prophet Muhammad)—operate similarly, though out of opposite social circumstances. In *Islam: The Religion of the Future*, for example, the

Egyptian Islamist Sayyid Qutb offers a world historical narrative about the rise and fall of civilizations due to religion and human nature. After describing the rise and fall of capitalism and communist society, Qutb writes, "All these [capitalist and communist] civilizations were cut off from the original source without which social orders, principles and values cannot survive: the source of belief issuing from God which gives comprehensive interpretation to existence, to the status of man and his objectives on earth. Hence, they [the Euro-American] were basically temporary civilizations, without roots attached to the depths of human nature."[15] In Qutb's account, human proximity to or distance from Islam explains history.

I should make it clear that I am not opposed to scholastic treatments of faith systems, or to examining them through history or even within a comparative framework. But that is not what is happening here. The problem arises not when a faith system is placed in history but when it is used to *explain* history. Thus arises the Grand Narrative. And with Aslan, Manji, and Hirsi Ali, the Grand Narratives they posit all describe a straightforward binary of a premodern Islam that has erected barriers for Muslims, hindering them from entering modernity. Moreover, these barriers—a rigid Ulama, intellectual sleights of hand like "closing the gates of ijtihad" and fabricating *ahadith*, or even the very faith itself—account for the political behavior of Muslims throughout the world and in world historical time.

Each of these three texts relies on its own Grand Narrative to prove its point, and it is worth examining what kinds of threads underpin their Grand Narratives to give them force to Western readers. Turning first to Hirsi Ali, we find a detail-driven memoir of a clearly turbulent life that involves survival in war-torn Somalia, flight to Saudi Arabia, refugee hardship in Kenya, oppression through female circumcision and forced marriage, and the remaking of a new life in the Netherlands. It is in many ways a compelling read. But perhaps the first thing to notice from the point of view of narrative is why we are drawn to the story. Part of the reason may lie in the structure of the work, which in fact replicates the American slave narrative in significant ways. Frederick Douglass titles the account of his life *My Bondage and My Freedom*; Hirsi Ali divides her story into "My Childhood" and "My Freedom." And like the slave narrative, hers is also one about achieving true consciousness under a system of oppression. In the slave narrative, the discovery of consciousness is generically inscribed in the act of learning how to write. With Hirsi Ali, it comes with going to school in the Netherlands.

Consider how she describes the vocational college preparatory classes that she was finally able to take. There, she tells us, she studied history voraciously, and the performance of naïveté is instructive of the move from blindness to vision, not just in language but also in political thinking. "That history book taught me Dutch," she writes. "The civics class, on the other hand, was full of terms I didn't understand, like *municipality* and *upper chamber*. I scraped through it. I failed the Dutch class by one point: I still couldn't write proper grammar. But because I had my Dutch equivalency exam, they let me enroll in Driebergen Vocational College anyway. By the skin of my teeth, I had made it."[16] Education and the Dutch language may bring consciousness to Hirsi Ali, but they also enable simplistic comparisons. "In February 1995," she writes, "there were huge floods across Holland. When Somalis are faced with catastrophic weather, drought and flooding, they all get together and pray. Natural disasters are a sign from God, to show humans they are misbehaving on earth. But the Dutch blamed their government for failing to maintain the dikes properly. I didn't see anybody praying."[17] When it comes to her education, she writes, "it seemed as if . . . everything I read challenged me as a Muslim. Drinking wine and wearing trousers were nothing compared to reading the history of ideas."[18]

The obscurant and anti-intellectual world of Islam functions as the slave system in Hirsi Ali's universe, and Muslims are guilty of enslaving themselves. Hirsi Ali's narrative makes this point repeatedly, and she liberally uses skin color to argue her point. Later, she begins work as a translator in the Dutch social welfare sector, and this experience further hardens her to the Muslims in her midst: "When I went to awful places—the police stations, the prisons, the abortion clinics and penal courts, the unemployment offices and the shelters for battered women—I began to notice how many dark faces looked back at me. It was not something you could avoid noticing, coming straight in from creamy-blond Leiden. I began to wonder why so many immigrants—so many Muslims—were there."[19] Later, she answers her question. "If Muslim immigrants lagged so far behind even other immigrant groups, then wasn't it possible," she asks, "that one of the reasons could be Islam? Islam influences every aspect of believers' lives."[20] Meanwhile, "By declaring our Prophet infallible and not permitting ourselves to question him, we Muslims had set up a static tyranny . . . we suppressed the freedom to think and to act as we chose. . . . We were not just servants of Allah, we were slaves."[21]

In the prototypical slave narrative, the former slave finds redemption in true Christianity. But Hirsi Ali's salvation from slavery, updated for today, comes not through Christianity but through atheism. As the Bible has the power to move the spirit in the slave narrative, *The Atheist Manifesto*, loaned to her by her boyfriend, becomes Ali's path to emancipation. But the emancipation she details is also not hers alone, for what would it matter if one Muslim gives up her faith? Hers is instead a broad prescription for all her coreligionists, and by the end of her narrative it is clear that she is lecturing all the Muslims of the world. If they are to enter modernity, they must give up God within their creed, not just individually but theologically. According the Hirsi Ali, Islam's salvation is atheism.

◆ ◆ ◆

Hirsi Ali's text is actually rich in detail about different social movements and political strife. It gives us large amounts of context, making it in fact a text of lost promise. The same cannot be said of Irshad Manji's *The Trouble with Islam*, a polemic rife with willful distortions, patent inaccuracies, and self-aggrandizing sanctimony. I will not bother to list these—there are far too many to think this a serious work worthy of such scrutiny—but we can look at its narrative tendency in a fashion similar to the ways of exploring Hirsi Ali's memoir.

Manji's is an epistolary text, full of Thomas Freidman–like platitudes and born out of disillusionment. "I have to be honest with you," she begins. "Islam is on very thin ice with me."[22] She proceeds to catalogue the manner in which she was schooled in a "madrassa" in Richmond, British Columbia, and how the experience traumatized her into action later in life. In her junior high school, she tells us, "dignity of the individual prevailed," but in her "madrassa," she "entered . . . wearing a white polyester chador and departed several hours later with [her] hair flattened and her spirit deflated."[23] "Islam" is the cause of this oppression, we are lectured again and again, just as Muslims are the cause of every tragedy she can muster. "The Muslims of East Africa treated blacks like slaves,"[24] she says. (And what about the Hindus of East Africa?) Muslims are responsible for the honor killings of Pakistan, the lack of independent women travelers in Malaysia, ethnic strife in Nigeria, and the Turkish nationalist genocide of Armenians of 1915. "Muslims did this!" she keeps intoning, as if every Muslim is individually responsible for the action of every other nominally Muslim person in the entire world and throughout time.

At the heart of Manji's polemic is the way in which Muslim and/or Palestinian "culture" squelches the individual.[25] She even draws parallels between the Prophet and bin Laden over the course of several pages, arguing that the Prophet "won decisive military victories through such primitive tactics as digging a ditch around his settlement, catching his opponents unawares, and crippling their combat-ready thoroughbreds," and then offering that "bin Laden's cavalry used box-cutters to attack a superpower."[26]

Such emotional blackmail is Manji's style; she goes to great lengths to posit Islam as a faith locked outside the gates of modernity due to its tyrannical anti-intellectualism. While the West is proudly freethinking, and Jews are the most freethinking of Westerners, for Manji, "mainstream Muslims . . . suppress their brain-power [with] the stated aim of the no-thinking rule."[27] She gets more specific. The Palestinians, in Manji's view, function as the ultimate expression of the failures of Islam, and the middle of her book is turned over to a narration of a six-day trip—paid for by a Canadian Jewish group—to Israel and the occupied territories. In Jerusalem, she encounters difficulty entering Al-Aqsa compound but freely visits the Wailing Wall. There, she writes, "I borrow a pencil and scrawl a request to God, then weave through the crowd to approach the wall. As I spend time in search of an unused crack that will clasp my prayer, I realize I'm holding up the Jews behind me. Still, I don't feel like an interloper [as the Palestinians have made her feel]. I feel at home. More viscerally than ever, I know who my family is."[28]

For Manji, Judaism stands as the ultimate expression of modernity and the culmination of the West. She presents Judaism as broad-minded, universal, and liberal to the core; this is especially evident in her narrative on the state of Israel. Judaism and Israel function as the antitheses to Islam, and as models to aspire to. She uses cultural-religious terms—Islam and Judaism—but it is really politics that drives her framework. Manji refuses to grant the Palestinians even basic rights. Instead, she imperiously lectures them about how they deserve their fate, due solely to the faults of their Muslim culture. In this bizarre narrative, where Islam is "irredeemably rigid" and "brain-dead,"[29] Judaism, in fact, even becomes the true Islam. She asks, "How many of us know the degree to which

Islam is a 'gift of the Jews'?"[30] And thus her self-label as a "Muslim Refusenik" takes on another dimension. "That doesn't mean I refuse to be a Muslim," she writes, explaining why she calls herself a refusenik. "It simply means I refuse to join an army of automatons in the name of Allah. I take this phrase," she continues, "from the original refuseniks—Soviet Jews who championed religious and personal freedom. Their communist masters refused to let them emigrate to Israel. For their attempts to leave the Soviet Union, many refuseniks paid with hard labor and, sometimes, with their lives."[31] For Irshad Manji, "Islam" can enter modernity. It just has to become Jewish.

♦ ♦ ♦

Turning to Reza Aslan's *No god but God,* we find a more complicated narrative, but one that nonetheless operates on a grand scale describing how Islam is well on the road to replicating Christianity. Aslan's book is full of the performance of partisan scholarship (he proudly accepts that he is writing an "apology" for Islam), and, insofar as it is a book about Islam as a faith, it is relatively unproblematic. (And I should add that Aslan's work is immeasurably more nuanced than Hirsi Ali's and Manji's, and that many of his public interventions are helpful. But this need not mean his book is beyond criticism.) The first half of the book travels over familiar territory. Here Aslan narrates the early days of Islam with control and sympathy and describes the religion's emergence within the social context of the Arabian Peninsula of that era.

More fundamental problems soon arise, however, and from two different directions. The first is the use of what Aslan calls the "story" of Islam to explain the subsequent history and politics of the Middle East and South Asia. (If this is "Islam's story," then where is Indonesia or Mali or Albania?) The second is the central conceit of the book, namely that Islam—like Christianity—is going through a reformation.

In fact, Aslan's book reads like a revisionist history of the Iranian revolution. The initial message of Islam was freedom and liberty, he tells us, but that message has, since the early days of the revolutionary message of egalitarianism, been hijacked by the clerics.

> Throughout Islamic history, as Muslim dynasties tumbled over each other, Muslim kings were crowned and dethroned, and Islamic parliaments elected and dissolved, only the Ulama, in their capacity as the link to the traditions of the past, have managed to retain their self-imposed role as the leaders of Muslim society. As a result, over the past fifteen centuries, Islam as we know it has been almost exclusively defined by an extremely small, rigid, and often profoundly traditionalist group of men who, for better or worse, consider themselves to be the unyielding pillars upon which the religious, social, and political foundations of the religion rest.[32]

The arrogance of this approach, summarizing the sweep of fifteen hundred years of human history within a few words, is at bottom breathtakingly simple. (Not to say historically untenable—what about popular Islam, for one thing?) The idea of a clergy tyrannically holding sway over the masses of people flies in the face of the complex and variegated ways that authority and state power have functioned throughout the history of the Muslim world.

But besides sounding very much like contemporary Iran, Aslan's view of a singular Ulama deciding the worldly fates of believers sounds a lot like the history of Christianity in Europe. In fact, in virtually every section one turns to in Aslan's book, the comparison to Christianity is drawn. Sometimes it is explicit, so the brief nine-year reign of Abbasid Caliph Mu'tasim is known only for its "inquisition."[33] Or when Aslan describes the umma, he writes that "put simply [the umma] is the Church in Islam."[34] Sufis are compared to Teresa of Avila, and are placed in opposition to the clerical order of the Ulama. Moreover, we are told that "Sufis" believe that

"God's very essence—God's substance—is love. Love is the agent of creation" and that they "understood Muhammad in the same way that many Christian Gnostics understood Jesus: as the eternal *logos*."[35] Sufis and the Indian reformer Sayyid Ahmed Khan, unsurprisingly, are the good guys in this narrative, peacefully opposed to the black-robed Ulama.

For a moment, consider Sufism with more than pacific new-age appreciation. Many of the often quite violent and often very hierarchical anticolonial struggles the Arab world witnessed—ranging from the Mahdi movement in Sudan to Abdel Kader in Algeria— were Sufi- led or -inspired, and they certainly complicate Aslan's narrative. The text does acknowledge Shah Wali Allah's political Sufism, but only to transition to political Islam and not to investigate the premise that Sufism could be more than private mysticism.[36] Aslan's examination of political Islam itself is preceded by a brief discussion of colonialism, which is put this way. "European ideals of secularism, pluralism, individual liberties, human rights, and, to a far lesser degree, democracy—that wonderful legacy of the Enlightenment that had taken hundreds of years to evolve in Europe—were pressed upon the colonized lands with no attempts to render them in terms the indigenous population would either recognize or understand,"[37] as if the ravages of colonialism are due to the stunted development of the colonized themselves.

These consistently drawn parallels between "East" and "West" structure Aslan's story. Of course, there is nothing wrong with analogy or drawing historical correspondences as a heuristic device. But a problem arises when analogy overwhelms the analysis to the point of emulation. In Aslan's narrative, it is as if "Islam" must follow the same world historical script as Christianity. Under such a weight, Islam will always fail, for the simple fact that Islam is not Christianity.

More troubling still is the manner in which politics is subsumed to the narrative of Islam, and from the opening pages of the book—a narration of how Aslan mediated and translated a sudden altercation between American missionaries and an irate Muslim conductor on a train in Morocco—to the ending, which refutes the "clash of civilizations thesis" in its analysis of the September 11 terrorist attacks, we are told that this book will explain not just a faith system but the paroxysms of the world. The violence of our age is due to a struggle over leadership, Aslan concludes, exactly as in the Christian past. "All great religions grapple over [authority]," he writes (so "lesser" religions don't?), "some more fiercely than others. One need only recall Europe's massively destructive Thirty Years' War . . . to recognize the ferocity with which interreligious conflicts have been fought in Christian history. In many ways, the Thirty Years' War signaled the end of the Reformation . . . and [led] ultimately to the doctrinal relativism of the Enlightenment. This remarkable evolution in Christianity . . . took fifteen vicious, bloody, and occasionally apocalyptic centuries. . . . And Islam has finally begun its fifteenth century."[38] In Aslan's narrative, one that is putatively about the world, responsibility becomes easy to assess. The "story" of Islam, with its incomplete reformation, is the sole cause of today's violence. "What is taking place now in the Muslim world is an internal conflict between Muslims," he writes, "not an external battle between Islam and the West. The West," he continues, "is merely a bystander."[39]

This is a false dichotomy if ever there was one—to be forced to choose between a civilizational clash and an internal civilizational civil war—for why can't it be neither? But the idea that the West is "merely a bystander" and, by extension, that "Islam" is a victimizer of the West ends Aslan's narrative. Moreover, it is the central thread that connects Aslan to Hirsi Ali to Irshad Manji. But surely this is ridiculous. The process of assigning political responsibility means assessing who, individually, does what to whom. It means grappling with the historical details of particular wars, state-building projects, specific colonial and postcolonial policies, the rise of secular nationalism, regionalism, military pacts, control over resources, globalization, and everything else. The narratives of Aslan, Hirsi Ali, and Irshad Manji, on the other hand, reduce politics to the spurious fact that Muslims are agents of Islam and only of Islam throughout the pages of history. Such epic civilizational narratives as these talk the language of political responsibility while obfuscating the same. To Western audiences, however, this is an oddly comforting story. It means that the world, meaning now the Western world, has been invaded by "Islam," an Islam that for centuries has been on the march to defeat individuality at every turn, is antimodern to the core, and has a totalitarian-like Comintern at its heart called "the Ulama." The truth for the proposition is made all the more "truthful" when it issues from the lips of Western Muslims. And the solution, if one can be found, is simplistically plotted as a stripped-down ijtihad, for ijtihad brings with it reformation, liberalism, and individuality.

Orientalism provides the means by which these narratives succeed, for it enables precisely this kind of wholesale summary of the complexity of human experience. It is Orientalism that endows one with the authority to proclaim the wish that "Islam" would become or emulate atheism, Judaism, or Christianity (or, in the case of Thomas Friedman, that Islam would finally just become Hinduism). But Orientalism does not account for the overarching structure of these three stories. In their repeated insistence of a system of tyranny defeating human liberty, these stories fundamentally replicate another narrative in our recent history, one similarly made more concrete by the collapsing of distance, since it is ex-fellow travelers who tell them. I am referring to familiar Cold War narratives published in the middle of the twentieth century, and particularly the confessional tales composed by ex-communists.

In 1949, Richard Crossman edited an influential series of essays with the title *The God That Failed*. Reprinted through the 1960s and, as Frances Stonor Saunders shows, supported by the

Congress for Cultural Freedom, a wing of the Central Intelligence Agency, *The God That Failed* features essays by André Gide, Richard Wright, Stephen Spender, Ignazio Silone, Arthur Koestler, and others who described their excited journeys into communism and their disillusioned return. The narratives in the book shared a good many characteristics, most notably that communism defeats every ounce of individuality, mainly by its collective belief that—as Arthur Koestler put it—communism is "the incarnation of the will of History itself."[40] Similarly, Ignazio Silone characterizes the history of the Communist International (sounding very much like these accounts of Islam) as "a history of schisms, a history of intrigues and arrogance . . . toward every independent expression of opinion."[41] In *The God That Failed*, communism is a bullying, antihuman pursuit recklessly imposing its idea of Truth on the world through brutality, as shown by Richard Wright, and murder, described by Stephen Spender.

It is far less important to adjudicate the truth of these claims than it is to connect old rhetorics of persuasion and argument to newer rhetorics, allowing us to see how certain tropes function in our society, how they are consistent, and how they differ. With this in mind, one crucial comparison arises. The failures of communism spelled out in *The God That Failed* were likened to the failures of organized religion, as the acolyte of Lenin was seen as being the same as the Catholic neophyte. "The strength of the Catholic Church," writes Crossman in his introduction, "has always been that it demands the sacrifice of [spiritual] freedom uncompromisingly, and condemns spiritual pride as a deadly sin. The Communist novice, subjecting his soul to the canon law of the Kremlin, felt something of the release which Catholicism brings to the intellectual, wearied and worried by the privilege of freedom."[42] Communism, like organized religion (especially Catholicism), flees from freedom and defeats the individual. The existence of this old narrative endows contemporary tales of "Islam" with the "truthfulness" on which they rest, because "our" violence, in this mythology, promotes liberty, while "their" violence is forever atavistic.

In *The God That Failed*, communism loses because it turns ideology into religion. In the hands of Hirsi Ali, Irshad Manji, and Reza Aslan, "Islam" fails because it has transformed a religion into ideology.

PART III

Muslims in Politics

The Rites and Rights of Citizenship

On Tuesday, September 6, 2011, I became a citizen of the United States. Almost ten years before, I was granted permanent residency. Between my green card and my naturalization certificate lies the seemingly endless first decade of the War on Terror.

I was in New York on September 11, 2001, but back then I was neither a permanent resident nor a citizen. And if you weren't a citizen, and you had a Muslim name, you couldn't help but think that your life was about to change for the worse. I was already teaching at CUNY's Brooklyn College, on a work visa. I had come to New York in 1990 from Canada to attend graduate school at Columbia University and, when I got the job at Brooklyn College, I transferred my student visa into a work visa and applied for a green card. My immigration attorney worked in Lower Manhattan, a block away from the towers, and he was among the first people I called to make sure he was fine. He was, thankfully. He was shaken up to be sure, and there was ash all over his building, he told me, but he was okay. His voice was breaking with emotion over the phone.

I remember many things about September 11, the solemnity mixing with the acrid smells in the air in particular, but also the tremulous anxiety surrounding Arabs and Muslims in the city in those days. The sweep arrests that John Ashcroft regularly announced on the airwaves in the first weeks following the attacks sent shudders through all the Arabs and Muslims I knew in the city. We would meet up regularly to trade FBI stories, which was weirdly consoling. There came a point when I realized that every Arab person I knew in New York had either been visited or knew someone who had been visited by the FBI. At that point, I was waiting for my green card to arrive, and when it did, on October 15, 2001, I felt my own personal sigh of national security relief. A green card may not carry the protections of citizenship, but it's a far less vulnerable condition than a work visa.

So much has happened in these ten years: the war in Afghanistan, the drumbeat to war in Iraq, the massive worldwide demonstrations in February and March 2003 to stop the war in Iraq, and the war itself. I remember the night it began, because I called my parents in Canada and surprised myself by crying into the receiver. There is the gulag of Guantánamo Bay, the sordid revelations of torture and abuse of detainees during the War on Terror, the arrests of thousands of immigrants following the attacks, the widespread spying on the Muslim community by multiple law enforcement agencies, other programs of the government that were pointed directly at the Muslim and Arab communities, and the exaggerated threats of homegrown extremism along with multiple cases of paid informants ensnaring gullible Muslims into dubious terrorist plots. Jose Pimentel is one example. Arrested in a sting operation involving both the FBI and the NYPD in late 2011, Pimentel is a man of questionable sanity. He told investigators he was followed around by a witch as a young boy in the Dominican Republic. As an adult convert to Islam, he tried to circumcise himself. He was known more for getting high and living off the two dollars a day allowance from his mother than for his political opinions. Here, as with others, the confidential informant assigned to the case (who smoked marijuana with Pimentel) provided the elements and know-how of the crime, showing that more frightening than the arrest is the length the government will go to produce its terrorism cases. In fact, Pimentel seems hardly scary when you look into the details.[1] His story is just sad.

There's more of course: the Bali terror attacks, the Madrid terror attacks, the London attacks, all completely horrific, immoral, and nihilistic. I remember the disgust my friends and I felt whenever

Osama bin Laden's face appeared on a screen, claiming to speak for the Muslim *umma* and the frustration we felt at being forced to feel that our only options were between bin Laden's fascism and Bush's imperialism. Then there is the populist anger that has grown louder against Muslims, mobilizing against mosques and pushing the phantasmic threat that the country is about to be overrun by sharia courts. So vitriolic and idiotic have these broadsides been that it has felt, at times, like a window was closing on Muslims in the United States.

What sustained me through it all, now that I reflect on it, was my lecturing. I would give talks to audiences across the country about civil liberties during wartime, about torture, about Islam, about the war, and the audiences were full of people who didn't want a murderous clash of civilizations but needed and wanted a lens through which they could understand this complicated world that they felt they had suddenly been thrust into. When I lecture in the Arab world, I often find myself telling my Arab audiences this about Americans. It's easy to caricature any people, and the caricature of Americans is that they don't know and don't care about the rest of the world, but that's not my experience. The Americans I have encountered, and continue to meet, throughout my travels have always been curious and generous. There is a minority, and it has grown more vocal and powerful and frightening since 2009, that either fears Islam beyond belief or, more likely, leverages a popular fear for its own agenda. The anti–Ground Zero Mosque movement of 2010 illustrates that well, as does the anti-sharia frenzy of 2011. But it's easy to fixate on a cartoon of your opposition, as they themselves prove.

The problem is magnified when government caters to the intelligence of fools. Loudmouth media braying constantly about the Muslim threat also creates huge cleavages in our culture. The Brookings Institution has released a survey on this. "Trust in Fox News is highly correlated with negative attitudes about Islam,"

Brookings found. "More than two-thirds (68 percent) of Americans who most trust Fox News for their information about politics and current events say that the values of Islam are at odds with American values. In contrast, less than half of Americans who most trust broadcast network news (45 percent), CNN (37 percent), or public television (37 percent) agree that Islam is at odds with American values."[2]

It's also not surprising that the picture changes when you try to take media and ideology out of the equation. Polling data show that if you know a Muslim personally, you're simply less likely to hold negative views of the religion.[3] In my day-to-day interactions with the people of this country, I see a sincere, inquiring, civil America, one that never seems to get represented in the mainstream. Muslim Americans know what I am talking about: the disconnect between the polls and the media coverage and the awkward relations with law enforcement on one hand, and the everyday warmth, generosity, and friendship from ordinary Americans on the other.

I could have applied for citizenship years ago, but bureaucracy has never been my strength and I did so only in January 2011. In May, I was granted my citizenship interview. I dutifully studied the hundred (easy) questions on American history, politics, and geography and was now wondering what to expect. What I didn't imagine was that the interview would start off like a scene from a Harold Pinter play. After my name was called, the citizenship officer first escorted me to his office, then shut the door, and next instructed me to sit down. I sat down.

"Now stand up," he said.

I stood up.

"Raise your right hand." I raised my right hand. He proceeded to swear me in. Then he told me to sit down again, which I did. (This was either exercise or an exercise in authority.) He asked me, "Is your name Moustafa Mohamed Bayoumi."

I knew the answer. Yes, I answered confidently.

"Do you want your name to be Moustafa Mohamed Bayoumi?"

This seemed like a trick question. I searched for a response. None came. He repeated the question, and I was silent. He became impatient.

"Do you want 'Mohamed' to be a part of your name?"

I couldn't think of an answer. What did this question mean? Was he kindly trying to suggest to me that "Mohamed" should not be my middle name? Maybe he was thinking it will cause me problems in today's United States? Or perhaps he himself holds the name Mohamed in disfavor? And why did I have to sit down and stand up and sit down again? Why was I breathing hard? Was I really that out of shape? I looked around. I was lost.

"I'm asking you if you want to change your name," he said, finally, and I later realized I was witnessing how self-reinvention is built into the American system. My full name had served me just fine in my life thus far, so I elected to keep it whole. But the whole exchange left me confused.

I wasn't being entirely irrational in my suspicions. There have been several lawsuits launched by Muslims because of unexplained delays in their petitions for citizenship. And in May 2011, NYU Law School and the Asian American Legal Defense Fund released a report titled "Under the Radar: Muslims Deported, Detained, and Denied on Unsubstantiated Terrorism Allegations."[4] There are real problems with the system. But I was fortunate that, despite a minor hiccup that required me to return for a second visit, I was granted my petition without any major problems.

The citizenship ceremony itself was revealing. During the processing part prior to the actual swearing in, we were given voter registration cards (available in four languages) and a woman representing the New York City Commission on Human Rights told us about her organization. She explained how the commission advocates for civil rights protections, and listed the various ways that people routinely encounter discrimination: in employment and in housing, because of their gender, appearance, or sexual preference, and due to their accent. "If you have an accent walking into this room, then, unless if you're less than ten years old, you're walking out of here with an accent!" she said, and everyone laughed, including the two Chinese—now Chinese Americans—on either side of me. She also told us that it was illegal to discriminate against someone because that person doesn't speak English, but she said it in English, which left me wondering whether this is the kind of knowledge that everyone, not just new citizens, needs to have.

The judge finally came in. We stood up and sat down (I'm good at this now), and she told us that despite what we hear about all the terrorism, crime, and poverty in the United States today, the country still holds the promise of a better life for us and our children. She explained how we now have the right to vote and to serve on juries, but she also encouraged us to exercise our other rights, naming our right to speak out and to get involved in the running of the country. Then we were given our certificates. Some people looked very happy. Most seemed in a hurry to get to work.

Why did I become a US citizen? The easy answer is that my life is here now, my green card was up for renewal, and I didn't have to give up my Canadian citizenship. But there is more to it.

The historian Rogers Smith writes that most people commonly believe that American citizenship is bestowed upon those who "subscribe to egalitarian, liberal, republican principles," what he terms the "latent" belief in what citizenship is. But, he argues,

> when restrictions on voting rights, naturalization, and immigration are taken into account, it turns out that for over 80 percent of US history, American laws declared most people in the world legally ineligible to become full US citizens solely because of their race, original nationality, or gender. For at least two-thirds of American history, the majority of the domestic adult population was also ineligible for full citizenship for the same reason. Those racial, ethnic

and gender restrictions were blatant, not "latent." For these people, citizenship rules gave no weight to how liberal, republican, or faithful to other American values their political beliefs may be.[5]

Smith is describing a history of very exclusive versions of citizenship, and during these same periods, the law sanctioned all kinds of official discrimination against various categories of people. We've moved beyond those kinds of blatant citizenship exclusions today, and all citizenships are by their nature exclusive anyway. But there is also something essentially inclusive about the American system, namely how the Bill of Rights speaks not of the rights of citizens but of the rights of "the people."

This means there is a professed value in the United States, one that seems to always be contested, of protecting vulnerable minorities, citizens or not, from the passions of the majority. I became a citizen because I believe the fight for preserving the rights of "the people" in the United States, not only other citizens, is worthwhile, and I can do that more effectively as a citizen of the country where I live. In that fight lies the defense of the American values of tolerance and respect. It also means that I can disagree with much of American foreign policy, as I do, and try to change it. Being a citizen of the United States doesn't mean that I'm any better or worse as a person. (Nor will I drop my Canadian "pardon me?" for the American "what?") It means that the United States has recognized me as part of its family, and I have recognized the American people as part of mine. And family relationships, as we all know, require work and communication. I will try to live up to my own professed ideals of fairness and equality for all. And I expect the United States to do the same.

Between Acceptance and Rejection

Muslim Americans and the Legacies of September 11

On September 11, 2010, the ninth anniversary of the terrorist attacks on the World Trade Center, I headed to Lower Manhattan to observe two demonstrations that had been called for that day. One was at City Hall Park, where people were assembling not only to remember the fallen but also to voice their support for the burning issue of the summer, namely the construction of a Muslim Cultural Center. First called Cordoba House, the center was later renamed Park51 and became popularly known as "the Ground Zero Mosque" (although it neither is at Ground Zero nor is a mosque). Two long city blocks—and a world—away was an anti-Park51 protest. The enormous difference between the two demonstrations pointedly illustrates how Muslim American life has precariously swung, and continues to swing, between poles of acceptance and rejection since 2001.

The pro-Park51 demo was peopled by a cross-section of New York City. It was noisy, disorganized, and apparently ad hoc. A quickly constructed stage anchored one end of the demonstration and speakers for a wide variety of political causes took the microphone to proclaim their belief in a multicultural America, opposition to bigotry and racism, criticisms of American imperialism, and support for workers' struggles in the city and around the world. The mood here was one of solidarity through people's differences. Multiethnic, multireligious, multiracial, young and old, the assembled group was made up of a wide swath of people who had all kinds of creative ways of wearing their jewelry, scarves, and piercings. In its multiplicity of people and causes, the demonstration seemed to be a pretty fair representation of New York City.

The anti-Park51 demonstration was something else entirely. News accounts estimated it was 50 percent larger than the pro-Park51 rally.[1] Organized by the right-wing group Stop the Islamization of America, this assembly was completely high-tech, with a large stage and a massive television monitor above that beamed in satellite feeds of former US ambassador to the UN John Bolton and other staunch conservatives to offer their "anti–Ground Zero Mosque" message. Men with suits and walkie-talkies were shuffling people and speakers around. The money behind the event was plainly evident, as was the difference in constituency. This group was overwhelmingly white and mostly older. American flags were everywhere, along with signs expressing the sentiment of the demonstration. Some were directed against the religion: "Hey Islam, we will never submit," read one. Another asked, "What would Jesus Do?" answering, "Have his throat slit by Mohammed." Many people held the same sign—the word "Sharia" written in bloodlike letters. Other signs attacked immigration policy: "Why give terrorists the rights of US citizens they are sworn to kill," "Terrorist Sleeping [sic] Cells in America are Muslims! Wake Up America!!!!," and "Illegal Aliens were Responsible for the 9/11 Attacks. The Solution is Simple. Close the Borders. No Immigration=No Terrorism" (in fact, none of the 9/11 hijackers entered the country illegally). Then there were the simple three-word signs: "No Victory Mosque," "No Obama Mosque," and "No Bloomberg Mosque." At the height of the demonstration were thousands of people yelling, "No Mosque! No Mosque!"

I've lived in New York City for twenty years and have attended my share of demonstrations, but this anti-Park51 demonstration felt different. It was raw and completely in-your-face. Directed not only at Muslims, the demonstrators' animus was also aimed at the few political leaders, such as Mayor Michael Bloomberg, who had come out publicly in support of Park51 by defending the constitutional principle of the free exercise of religion. Opponents of Park51, however, weren't buying it, and the zeal of their passions against Muslims illustrated how much being a Muslim in America today is to embody, quite literally, some of America's most contested political and cultural debates. I came home depressed.

Sociological Dilemma

Before 9/11, most Americans probably thought very little about their Muslim neighbors. Despite a history that stretches back to the days of slavery—sizeable numbers of Africans enslaved in the United States were Muslim[2]—Islam was rarely considered an American religion. The rise of the Nation of Islam and the spectacular life and death of Malcolm X meant that when Islam in America did register on the national psyche, it was most likely seen as one part of the African American struggle for civil rights and recognition of their long history. Today, everything is different. Muslim Americans are now viewed as immigrant outsiders and have become regular topics of conversation on television news and talk radio shows, subjects of investigation by research institutes, reasons for people to organize and demonstrate, and the concern of law enforcement and government policymakers. In short, Muslims in America have become a sociological dilemma.

As troubling as it is for a religious community to become scientifically interesting, it is equally true that Muslim Americans have also been warmly received by many of their fellow Americans, who have often sought them out to understand their faith and predicaments and to protect their civil liberties when threatened. Muslim Americans too, from young people to the major national organizations, have understood the responsibilities of communicating who they are to the wider public and have since September 11 spoken in a more American idiom about their dilemmas (including loudly condemning terrorism, despite protestations to the contrary).[3] They now often seek alliances and coalitions with other religious and minority groups in the country. They regularly hold open houses at their mosques and Islamic centers to facilitate communication with non-Muslims. And campus-based Muslim student associations around the country sponsor Islam awareness weeks to represent themselves—rather than be represented by the media—to larger publics. Since 9/11, the general public has also shown an interest in understanding Islam and Muslims. For a while, the Qur'an was even a best seller.

Despite these fine efforts on the part of both Muslim and non-Muslim Americans, full acceptance of Muslim Americans seems less assured today than ever. According to an annual *Washington Post*–ABC News poll, approximately 39 percent of Americans held unfavorable opinions of Islam in 2001. Dipping for a few years, the number rose to 46 percent in 2006. In 2010, it reached 49 percent.[4] The *Economist* took a poll when the Park51 debates hit their stride, finding that 55 percent of Americans held negative opinions of Islam.[5]

This growing animosity surprises many Muslim Americans, since for many years following 9/11 popular anger was not the primary problem confronting their communities; religious and national-origin profiling was their true concern. While it is true that the number of reported hate crimes against Muslim Americans skyrocketed in the first six months after 9/11 (and still have not returned to pre-9/11 levels), perhaps the greatest reverberation for Muslim Americans in the decade following 9/11 came from large-scale arrests across the nation. Hundreds of immigrants were rounded up in the months after the terrorist attacks, often on flimsy evidence or simply on the basis of national origin. Law professor David Cole estimates that more than five thousand individuals were arrested, the vast majority of them deported after spending months in detention.[6] One Palestinian man was arrested while driving four miles over the speed limit. He spent four months in jail before being deported.[7] Another Algerian man, arrested in September 2001 and cleared of any terrorism connection by November 2001, spent nearly five years in detention.[8] Eighty days was the average, according to the Justice Department's inspector general, who criticized post-9/11 detention practices in two lengthy reports.[9]

As difficult as this was for the community, it could have been worse. David Ayers, US Attorney General John Ashcroft's chief of staff, had proposed house-to-house searches in parts of the country with large Muslim communities. He was opposed by James Ziglar, then commissioner of the Immigration and Naturalization Service, who stood his ground by reportedly telling Ayres, "I know you're not a lawyer, but we do have this thing called the Constitution."[10] Without Ziglar's support, the proposal died in the water.

Other law enforcement initiatives that specifically targeted Muslim immigrants in the United States did survive. These included the special registration program, which required all adult male visitors to the country from twenty-four Muslim-majority countries (and North Korea) to register their whereabouts with the government (see Chapter 3), and the Absconder Apprehension Initiative, where the government sought to deport immigrants who had absconded on a deportation order and, in doing so, prioritized immigrants from Muslim-majority nations. Additional initiatives included "voluntary" interviews with Arab and Muslim immigrants in the country, warrantless wiretaps, extended use of the material witness statute (that many in the legal community see as an abuse of the law), the deployment of spies and informants into Muslim communities, and microscopic scrutiny of charities and charitable giving.[11]

These various initiatives, strung together in a short span of time, led often to feelings of being under siege by the authorities in many Muslim American communities. In 2006, the Vera Institute of Justice, an independent nonprofit organization dedicated to examining law enforcement strategies, was commissioned by the Department of Justice to study how changes in policing since 9/11 had affected Arab American communities (the conclusions would apply generally to many Muslim American communities). Their report "confirmed that September 11 had a substantial impact on Arab American communities," drawing attention to worries about overzealous policing. "Although community members also reported increases in hate victimization," the report stated, "they expressed greater concern about being victimized by federal policies and practices than by individual acts of harassment or violence."[12]

Since the inception of these discriminatory policies, the Muslim American community has also found many allies and defenders of their rights, including the American Civil Liberties Union, the Center for Constitutional Rights, Amnesty International, Human Rights Watch, and other local organizations and individual attorneys. The support offered to the community illustrated a divided reaction on the part of the country. On the one hand, government initiatives, specific immigration policies, and law enforcement strategies were aimed directly at the larger Muslim American community. On the other hand, significant sectors of civil society offered substantial resistance to the targeting of Muslims on the basis of due process and equal treatment under the law.

Divided Cultural Front

The cultural front is similarly bifurcated. Wildly successful television shows like 24 showed a nation spellbound by the threat of homegrown terrorism. In season four, 24 depicted a harsh, duplicitous world where an ordinary Muslim Middle Eastern family in Southern California is called into action as a "sleeper cell" to perform a terrorist act in the United States. The Showtime series *Sleeper Cell* also depicted ordinary Muslims, this time from various backgrounds, ready and willing to follow their charismatic leader in attacking US citizens. The film *Traitor* (2008), starring Don Cheadle, had a similar storyline.

But films with other narratives also succeeded in portraying Muslim life in the United States through broader lenses. In a film about the friendship between an aging college professor and a young Arab immigrant drummer, the 2007 independent feature *The Visitor* sensitively depicted the realities of immigration detention, something rarely explored through film. Also in 2007, the WB Network carried the comedy show *Aliens in America* for one season, which rather brilliantly chronicled a Pakistani exchange student's life in Wisconsin during the age of terror. And in February 2010, Bill Cosby endorsed Katie Couric's call to model a television show about a Muslim American family after *The Cosby Show*, a popular sitcom that aired in the mid-eighties and greatly contributed to the decrease in discriminatory attitudes aimed at African Americans.[13]

These are seemingly positive signs of acceptance, though as Evelyn Alsultany warns, even sympathetic representations in a multicultural mode can work to reinforce racism and deflect attention away from state repression.[14] Nevertheless, celebrating more complex representations of Muslims in the American cultural scene may be premature. Anger and suspicion against Muslim Americans are growing, and the dominant narrative about Muslim Americans seems to be changing. The American Muslim community had often been compared favorably to its European counterparts. American Muslims were seen as well assimilated and not a threat to public order (unlike Europe's recent Muslim immigrants, the story went), feeding the US image of itself as a successful immigrant-absorbing nation and notions of American superiority over Europe. A 2007 study by the Pew Research Center, called *Muslim Americans: Middle Class and Mostly Mainstream*, confirmed the idea of Muslim American integration, by both its title and its findings.[15]

But that story is receding while another—the fabulous story that American Muslims are on a "stealth jihad" to usurp the US Constitution and impose Islamic law on the land—is quickly taking its place. This most recent narrative about Muslim Americans, which fueled the opposition to Park51, is expressed much less in the language of national security and far more through the language of cultural domination. In what is really a nonissue, Oklahomans voted overwhelmingly in November 2010 in favor of a state constitutional amendment that would ban the use of sharia law in their courts. Voters there were reacting to a well-funded campaign and to what Republican State Representative Rex Duncan has called "a war for the survival of the United States."[16] The Oklahoma State legislature was in fact kicking off a national movement of introducing similar legislation in a majority of the states across the country.

Similarly, recent antagonism to mosques is not limited to the area around Ground Zero. The Pew Center on Religion published a report in September 2010 that found that at least thirty-five mosques around the country have faced opposition over the past two years.[17] In one California case, mosque opponents were advised to bring dogs to their demonstration since, as the leader of their group stated, Muslims "hate dogs."[18] Meanwhile, Terry Jones, a fringe religious leader in Florida, garnered international coverage for his plans to burn Qur'ans on September 11, 2010, and was talked out of the idea by Secretary of Defense Robert Gates, no less. In March 2011, however, Jones staged a "mock trial" of the Qur'an, which culminated in his public burning of the holy book, igniting deadly protests in Afghanistan.[19] Conservative talk show host Bill O'Reilly appeared on the popular daytime television show *The View* on October 14, 2010, where he stated that "Muslims killed us on 9/11," causing two of the hosts, Whoopi Goldberg and Joy Behar, to walk off stage in anger. During the 2010 election season, the Tea Party Nation called on its supporters to oust African

American Congressman Keith Ellison from his seat because he is Muslim.[20]

It would seem that the fear of terrorism, commonly (and regrettably) associated with Islam, is being usurped by a very popular fear of Muslims in general. Acceptance of Muslim Americans, a counterweight to these suspicions for many years, may also be receding. The questions are not just why this has happened, but why it has taken nine years for this dramatic change to occur and if it will remain.

One answer could be that the Muslim American community has itself become increasingly radical. The lunatic ravings of Yemeni-American firebrand Anwar Al-Awlaki, telling Muslim Americans to rise up against their government, certainly don't help. Popular suspicion may also be stoked by a few high-profile arrests of "home-grown" terrorists. (Many, though not all, of these cases are "sting" operations run by the FBI.) Representative Peter King (R-NY) has gone so far as to hold congressional hearings about the radicalization of American Muslims.

Yet, a 2010 study by the Triangle Center on Terrorism and Homeland Security found that the number of Muslim Americans involved in terrorist activities is miniscule compared to the size of the community, labeling the problem of Muslim American home-grown terrorism "a serious, but limited, problem."[21] Forty percent of Muslim domestic terrorism suspects since 2001 have been turned in by fellow Muslims,[22] and law enforcement officials from around the country vocally contradict King's claim of Muslim noncooperation.[23] Greg Sargent, a *Washington Post* columnist, calls King's hearings "buffoonery."[24]

Nativism and Paranoia

There may be better places to search for explanations for today's climate, including American traditions of nativism. As John

Higham's classic work *Strangers in the Land: Patterns of American Nativism, 1860–1925* makes abundantly clear, Catholics, Germans, Blacks, Jews, Asians, political radicals, and immigrants of all sorts have all been vilified by a doctrine known variously as Know-Nothingism, 100 Percent Americanism, or the Anglo-Saxon ideal. "Nativism," Higham writes, "was a defensive type of nationalism, but the defense varied as the nativist lashed out sometimes against a religious peril, sometimes against a revolutionary peril, sometimes against a racial peril."[25]

Muslim Americans today are cast as the latest villains in the grand nativist epic about the downfall of the United States. And while nativism offers a clue into explaining anti-Muslim feeling in the United States today, we can better understand the situation by turning to a related phenomenon that Richard Hofstadter identified in 1964. In his classic essay on political paranoia, Hofstadter argues that a recurring motif in American conservative discourse is a "paranoid style" of politics. He uses the term "paranoid" because he believes it best describes "the heated exaggeration, suspiciousness, and conspiratorial fantasies" of the right.[26] As Higham does, Hofstadter reaches back into the nineteenth century to provide a genealogy of his subject, but he is most interested in the Cold War politics of his age. The "paranoid style" was evident everywhere Hofstadter turned. He quotes Joseph McCarthy, who believed he was surrounded by "a conspiracy on a scale so immense as to dwarf any previous such venture in the history of man."[27] This paranoid disposition is driven by "catastrophe or the fear of catastrophe," which "is most likely to elicit the syndrome of paranoid rhetoric."[28] The paranoid style of American politics propels the fear and loathing of American Muslims today. The irrational panic that sharia law is on the cusp of conquering the nation has its roots in the Cold War conservative belief that the minions of the Soviet Union were deeply entrenched in the American ruling class and ready to turn on a ruble.

The modern anti-Muslim crusader in the United States believes that Islam is on the march in the country, and they are the last resistance. Just as immigration in the past left the nation nearly defenseless to the true and existential threats of the hour, so too does politically correct multiculturalism today. They believe that the conspiracy itself reaches high into the upper echelons of the ruling class, sometimes including President Obama himself. This may help explain why 24 percent of the electorate (and 46 percent of the GOP) in 2010, according to *Time*, believed that the president is a Muslim.[29]

There is certainly a kind of implied racial coding going on here—being Muslim also means that Obama is simply not one of "us"—but the feeling that a cabal of international socialists and Muslims have or are ready to take over the country is implicit in much right-wing rhetoric today, from Republican leader Sarah Palin's exhortation to "take our country back" (from what exactly?) to the demands to see Barack Obama's birth certificate and the labeling of Park51 as the "Obama Mosque."

Hofstadter's words sometimes sound eerily contemporary, making the connection between past paranoia and today's sentiments even clearer. "The modern right wing," he writes,

> feels dispossessed: America has been taken away from them and their kind, though they are determined to try to repossess it and to prevent the final act of subversion. The old American virtues have already been eaten away by cosmopolitans and intellectuals; the old competitive capitalism has been gradually undermined by socialist and communist schemers; the old national security and independence have been destroyed by treasonous plots, having as their most powerful agents not merely outsiders and foreigners but major statesmen seated at the very centers of American power. Their predecessors discovered foreign conspiracies; the modern radical right finds that conspiracy also embraces betrayal at home.[30]

It has lately become commonplace to argue that former President George W. Bush had been more respectful toward Islam than Obama, explaining why passions against Muslims only recently exploded. But this misses the point. Conservatives are driving today's anti-Muslim agenda, but under Bush's leadership, their notion of an imminent takeover of the United States government made little sense (that was left to Michael Moore's film *Fahrenheit 9/11* [2004], which illustrated a kind of paranoia of the left). On those few occasions when Bush did speak out for Muslim Americans and against hate crimes, the underlying point, as influential sociologist Max Weber would see it, was the state's monopoly on violence. The fact is that until recently, the American Muslim community was most concerned about state repression and racial profiling. Now, they have racial profiling *and* inflamed populist fear and anger to worry about.

Fear and Loathing of Islam

Something's gone terribly wrong.

In August 2007 the New York Police Department released a report called "Radicalization in the West: The Homegrown Threat," claiming that the looming danger to the United States was from "unremarkable" Muslim men under thirty-five who visit "extremist incubators." The language sounds ominous, conjuring up *Clockwork Orange*-style laboratories of human reprogramming, twisting average Muslims into instruments of evil. And yet what are these "incubators"? The report states that they are mosques, "cafes, cab driver hangouts, flophouses, prisons, student associations, non-governmental organizations, hookah (water pipe) bars, butcher shops and book stores"—in other words, precisely the places where ordinary life happens.[1]

But the report wasn't based on any independent social science research, and actual studies clearly refuted the very claims made by the NYPD. The RAND Corporation found that the number of homegrown radicals here is "tiny." "There are more than 3 million Muslims in the United States, and few more than 100 have joined jihad—about one out of every 30,000—suggesting an American Muslim population that remains hostile to jihadist ideology and its exhortations to violence," RAND's 2010 report found. "A mistrust of American Muslims by other Americans seems misplaced," it concluded.[2] In 2012, an analysis by the Triangle Center on Terrorism and Homeland Security also described the number of American Muslims involved in domestic terrorism since 2001 as "tiny." "This study's findings challenge Americans to be vigilant against the threat of homegrown terrorism while maintaining a responsible sense of proportion," it said.[3] And a 2011 Gallup survey found that American Muslims were the least likely of any major US religious group to consider attacks on civilians justified.[4]

Every group has its loonies. And yet the idea that American Muslim communities are foul nests of hatred, where dark-skinned men plot Arabic violence while combing one another's beards, persists. In fact, it's worse than that. In the past few years, another narrative about American Muslims has come along, which sows a different kind of paranoia. While the old story revolves around security, portraying American Muslims as potential terrorists or terrorist sympathizers, the new narrative operates more along the axis of culture. Simple acts of religious or cultural expression and the straightforward activities of Muslim daily life have become suspicious. Building a mosque in Lower Manhattan or in Sheepshead Bay, Brooklyn, or in Murfreesboro, Tennessee, becomes an act of "stealth jihad." Muslims filing for divorce invokes the bizarre charge of "creeping Sharia." A dual-language Arabic-English high school in New York is demonized as a "madrassa." Even the fact that some Butterball turkeys are "halal" was enough to fire up the bigotry last Thanksgiving, the most American of holidays.[5]

What happens when ordinary life becomes grounds for suspicion without a hint of wrongdoing, when law enforcement premises its work on spying on the quotidian and policing the unremarkable, and when the everyday affairs of American Muslim life can so easily be transformed into nefarious intent? Something has gone terribly wrong for American Muslims when, more than a decade after the terrorist attacks of September 11, anti-Muslim sentiment in the United States continues to grow, reaching about half of the population, according to polls. In fact, the idea that American Muslims are to be feared or loathed or excluded from the United States is not only present but being actively promoted by significant and influential sectors of American society.

· · ·

In September 2011, *Wired* broke the story that the FBI was telling its counterterrorism agents in training that mainstream American Muslims are probably terrorist sympathizers, that the Prophet Muhammad was a "cult leader," and that the religiously mandated practice of giving charity in Islam is no more than a "funding mechanism for combat." The training materials, which stated that FBI agents had the "ability to bend or suspend the law and impinge on freedoms of others," identify other insidious techniques Muslims use for promoting jihad, including "immigration" and "lawsuits"—in other words, the ordinary uses of the American political system. The revelations forced the FBI to remove 876 pages from its manuals.[6]

Another egregious example that came to light around the same time was that the NYPD, as part of its training, was screening *The Third Jihad*, a film that claims "the true agenda of much of Islam in America" is "a strategy to infiltrate and dominate" the country. The film ran on a continuous loop for somewhere between three months and a year of training and was viewed by at least 1,489 officers.[7] Yet another example involved Army Lt. Col. Matthew Dooley, who taught a course at the Pentagon's Joint Forces Staff College that informed senior officers that the United States would have to fight a "total war" against the world's Muslims, including abandoning the international laws of war that protect civilians (deemed "no longer relevant"), and possibly applying "the historical precedents of Dresden, Tokyo, Hiroshima, Nagasaki" to destroy Islam's holy cities of Mecca and Medina. Claiming "Islam is an ideology rather than solely a religion," the class taught that the United States was "culturally vulnerable" to this threat because of its "'judeo-christian' [*sic*] ethic of reason and tolerance." Only in the wake of the revelations did the Pentagon cancel the course and relieve Dooley from his teaching assignment.[8]

The consequences of these efforts to promote anti-Muslim beliefs and sentiments influence how American Muslims practice their faith, engage with their neighbors, cooperate with law enforcement, work at their jobs, and study at school. Anti-mosque activity, according to the ACLU, has taken place in more than half the states in the country.[9] And American Muslims, who make up 1 to 2 percent of the population, account for more than 20 percent of religion-based filings with the Equal Employment Opportunity Commission.[10]

There is legitimate concern about future acts of terrorism in the United States. But there is also plenty of reason to be skeptical of many of the plots that the FBI has disrupted, which are usually scripted by a paid informant, often with a criminal record himself. In one such case, that of the Newburgh Four, the judge explained this clearly during the sentencing phase of the trial and after the nearly indigent men had been found guilty of planning to shoot down military airplanes and blow up two synagogues in Riverdale, New York. "I believe beyond a shadow of a doubt that there would have been no crime here except the government instigated it, planned it and brought it to fruition," US District Judge Colleen McMahon said, adding, "That does not mean there was no crime." The four men were sentenced to twenty-five years in prison, the minimum sentence allowed under federal guidelines.[11] Needless to say, the publicity these "plots" receive feeds the anti-Muslim fervor.

Media coverage plays a major role in ramping up anti-Muslim attitudes, for a very simple reason: 62 percent of Americans, according to a 2010 *Time* magazine poll, say they have never met a Muslim.[12] (If you do know a Muslim, you're less likely to harbor anti-Muslim feelings, polls also show.)[13] Absent ordinary personal contact, most Americans will get their views of Islam through television, cable news, talk radio, the Internet, and really bad action movies. Because the counterweight of personal contact is missing, Muslim attitudes are easily ventriloquized and distorted, and

Muslims themselves often rendered mute or suspect. The myth that American Muslims haven't spoken out against terrorism, for example, continues to haunt the community, even though they do so loudly and repeatedly.

Republican politicians, meanwhile, were falling all over themselves to vilify Muslims during the 2012 presidential primary. Herman Cain proclaimed that "a majority of Muslims share the extremist views," initially vowing not to appoint any Muslims to his cabinet. Rick Santorum endorsed religious profiling, saying that "obviously Muslims would be someone [sic] you'd look at." Newt Gingrich compared Muslims to Nazis in 2010, when he opposed building an Islamic center in Lower Manhattan. "Nazis don't have the right to put up a sign next to the Holocaust museum in Washington," he said. And, in 2007, Mitt Romney said, "Based on the numbers of American Muslims [as a percentage] in our population, I cannot see that a cabinet position would be justified. But of course, I would imagine that Muslims could serve at lower levels of my administration."[14] Whatever happened to the matter of qualifications? But hey, if you're a Muslim, that's all you'll ever be. Romney has hired Walid Phares, part of the active anti-Muslim network, as a foreign policy adviser, and GOP voters continue to consider that President Obama is a Muslim in large numbers (52 percent of Mississippi GOP members thought so in March 2012).[15]

It gets stranger still. When media portrayals of everyday American Muslim life are produced, the very ordinariness is attacked as a lie. TLC's show *All-American Muslim* premiered in November to favorable reviews. The show, which focused on five Lebanese-American Shi'i Muslim families in the Dearborn, Michigan, area, was a bit of a yawner for racy reality TV, but it was a useful kind of ethnography for Americans unfamiliar with the stuff of daily American Muslim life. Immediately, the organized anti-Muslim network kicked into gear. The Florida Family Association, basically a one-man show run by David Caton, led a boycott of the show via email that was quickly picked up by the extreme right-wing anti-Islamic blogosphere, and led to Lowe's and Kayak.com pulling their ads. Caton's email read, "The show profiles only Muslims that appear to be ordinary folks while excluding many Islamic believers whose agenda poses a clear and present danger to liberties and traditional values that the majority of Americans cherish."[16]

Follow the logic. The only thing accepted as "normal" for a Muslim is to act like an extremist. Ordinary Muslim folk appearing to live ordinary Muslim lives? That's just plain suspicious.

The same belief drives the NYPD's surveillance of American Muslim communities. Police Commissioner Raymond Kelly informed American Muslim audiences in 2007 that the radicalization report of that year was "never intended to be a policy prescriptive for law enforcement actions," but we now know he was lying. Meanwhile, we also know how American Muslims who were not suspected of any wrongdoing were spied on in New York and beyond by the NYPD, with the CIA's help. (See the introduction for more.) Undercover officers chatted up bookstore owners, played cricket with Muslims, and uncovered such unsavory things as a travel agency on Atlantic Avenue in Brooklyn, where an officer "observed a female named 'Rasha' working in the travel agency, she recommended the 'Royal Jordanian Airline.'"[17]

The department also spied on Muslim college students throughout the Tri-State Area, including at Brooklyn College, where I teach. Soheeb Amin, president of the college's Islamic Society, told me that the AP reports were more of a confirmation than a revelation. "We know that there are people who are looking for excuses to get you in trouble for your religion," he noted, and so he has adjusted. "I don't talk about politics. I don't talk about anything controversial. I don't do anything that can raise suspicion." Like many American Muslims, he feels his rights to practice his religion and express his ideas have been compromised. He told me he prays the mandatory five daily prayers, "but now I know that there are

NYPD reports that mention that people prayed four times a day, and I guess five is worse than that," he added, only half-joking.

◆ ◆ ◆

Does this mean that the United States is an Islamophobic country? Of course not. Large support for American Muslims exists in many quarters. Polls may suggest that about half the population is anti-Muslim, but that leaves half that isn't. In many quarters of the country, there is genuine, not suspicious, interest in American Muslims and the realities they face, as evidenced by the fact that TLC produced *All-American Muslim*. Aasif Mandvi's contributions to *The Daily Show* routinely deflate the power of this contemporary prejudice, and libraries, museums, classrooms, and houses of worship across the country now regularly include Muslims and Islam in their programming in an attempt to further understanding and combat bigotry.

American Muslims have responded to events over the past decade and the expansion of an anti-Muslim network largely by being more, not less, visible. The number of mosques grew 74 percent over the past decade, despite the opposition Muslims sometimes confront in their construction.[18] Even if a 2011 poll found that 48 percent of American Muslims reported experiencing discrimination in the previous twelve months, they also showed more optimism than other Americans in the poll that their lives would be better in five years (perhaps, in part, because of today's discrimination).[19] The guiding belief in the American Muslim community today is that the country will recognize that Muslims have always been and will continue to be a part of America.

An ordinary life is more meaningful than it sounds. It signifies being able to live your life as you define yourself, not as others define you, and being able to assume a life free of unwarranted government prying. In fact, ordinariness is the foundation of an open society, because it endows citizens with a private life and demands that the government operate openly—not the other way around, which is how closed societies operate.

There is a real danger that the same tools that enable today's Islamophobia will continue to migrate and expand with little or no public outcry. The FBI deployed a strategy of sting operations against Occupy protesters that was eerily familiar to that used against American Muslims, to little outrage.[20] The president enacted a law that allowed for the indefinite detention of American citizens, and after a federal judge struck it down as unconstitutional, Congress rushes in two days later to try to keep it on the books.[21] American citizens can be assassinated by presidential decree, making a mockery of due process. Forget the Muslims. This mission creep is as good a reason as any to pay attention to Islamophobia today—because when the ordinary affairs of the United States include such actions, the stakes are nothing less than extraordinary.

The Oak Creek Massacre

The tragedy of the shooting in Oak Creek, Wisconsin, on August 5, 2012, is enormous. Six innocent people were gunned down in a Sikh temple by a white supremacist—but they weren't innocent because they were Sikh, they were innocent because, well, *they were innocent*! Had Wade Michael Page walked into a mosque and begun shooting Muslims, the victims of his rampage would have been no more deserving of death.

It's true that we don't know Page's precise motivations, but in all likelihood it wasn't Sikhophobia, a term barely known in the United States. It was Islamophobia. That's why to say that Page made a "mistake" in targeting Sikhs, as many have reported, or that Sikhs are "unfairly" targeted as Muslims, as CNN stated,[1] is to imply that it would be "correct" to attack Muslims. Well, it's not, and even if this is an error embedded in the routine carelessness of cable news, we need to be attentive to the implications.

Immediately following the massacre, there was plenty of media coverage about the Sikh religion and its origins and practices. Knowledge is always welcome over ignorance, but what we really need to educate ourselves about is the way racism operates in this country and its deadly character. The facts are not consoling. According to the Southern Poverty Law Center (SPLC), the extreme right wing grew "explosively" in 2011 and for the third year in a row. That year the SPLC tracked 1,018 hate groups, up from 602 in 2000, the year that Page is reported to have appeared on the Neo-Nazi scene. The number of hate groups, in other words, almost doubled in twelve years, and that growth accelerated after the election of Obama.[2] The targets have also expanded. White supremacists have always been obsessed with Jews, blacks, and the LGBT community as their objects of hate. And about a decade ago, Jews and blacks were Page's main villains, according to Pete Simi, who interviewed him in 2001. But things have changed since then.[3] What continues to be underappreciated is how the hatred of Muslims has become a major motivating and mobilizing force in this putrid scene.[4]

Meanwhile, polemicists like Sam Harris, magazines like *Commentary*, politicians like Peter King, and loony bloggers like Pamela Geller and Debbie Schlussel have been screaming at the top of their lungs for years that there is no such thing as Islamophobia. As Laila Lalami points out,[5] they talk only about "Islamophobia"—the word set off in scare quotes, as if Muslims have devised some sort of plot to exploit the liberal guilt of Americans through political correctness, the fallback term right-wingers constantly throw out for anything they don't like.

But Islamophobia is real. Not only does it exist but it's an increasingly toxic part of the political discourse of this country. To think that the compulsive hatred and fear of Muslims is reserved for the extreme right is to wall oneself off from how mainstream conservative discourse participates in this paranoid obsession that the old America is being nefariously and surreptitiously taken away from them. At bottom, this is an anxiety about the loss of privileges and power, quite likely related though not exclusively driven by downward economic mobility. (The *New York Times* offered the suggestive detail that property Page owned in North Carolina was foreclosed on in January.)[6] Whatever the causes, the form that this hatred takes is cultural, and Muslims, Mexicans, nonwhite immigrants, really anyone who isn't "American" by the most conservative definition becomes suspect.

Still, it is Muslims who are now some of the biggest villains in this story of decline, as the well-funded Islamophobic network pushes the paranoid fantasy that sharia law is about to usurp the Constitution or, even more simply, that Islam is not a religion at all but a "cult."[7] One day after the Oak Creek shooting, the mosque of Joplin, Missouri, was burned to the ground by Jedidiah Stout (who also attempted to burn down the Planned Parenthood center in Joplin).[8] In this climate, anyway, mosques are seen not as American places of worship but as temporary hotels for perpetual foreigners and fiery incubators for terrorism. But the statistics show another story. As reported by Liz Goodwin at *Yahoo News,* "Between 1980 and 2001, non-Islamic American extremists carried out about two-thirds of all terrorism in the United States, according to FBI statistics cited by the Council on Foreign Relations. Between 2002 and 2005, that figure jumped to 95 percent. In the ten years following 2001, only 6 percent of terrorist acts in America have been the work of Islamic extremists."[9]

Yet Islamophobia is not solely the domain of the extreme right wing. It was also part of the Republican campaign for president in 2012. One of Mitt Romney's foreign policy advisers was Walid Phares, part of the active anti-Muslim network.[10] Michele Bachmann sent a letter urging the Justice Department to investigate Hillary Clinton's adviser Huma Abedin, among others, for "the deep penetration in the halls of our United States government" by the Muslim Brotherhood.[11] Peter King held show trials falsely accusing Muslim Americans of radicalization and sedition.[12] And, as late as 2012, one in three Republicans *still* believed Obama is a Muslim.[13] Oh, brother!

Meanwhile, the current Democratic establishment shouldn't be absolved of its sins. The Pentagon and the FBI have all promoted the most extreme, pernicious, and twisted views about civilizational conflict with Muslims, and the FBI actively sends spies and informants into the community, often ensnaring vulnerable idiots in bogus plots. Authorities then announce the scripted arrests in ominous tones, further ramping up fear about Muslim Americans.

Or here's another example. In September 2011, Bruce Norum, the top federal immigration official in Montana, forwarded a virulently racist chain email to immigration attorney Shahid Haque-

Hausrath that read, "I want you to leave. I want you to go back to your desert sandpit where women are treated like rats and dogs. I want you to take your religion, your friends, and your family back to your Islamic extremists, and STAY THERE!"[14] This is the man who holds the power to arrest, detain, and deport immigrants in Montana. One would think this would be evidence that Norum's not quite capable of performing his duties without bias and therefore must have lost his job. Instead, he was simply suspended from his duties for eight months.

And then there's Michael Bloomberg. Under his watch, the NYPD has been engaged in a massive spying campaign against New York's Muslim American community that included compiling huge amounts of information on ordinary Muslims going about their regular activities at school, on the streets, and while shopping, eating, and praying. As is abundantly clear from the reporting on this issue, probable cause didn't drive this surveillance. Ethnicity and religion did. By not repudiating the program, the mayor and the NYPD sent a clear message to the country that mosques and Muslims are not to be trusted. And yet, while properly paying a condolence visit to the city's biggest Gurdwara, the mayor proclaimed, "No matter who you are, no matter where you're from, no matter what religion you profess, you have a right to be safe in your homes, in your places of worship, on the streets of New York City."[15] He offered no hint of recognition that his NYPD surveillance programs chips away at the security of Muslim New Yorkers.

What we need to recognize is the way that the hatred, fear, and suspicion of Muslims has seeped so effortlessly into our culture. Under the guise of common sense, the vilification of Muslims is normalized and naturalized by a broad swath of the population, including leading politicians, law enforcement officials, petty bureaucrats, and the media. Wade Michael Page was a racist, bigoted extremist. But the Islamophobia that drives people like Page is not exceptional. It's part of our mainstream.

11

White with Rage

In August 2008, my book *How Does It Feel to Be a Problem? Being Young and Arab in America* was published by Penguin Press. A few months later, Barack Obama was elected president of the United States. Despite my own delusions of importance as a writer, I must admit that there is no direct connection, but the facts are related nevertheless. Since my book is largely about how Arab Muslim Americans had survived the erosion of their civil rights after the terrorist attacks of September 11, 2001, the election of Obama, a constitutional lawyer and community organizer, is significant. His presidency seemed to promise a new era of racial justice in American politics, what many have called the arrival of a "postracial" age in the United States. But in the years since Obama became president, Muslim Americans have witnessed something new and far from a nirvana of coexistence, namely the rise of an angry, populist movement across the nation that is opposed not just to the free exercise of their religion, but sometimes to their very presence in the country. How did this happen?

Before answering this question, it's worth reflecting on what life for Muslim and Arab Americans was like under George W. Bush's administration, the period that had inspired me to write my book. It's no exaggeration to say that prior to the terrorist attacks of September 11, Muslim and Arab Americans registered very little on the daily radar of most Americans. We were largely an invisible minority, and if Americans thought about us at all, they conjured angry overseas mobs, swarthy terrorists, or gluttonous oil sheikhs, in other words the stock pictures of the Orientalist imaginary. With a few exceptions, such as the 1998 film *The Siege*, contemporary

American popular culture almost never represented us in America, let alone as Americans. If we were present, it was as relatively harmless and isolated individuals. The cross-dressing Corporal Klinger, played by Lebanese American actor Jamie Farr, on the TV show *M*A*S*H* was probably the best known Arab American on television, and if you asked someone to name a Muslim American, you would probably hear an answer either of Muhammad Ali, now comfortably celebrated, or Malcolm X, who was killed long ago. But after September 11, the idea that Muslims and Arabs were actually living next door became a major source of terrorist anxiety. Immediately following the attacks, vigilante violence skyrocketed against Arabs, Muslims, and anyone who resembled "a Muslim," which generally meant brown skin or something wrapped around one's head. Almost overnight, we had become a shadowy community to be afraid of.

The Bush administration helped fuel this anxiety. While it is true that six days after the terrorist attacks President Bush visited the Islamic Center of Washington, DC, where he spoke out against vigilantism and told the country that "the face of terror is not the true faith of Islam . . . Islam is peace,"[1] the actions of his administration spoke louder than his words. The FBI had asked the public for help following the terrorist attacks and established a hotline for callers. Within just seven days, the bureau received over ninety-six thousand tips or potential leads from a nervous public.[2] For weeks after the attacks, Attorney General John Ashcroft would announce the number of people arrested in connection with the investigation, which reached over a thousand, in what seemed like an obvious attempt to tell the American public that they were working the case hard, especially after having failed to thwart the attacks in the first place. As it turned out, none of those arrested after September 11 had anything to do with al-Qaeda. (Zacarias Moussaoui, the so-called twentieth hijacker, had been arrested on August 16, 2001.) In an October 2001 speech to the nation's mayors, Ashcroft proffered the suggestion that terrorism was limited to immigrants to the United States. "Let the terrorists among us be warned," he intoned. "If you overstay your visa even by one day, we will arrest you."[3] And in 2002, the government announced its new "Operation Tips" program, wherein it aimed to recruit letter carriers and couriers, utility company workers, cable TV installers, and others whose jobs provided access to private homes, as amateur spies who were to report "suspicious" activity to the government. Only after loud public opposition—since in this case it was not just the rights of immigrants, Arabs, and Muslims that were being violated—was the program cancelled.[4]

Other law enforcement policies played out similarly. On September 11, 2002, the government began a program of "special registration" that required nonimmigrant men from twenty-five Muslim-majority countries to register their whereabouts in the country (see Chapter 3). Then, there was heightened immigration enforcement that directly targeted Arab and Muslim communities, the deployment of spies and use of informants in the community, wiretaps without court warrants, the abuse of the material witness statute (keeping people in jail longer than they should have been), the extended examination of Muslim charities, and more. All of these policies were corrosive on the human level for Arab and Muslim Americans, ultimately breaking down all trust between people as well as alienating the communities from law enforcement.

Almost all these programs fueled the media for years after the September 11 attacks. And as we were transformed from invisibility to hypervisibility, we now occupied that zone in the American imagination traditionally reserved for enemies and subversives. But the random acts of vigilante violence notwithstanding, the new focus on us didn't translate into grassroots movements of opposition during these years. Why should it have? The Bush administration was announcing to the public that it was taking care of the supposed threat we posed so they didn't have to. The only time the

American public became highly agitated about a related issue was when, in 2006, the Bush administration proposed selling the management of major American shipping ports to Dubai Ports World, a company based in the United Arab Emirates. After having been told for years by their government that Arabs and Muslims were to be feared, the American public decided this was a contradiction too big to bear. The outcry was loud and obnoxious, and Dubai Ports World eventually sold their American port management business to AIG.

With this newfound scrutiny came an almost complete lack of understanding of the texture of our lives. What often took its place was the most simplistic stereotyping of Muslims or an almost willfully ignorant knowledge about Islam, even from top government officials. Dale Watson, the FBI's top intelligence official during and after the terrorist attacks, was asked if he could describe the difference between Sunni and Shiʻi Muslims. "Not technically, no" was his response.[5] Just prior to the invasion of Iraq in 2003, even President Bush reportedly had to be schooled on the elementary fact that that practitioners of Islam fell into two main sects.[6] We Muslims and Arabs were constantly talked about, but rarely heard from, and the discussions about us were shallow, presumptuous, and dangerous. Since few Americans had any real knowledge about Islam or the Arab world, gross generalizations and bigoted statements flew easily and unchallenged across the airwaves.

"He's an Arab"

I decided sometime in 2004 that I would attempt, in my own small way, to counteract this terrible and growing tendency toward dehumanizing Arab and Muslim Americans by writing a book. I sought to fill the emptiness of the stereotype with the stuff of human life, and the best way to do that, I surmised, was to ground my research in a specific geography and with a particular group of people.

I chose to write about Brooklyn, New York, home to the largest number of Arab Americans according to the 2000 US census, and where I live. I also chose to write about primarily young Arab Muslim Americans in their early twenties, since it seems to me that to be young and figure out your place in the world is already difficult, but to do so with a growing hostility from society around you is even more trying. I had a sense of the kind of stories I wanted to write about. They were the ones I was hearing from friends and occasionally reading about, but I didn't go specifically looking for the stories that ended up in my book. Instead, I visited mosques and community centers, talked to friends and had them ask their friends, consulted with lawyers, and spread the word that if anyone wanted to tell me a story, I would offer a sympathetic ear. Writing the book became my own journey through twenty-something Arab America.

What I discovered was a generation that took its responsibilities to represent itself very seriously. This was particularly true among the more devout Muslims. Pious Muslim women told me repeatedly, for example, that wearing a headscarf was not done solely for reasons of religious virtue but was also motivated by the need to represent themselves and not let others represent them. The headscarf became a symbol of religious pride and an opportunity for non-Muslims to ask the young women questions about the faith, and many had developed an index of answers to the questions. I found a lot of anxiety among young Muslim men in particular regarding their own employment prospects. They worried, not without reason, that all the negative sentiment expressed toward Muslims and Arabs would narrow their chances to land jobs. I also heard about a few blatant acts of vigilante violence, but many more people underscored to me the support they had from neighbors and friends.

Then there were stories about the government. After the September 11 attacks, Arab and Muslim communities in and around

Brooklyn felt besieged by the various government policies and law enforcement initiatives that singled them out. Lawyers complained to me about the difficulties they had finding clients in the immediate aftermath of the attacks. I interviewed one young Syrian American woman whose family was detained for three months after the attacks and then were just as suddenly released. The father of another young Palestinian man had been arrested in a sting operation and was sitting in jail awaiting deportation, so the young man had been forced to assume a new role not just in life, but within his family too. And so on. A 2006 study by the Vera Institute of Justice, an independent nonprofit organization dedicated to examining law enforcement strategies, reached similar findings.

The social consequence of this kind of government scrutiny was what I was mostly interested in documenting, and it was fascinating to hear stories from Arab American shopkeepers about the support they received from their neighbors, or to witness the active involvement of human rights advocates in the affairs of the community, or to hear about churches and synagogues that were pursuing interfaith efforts to get to know their Muslim neighbors better. In the face of government repression bearing down on an essentially vulnerable community, active resistance was found among key elements of American civil society, operating with integrity and sometimes very effectively to counteract the rampant scapegoating.

And so it seemed reasonable to believe that the civil rights of Arabs and Muslim Americans would again be if not completely restored, at least not made into a political football to score easy points with by the time Barack Obama was elected president. After all, at the Democratic National Convention of 2004, Obama (then a Senate candidate) had spoken out unambiguously for the civil rights of Arab Americans. "If there's an Arab-American family being rounded up without benefit of an attorney or due process, that threatens my civil liberties," he said to wide applause.[7] And by

2008, the American public was growing tired of George W. Bush, who was serving out his second term, and of the wars overseas. The government's disastrous response to Hurricane Katrina signaled to many that the administration was arrogantly out of touch with the needs of its people, and the sudden near collapse of the banking system translated into a loss of confidence in Republican economic policies. Change was in the air.

Then again, just being Muslim or Arab American became a major political issue in the 2008 presidential election. John McCain, the Republican candidate for president, tried to dress down a woman at a Town Hall meeting who said she couldn't "trust" Obama because "he's an Arab." McCain responded by saying, "No Ma'am. He's a decent family man, citizen, that I just happen to have disagreements with," as if being a decent family man is the opposite of being an Arab.[8] Meanwhile, the Obama campaign, which had moved two women in hijab out of camera during a campaign stop, called the repeated allegation that Obama was a Muslim a "smear," as if being a Muslim was the equivalent to being a criminal. Still, I was optimistic that these could be chalked up to the dying breaths of political opportunism at the expense of Muslim Americans.

Boy, was I wrong, and not just because the Obama administration has followed, and in many cases even expanded, the same harmful policies as its predecessor on civil rights issues. Under Obama, the government has relied more on its dubious use of spies and informants within the Muslim American community, authorized killing American citizens without due process through its now common tactic of drone strikes, deported unauthorized immigrants at a far greater rate than George W. Bush, grown the surveillance state massively, protected its own legally questionable actions by invoking the State Secrets Protection Act, and much more.

Although the Obama administration speaks in a far less aggressive rhetoric when implementing these terrible policies, the popular climate since 2008 for Arab and Muslim Americans nevertheless

has neither improved nor stayed the same but generally gotten precipitously worse. About half the American population harbors negative feelings toward Muslims, according to polls. Opinions are one
thing, actions are another, and in the past few years in the United
States, a right-wing anti-Muslim activist core has mobilized against
a perceived "Islamic threat" on American values and the American
system in ways they hadn't prior to 2008, often through legislation
in state legislatures making it illegal to consider sharia (Islamic legal
principles)—or sometimes referred to simply as "foreign law" in
the legislation—in state courts. The Republican National Platform
of 2012 contained almost identical language, and such legislation
has been introduced in at least thirty-two state legislatures, even
though in the American legal system the Constitution necessarily
takes precedence over any other law. But much of the anti-Muslim
agitation is about phantom threats anyway.

Nor is the putative threat of sharia law usurping the Constitution the only anti-Muslim agitation in the American public sphere.
Legislators actively promote the idea that Muslim Americans are
fifth-column infiltrators, poised to take over the country in the
name of Islam. In the summer of 2012, five Republican lawmakers
sent a letter to the Justice Department claiming their "serious security concerns" of the "deep penetration in the halls of our United
States government" by the Muslim Brotherhood.[9] (Other Republicans dismissed the allegation for what it is: ludicrous.) Peter King,
a Republican congressman from New York and chairman of the
Homeland Security Commission, held five public hearings about
radicalization in the American Muslim community, even though
all the serious social science on this question shows that American
Muslims overwhelmingly reject extremist ideology.

Fear Inc.

Something has changed in America. When my book was published, it was rare to see large numbers of Americans on the streets protesting Muslim Americans exercising their right to practice their religion. In the last couple of years, however, we have seen raucous anti-Muslim protests around the country, from Tennessee to New York, from California to Michigan. In the minds of many, it seems, a new narrative has taken hold, one that operates more along the lines of culture than through the threat to national security. Acts of cultural and religious expression, and even just the ordinary activities of Muslim Americans, have now become suspicious on another level beyond imminent violence. Just being Muslim is now seen as a threat to the very culture of America.

And so we return to the question regarding the origin of this change. Is this new populist agitation against Muslim Americans the logical outcome of a decade-long War on Terror that shows little sign of ending? Is it due to the dogged persistence of Orientalist clichés that never seem to die but multiply into new formulations? Is it because of a few high-profile arrests of Muslim American terrorism suspects in the United States in recent years? Is it a consequence of an American foreign policy that depends upon demonizing its overseas enemies? And has this demonization of Muslims abroad traveled back, like a chicken coming home to roost, to American Muslims? Or is the rise of populist anger at Muslim Americans pushed by a small group of right-wing ideologues who wish to goad the US population to the right of the political spectrum for specific foreign policy goals—often connected to American intervention in the Muslim-majority countries and support for Israel's policies against the Palestinians?

The Center for American Progress, a liberal think tank in the United States, has supplied good evidence for this last answer. In August 2011, the center published *Fear Inc.: The Roots of the Is-*

lamophobia Network in America, which argues that the rise of Islamophobia in the United States is connected to "a small, tightly networked group of misinformation experts guiding an effort that reaches millions of Americans through effective advocates, media partners, and grassroots organizing." The report actually identified the key players in this Islamophobic network, as well as the more than forty million dollars paid out by seven foundations over ten years to support their detestable mission.[10] While there is likely some truth to this reason, and all of the reasons, I think many miss the bigger picture. *Fear Inc.*, for example, makes a convincing case, but it also assumes that people can be directed to act by the network and not by their own desires or for their own reasons.

Maybe there is another motivation. Perhaps this rising populism has less to do with Muslim Americans specifically and more to do with the changing demographics of the United States. Put another way, perhaps the anger directed at us is at least as much a symptom of a general malaise that some Americans feel about their changing fortunes and dwindling stature as it is about specific foreign policy objectives or a kind of classical anti-Muslim bigotry. The phantom fears surrounding Muslim America may be driven by an anxiety held by an older, white, and Christian America that is nervously confronting the end of its majority in American politics. And the fact that this populism has risen to prominence after 2008, that is to say after the election of Barack Obama, is no coincidence. Obama symbolizes to them the beginning of the end of their historic privileges.

Actually, their fears are not unfounded. In 2008, the US Census Bureau projected that in 2042 the population of the country would be majority minority, that is to say, white Americans would then constitute less than 50 percent of the population. (Currently minorities account for about 37 percent of the population.)[11] In some ways, we are almost already there. The Census Bureau revealed in July 2011 that more than half of the babies born in the country be-

longed to current minority groups,[12] and in October 2012 the Pew
Forum on Religion and Public Life released a study showing that
Protestants now account for less than half of the population—as
opposed to forty years ago when they made up about two-thirds
of the nation.[13]

The racial, religious, and ethnic transformation the United
States has been experiencing since the immigration laws changed
in 1965, when the door was opened to non-European immigrants,
is indeed profound. In some ways, this transformation is even more
significant to an American identity based on whiteness than the
end of slavery or the end of segregation in the United States. Those
watershed moments in American history meant that the majority
lost much of its ability to impose its will on a minority. This time,
however, the concept of a majority in society will itself become
outdated.

Even though Muslim Americans account for somewhere between 1 and 2 percent of the population, our oft-remarked-upon
and exaggerated difference from the majority matters to those who
worry about the disappearance of an America they feel they know.
Maybe this is why we repeatedly hear the fears that Muslims are
taking over America, an impossibility considering our numbers
and influence. The fact that it is far more socially acceptable to
express negative opinions about Muslims than virtually any other
racial, religious, or ethnic group also suggests that much of the hostility directed at us could be a displacement for general feelings of
impending usurpation from a position of privilege. What else explains the strange and enduring allegation that President Obama is
actually a Muslim, which becomes another way of saying that the
African American Obama is not one of "us," as "Muslim" becomes
a stand-in for many kinds of otherness?

We don't have to take the idea of a "white America" too literally here either. Race and racial thinking is the long tragedy of the
American drama, and any talk of white identity may invoke older

images of hoods and burning crosses. But that's not how the current anxiety about losing a place of privilege in the nation expresses itself today. It's more a feeling of social melancholy expressed in many ways, from anti-immigrant movements like the Minutemen to the rise of the Tea Party, and frequently channeled on Fox News. Behind the anger, one often hears a pervasive sense of loss. When a Muslim community on Staten Island wanted to build an Islamic Center in 2010, they met with opposition from their neighbors, and the mournful feeling that the old America was slipping away was expressed by one protestor: "We just want to leave our neighborhood the way it is—Christian, Catholic."[14]

The *Atlantic* recognized this cultural anxiety about the changing demography in the United States when it published an article in 2009 called "The End of White America?" The article quotes sociologist Matt Wray, who studies whiteness in America today: "Following the black-power movement, all of the other minority groups that followed took up various forms of activism, including brown power and yellow power and red power. Of course the problem is, if you try and have a 'white power' movement, it doesn't sound good." The article continues, "The result is a racial pride that dare not speak its name, and that defines itself through cultural cues instead—a suspicion of intellectual elites and city dwellers, a preference for folksiness and plainness of speech (whether real or feigned), and the association of a working-class white minority with 'the real America.'"[15] Anti-Muslim populist agitation—politically permissible in ways that mobilizing against other minorities simply isn't—adopts similar characteristics that likewise work to build a culture of pride in that same white, Christian America that now feels anxiously under siege. These include suspicions of a "politically correct" elite (that is, in this case, forcing Muslims onto average Americans), a direct alignment of Christian with American values, and a sense that this populist vanguard is the last, best defense of the "real" America.

The Browning of America

At the very fringes, an explicit "white power" movement does in fact exist in the United States, and according the Southern Poverty Law Center, which tracks domestic hate groups, "white power" and other right-wing extremist groups have grown "explosively" in recent years. (I discuss this more in Chapter 10.) And yet the "white power" movement is only the most extreme example of a narrative of discomfort between an older version of America and a new multicultural, multiethnic, and multifaith America, but the fretful sentiment is commonly found among large swaths of the population. The best evidence for this, particularly when considering attitudes toward Muslim Americans, is found in a 2011 study coproduced by the Brookings Institution and the Public Religion Research Institute titled *What It Means to Be an American: Attitudes in an Increasingly Diverse America Ten Years after 9/11*.[16] The researchers polled 2,450 adult Americans on a variety of pressing political questions surrounding immigration and identity, and the results are intriguing, particularly because the study took age, education, and political leaning into account. While it was not solely concerned with American attitudes toward Muslims, the study did consider many questions about American attitudes to Islam; the results clearly show that suspicion of Muslims divides along political and generational lines. (The study did not quantify responses by race.)

According to the poll, older Republicans specifically, not the public generally, are the most predisposed to be suspicious. Fewer than half of the Republicans surveyed held favorable views of Muslims, compared with about two-thirds of the Democrats, and younger Americans (eighteen- to twenty-nine-year-olds) had twice as much social interaction with Muslims compared to their seniors. Nearly two-thirds of Republicans say that the values of Islam are at odds with American values and that trust in Fox News correlates highly with negative attitudes about Islam. Significantly, the number of Republicans that perceives a conflict between American values and Islam (63 percent) is in the same ballpark as of Republicans who also see immigrants generally as threatening American customs and values (55 percent). Through its many questions, the poll confirms the view that those holding the most ardent anti-Muslim attitudes come mainly from a very specific, generally older, and highly conservative segment of the population, precisely the ones who would feel most threatened by the browning of America.

It may not seem so, but this is ultimately good news. For one thing, the current generation of younger Americans, the most religiously and ethnically diverse in the nation's history, tends to be less opposed to Muslim Americans than their senior counterparts, though 23 percent of younger Americans still bewilderingly believe that American Muslims are trying to establish sharia law in the land. While it's always possible that people's opinions change as they age, the overall trends in the survey strongly suggest a society of more rather than less inclusion.

More important in the short run is the recognition that we don't have to assume a "clash of civilizations" confrontation every time a conflict with Muslim Americans arises. We can and should be thinking about politics in context, and that means thinking carefully and deeply about what the cleavages in American society currently are and from where they derive. We need not believe that large numbers of Americans are and will forever be opposed to Islam and Muslims.

But the bad news is not absent either. Anti-Muslim agitation is a political reality in the United States today, and it needs far more attention than it is currently being given. It's also entirely reasonable, unfortunately, to expect more resentment, elevated anxiety, and the increased possibility of violence in the years to come, as the demographic changes in the country become even more evident. If and when more violence arrives, the challenge will be the same as it was with the September 11 attacks. We shouldn't rush to judgment, we shouldn't look for easy scapegoats, and we shouldn't blame an entire religion or race for the actions of a few. What we need to invest in, now and in the future, are more complex ways of thinking about American society and better ways of achieving a society that provides justice for all. And when that day comes, *How Does It Feel to Be a Problem?*, instead of being about current affairs, will become a book about history.

PART IV

Muslims in Culture

12

My Arab Problem

In August 2010, I briefly occupied a small corner of the culture wars, and I felt like a fish in a fishbowl. Everybody was staring at a distorted image of me, and all I could do was blink and blow bubbles.

I teach at Brooklyn College, where the undergraduate writing program has for the past several years assigned a "common reading" to all incoming freshmen. In 2010, the program selected my book *How Does It Feel to Be a Problem? Being Young and Arab in America*, in which I tell the stories of seven Arab American men and women, all in their twenties and living in Brooklyn, coping in a post-9/11 world.

The criteria for the common reading are that the book should preferably be set in New York City, have a significant immigration component (since many of our students are themselves immigrants or come from immigrant backgrounds), and be in the form of life stories. It should be by a living writer, since the author is invited to the campus to talk with students. My book fit the bill. (Previous readings have included Frank McCourt's *Angela's Ashes* and Jonathan Safran Foer's *Extremely Loud and Incredibly Close*.)

Everything was fine until about a week before classes began. That's when the chair of my department called me to report that the college had received a small number of complaints from alumni and an emeritus faculty member about the selection. She assured me that the college was standing by its decision, which the dean of undergraduate studies subsequently reiterated. But I knew that in today's wired world, administrators worry about complaints hitting the Internet and going "viral." And that's exactly what happened.

The tempest ensued when Bruce Kesler, a conservative California-based blogger who is a Brooklyn College alumnus, labeled me a "radical pro-Palestinian" professor in one of his posts and called the book's selection an "official policy to inculcate students with a political point of view." He said he was cutting out a "significant bequest" to the college from his will.[1] (He didn't mention how significant his bequest would have been.) In another letter, posted on a different blog under the title "Brooklyn College-Stan," a retired Brooklyn professor wrote that assigning my book "smacks of indoctrination" and "will intimidate students who have a different point of view."[2]

My first reaction was one of disbelief. Wow, I thought, is my writing really that powerful? But on closer inspection, it became clear to me that my detractors hadn't actually read the book. Next I realized how insulting those objections were to our students, suggesting that they are unable to form independent judgments of what they read.

I hoped the noise would fade, but within days, tabloid news media had grabbed the issue from the right-wing blogosphere. Articles appeared in New York's *Daily News*, the *Jewish Week*, and *Gothamist* and were picked up by the *Huffington Post* and *New York Magazine*. The *New York Post* ran an op-ed by a retired history professor at City College who deftly illustrated that one need read only a book's Amazon.com page to reach conclusions about it. The op-ed called the selection of my book a "scandal" and claimed that it paints "New Yorkers in particular as completely Islamophobic" (patently untrue).[3] I received calls at home from television news shows, and the local Channel 11 even broadcast my picture, calling me "this guy!" in the teaser.

I was ready to hide behind a piece of coral. Both the *New York Times* and the *New Yorker* pointed out that the controversy was driven almost entirely by off-campus conservatives, but it didn't matter. Now I—not those manufacturing the storm—had become the controversial one, and Brooklyn College was not advancing a liberal education by having students read a book about the post-9/11 life experiences of young Arab Americans, but was, rather, "pushing" an "anti-American, pro-Islam" book, at least according to *RightWingNews*.[4]

I was getting a very personalized education about how all things Muslim are at the center of today's culture wars. I might have found the fracas amusing were it not unpleasant to be called all kinds of names in public. I certainly didn't recognize my book or myself in the descriptions being tossed about. I mean, the only radical organization I belong to is the Park Slope Food Coop (from which, I must confess, I've been suspended several times).

My surprise at being at the center of a controversy, even a trumped-up one, wasn't based on naïveté. Rather, it came from the fact that the book had been out for two years already without sparking a storm. The *Wall Street Journal* profiled it and me in 2008. *Publishers Weekly* gave it a starred review (no doubt with an invisible crescent surrounding that star), CNN and NPR interviewed me about the book, and Francine Prose reviewed it favorably for *O Magazine*. Vermont's Johnson State College selected the book for its common reading in 2009 without any pushback that I'm aware of, and I had already spoken about it at a number of high schools and colleges, in the United States and Canada, and in front of church leaders, a Jewish congregation, and several community groups. The book even won a 2008 American Book Award (not an anti-American Book Award). (The book has subsequently been selected as the common reading at more than a dozen colleges around the country.)

Opposition to my book seems more symptomatic of our moment than produced by its contents. And Brooklyn College's reading list isn't the only one under attack. The Texas State Board of Education voted in 2010 to limit references to Islam in their high school textbooks, even though, as the Associated Press noted, "the resolution cites world-history books no longer used in Texas schools."[5] According to the Texas Freedom Network, which advocates for religious freedom, the resolution was "based on superficial and grossly misleading claims," including allegations that the textbooks "whitewash" Islam while vilifying Christianity, and that Arab investors are taking over the American publishing industry.[6] (That accusation was based on a 2008 decision by Dubai's royal family to invest heavily in a company that owns Houghton Mifflin Harcourt; but the family lost its stake in the company in 2010.)[7]

In other words, the Texas resolution is another attempt to create a controversy where there is none. It's contrived to give the idea that Islam is on an ideological march in this country, and that opponents of such nefarious plots are America's noble defenders. The fact that this bears little relation to reality is immaterial, and those who venture to point out as much are attacked as duped liberals or ideological warriors for political correctness.

Understanding this topsy-turvy world, where assailants driven by ideology paint their targets as the ideological ones, also explains the rhetoric around Park51, the so-called Ground Zero Mosque (not at Ground Zero and not a mosque). Here the flip comes mostly around the words "tolerance" and "sensitivity." Park51's opponents, like Sarah Palin, claim that their opposition is based not on bigotry—though it's hard to see how they aren't equating all Muslims with terrorism—but on the project's being blithely "insensitive" to the memory of September 11.[8] That argument is a sleight of hand, though. It shifts the burden of sensitivity away from the opponents and heaps it onto the weaker party, making the Muslim Americans exercising their constitutional rights appear as the intolerant ones.

We have seen this kind of shadow play before. When the New York City educator Debbie Almontaser opened a dual-language Arabic-English public high school in New York in 2007, she was immediately attacked personally, and the very idea of teaching Arabic (prioritized, incidentally, as a "national-security language" by the US Department of Education) was maligned. The conservative columnist Daniel Pipes wrote that "Arabic-language instruction is inevitably laden with Pan-Arabist and Islamist baggage," thus finally explaining the legions of Islamist Arab Christians in the world.[9]

What is going on here? As soon as Muslims such as Debbie Almontaser, Imam Feisal Abdul Rauf, or myself are on the cusp of entering the mainstream fully (through a school, a center, or a common reading), we are hit with a wave of opposition attempting to render us or our work invisible. Never mind that we are, by all reasonable accounts, downright moderates on the political spectrum. The trick is simply to attach the word "radical" in front of a Muslim name, and, like a magician, make the actual person disappear in a cloud of suspicion.

If you happen to be the president of the United States, "First Muslim" will suffice.

At a time when the *Economist* reports that 55 percent of Americans hold unfavorable views of Islam, and *Time* found that nearly one-third of Americans say Muslims should not be permitted to run for president (too late!), I would like to think that the opposition to our work illustrates the need for it even more profoundly.[10] Knowledge about Arabs and Islam is woefully inadequate. Projects like the dual-language school, Park51, and a common reading of my book can help Americans experience the Arabic language, Islam, or Arab American youth culture through a kind of empathy, which is a far greater threat to the culture wars than even sympathy is. Sympathy asks for charity; empathy produces understanding.

Ideology, on the other hand, blinds people to the point where they won't even admit the experiences of others. To be invisible means to be twisted beyond recognition, to have others speak for you, or simply to be not seen. Borrowing from Ralph Ellison, it is as though we Muslim and Arab Americans have been surrounded by mirrors of hard, distorting glass. When our opponents approach us, they see only our surroundings, themselves, or figments of their imagination—indeed, anything and everything except us.

Today's culture wars are being fought on a terrain ravaged by the worn debates around liberal education, the poverty of a political discourse fomented by the web, the unrelenting vilifications of Islam and Muslims, and the zero-sum game by which the politics of the Middle East are too often played in the United States. In the wings is the Israeli-Palestinian conflict. Part of the opposition to me may stem from another book, *Midnight on the Mavi Marmara*, that I had just edited about the Israeli attack on the Gaza flotilla in May 2010. (As I make clear in my introduction, I'm a believer in coexistence, in favor of a negotiated settlement, and opposed to terrorism and occupation.) But criticism or acceptance of the Israeli government's actions shouldn't determine acceptable speech in the United States. Anyway, students were not assigned that book.

Or maybe there's another source of the animus against me. Back in May 2010, I published a short essay in the *New York Times Magazine* describing my experiences as an Arab extra on the set of *Sex and the City 2* (reproduced here as Chapter 4). I was mildly critical of the movie for the way it used the Middle East, yet again, as an exotic stage for American pop-culture fantasies. Maybe that set some people off. After all, the show has a lot of hard-core fans.

13

Disco Inferno

Yasir al-Qutaji is a thirty-year-old lawyer from Mosul, Iraq. In March 2004, while exploring allegations that US troops were torturing Iraqis, Qutaji was arrested by American forces. News accounts describe how he was then subjected to the same kinds of punishment he was investigating. He was hooded, stripped naked, and doused with cold water. He was beaten by American soldiers who wore gloves so as not to leave permanent marks. And he was left in a room soldiers blithely called The Disco, a place where Western music rang out so loud that his interrogators were, in Qutaji's words, forced to "talk to me via a loudspeaker that was placed next to my ears."[1]

Qutaji is hardly the only Iraqi to speak of loud music being blared at him, and the technique echoes far beyond Mosul. In Qaim, near the Syrian border, *Newsweek* found American soldiers blasting Metallica's "Enter Sandman" at detainees in a shipping crate while flashing lights in their eyes.[2] Near Fallujah, three Iraqi journalists working for Reuters were seized by the Eighty-Second Airborne. They charged that "deafening music" was played directly into their ears while soldiers ordered them to dance.[3] And back in Mosul, Haitham al-Mallah described being hooded, handcuffed, and delivered to a location where soldiers boomed "extremely loud (and dirty) music" at him. Mallah said the site was "an unknown place which they call 'the disco.'"[4]

Disco isn't dead. It has gone to war.

And it's everywhere: Afghanistan, Guantánamo Bay, Abu Ghraib, anywhere touched by the War on Terror. In Afghanistan, Zakim Shah, a twenty-year-old Afghan farmer, was forced to stay awake while in American custody by soldiers blasting music and shouting at him. Shah told the *New York Times* that after enduring the pain of music, "he grew so exhausted . . . that he vomited."[5] In Guantánamo Bay, Eminem, Britney Spears, Limp Bizkit, Rage Against the Machine, Metallica (again), and Bruce Springsteen ("Born in the U.S.A.") have been played at mind-numbing volumes, sometimes for stretches of up to fourteen hours, at detainees.[6] And at Abu Ghraib, Saddam Salah al-Rawi, a twenty-nine-year-old Iraqi, told a similar story. For no reason, over a period of four months, he was hooded, beaten, stripped, urinated on, and lashed to his cell door by his hands and feet. He also talked about music becoming a weapon. "There was a stereo inside the cell," he said, "with a sound so loud I couldn't sleep. I stayed like that for twenty-three hours."[7]

Whatever the playlist—usually heavy metal or hip-hop but sometimes, bizarrely, Barney the Dinosaur's "I Love You" or selections from *Sesame Street*—the music is pumped at detainees with such brutality to unravel them without laying so much as a feather on their bodies.[8] The mind is another story, and blasting loud music at captives has become part of what has now entered our lexicon as "torture lite." Torture lite is a calculated combination of psychological and physical means of coercion that stop short of causing death and pose little risk that telltale physical marks will be left behind, but that nonetheless can cause extreme psychological trauma. It's designed to deprive the victim of sleep and to cause massive sensory overstimulation, and it has been shown in different situations to be psychologically unbearable.

Clearly, torture music is an assault on human rights. But more broadly, what does it mean when music gets enrolled in schools of torture and culture is sent jackbooted into war? With torture music, our culture is no longer primarily a means of individual expression or an avenue to social criticism. Instead, it is an actual weapon, one that represents and projects American military might. Cultural differences are exploited, and multiculturalism becomes a strategy for domination. Torture music is the crudest kind of cultural imperialism, grimly ironic in a war that is putatively about spreading "universal" American values.

Yet the first reaction torture music inspired among Americans was not indignation but amusement. Finally, dangerous terrorists—like everyone else—will be tortured by Britney Spears's music! Most commentators saw it this way, particularly after *Time* reported that Christina Aguilera's music was droned at Mohammed al-Qahtani, another alleged twentieth 9/11 hijacker (like Zacarias Moussaoui), at Guantánamo. The *Chicago Tribune*'s website compiled readers' favorite "interro-tunes" (the winner was Captain & Tennille's "Muskrat Love"). The *New York Sun* called it "mood music for jolting your jihadi," and a Missouri paper wrote cheekily that Defense Secretary Donald Rumsfeld had "approved four of seven stronger coercive tunes but said that forcing the prisoner to view photos of Aguilera's Maxim magazine photo shoot—in which she poses in a pool with only an inner-tube to cover her ferret-like figure—would fall outside Geneva Convention standards."[9]

Thus, torture lite slides right into mainstream American acceptance. It's a frat-house prank taken one baby step further—as essentially harmless, and American, as an apple pie in the face. It's seen as a justified means of exacting revenge on or extracting information from a terrorist—never mind that detainees in the War on Terror are mostly Muslims who were in the wrong place at the wrong time.

"Without music, life would be an error," writes Nietzsche, but for Muslim detainees, it's the other way around.[10] Mind-numbing American music is blasted at them with such ferocity that they will believe their lives are a mistake.

✦ ✦ ✦

Torture music has a history. In 1997, while considering the regular Israeli use of the practice, the United Nations Committee

Against Torture explicitly qualified it as torture and called for its ban. In 1978 the European Court of Human Rights confronted a similar technique employed by Britain in the early 1970s against Irish detainees, although in the British rendition, it was loud noise instead of music that was wielded against detainees. This was one of the so-called Five Techniques, scientifically developed interrogation practices that also included wall-standing, hooding, sleep deprivation, and withholding of food and drink. While the court stopped short of calling this torture, it did label it "inhumane and degrading" and found that the Five Techniques were breaches of the European Convention on Human Rights. Britain promised never to employ them again. (Questions have since been raised about British troops "hooding" prisoners in Iraq.)[11]

In fact, the Five Techniques never disappeared. All five and a few more have materialized as an orchestra of effects in the prosecution of the War on Terror. Attorney Jonathan Pyle and his law partner, Susan Burke, have interviewed scores of Iraqis for a class-action suit against private contractors for their alleged roles in abusing Iraqis. They report that Iraqis repeatedly describe the same kinds of abuse—being hooded and handcuffed, sealed in containers, doused with cold water, subjected to strobe lights, and blasted with brutally loud music. And according to the Fay report, one of the government's many investigations of the Abu Ghraib scandal, sleep adjustment was brought to Iraq with the 519 Military Intelligence Battalion from Afghanistan.[12] Shafiq Rasul, a British citizen who was imprisoned for two and a half years, says he endured similar treatment in Guantánamo after October 2002.[13] Citing a source familiar with conditions at Guantánamo, Physicians for Human Rights described how the "deprivation of sensory stimulation on the one hand and overstimulation on the other were causing spatial and temporal disorientation in detainees. The results were self-harm and suicide attempts."[14]

With a little imagination, it's not hard to see exactly how. Of Britain's Five Techniques, noise was considered the hardest to suffer. In his book *Unspeakable Acts, Ordinary People*, John Conroy describes the "absolute" and "unceasing" noise that the Irishmen who were first subjected to the Five Techniques endured. While the other four techniques were clearly terrifying, the noise was "an assault of such ferocity that many of the men now recall it as the worst part of the ordeal."[15]

A US military program confirms Conroy's observation. In July 2005, the *New Yorker* reported on the SERE program (Survival, Evasion, Resistance, and Escape), a course that trains soldiers to withstand interrogations by subjecting them to the harsh treatment they could expect if captured. (The article suggests these counter-interrogation techniques have been twisted and turned into policy at Guantánamo.) Soldiers often believe the interrogation part of their program will be the most difficult, but according to the article, "the worst moment is when they are made to listen to taped loops of cacophonous sounds. One of the most stress-inducing tapes is a recording of babies crying inconsolably. Another is a Yoko Ono album."[16]

Such distress noises (called "horror sounds" by one ex-detainee)[17] have been reported in Afghanistan and Guantánamo. Erik Saar, a former Gitmo translator, describes in his book *Inside the Wire* how Qahtani "was subjected to strobe lights; a loud, insistent tape of cats meowing (from a cat food commercial) interspersed with babies crying; and deafening loud music—one song blasted at him constantly was Drowning Pool's thumping, nihilistic metal rant 'Bodies' ('Let the bodies hit the floor . . .')."[18]

Ex-interrogators at Guantánamo's Camp Delta described their methods to the *New York Times*. These included shackling detainees to the floor, cranking up the air conditioning, and forcing them to endure strobe lights with rock and rap music playing at mind-numbing volumes for unbearably long sessions. "It fried them," one said. Another admitted that detainees returned "very wobbly. They came back to their cells and were just completely out of it."[19]

This is when the mind begins its rebellion against the body. After you end up "wobbly" or "fried," a severe posttraumatic stress disorder commonly results. Patrick Shivers, one of the Irish victims of the Five Techniques, developed a lasting and severe hypersensitivity to noise to the point where he was "disturbed by the sound of a comb placed on a shelf in his bathroom."[20]

In Iraq we can hear about the beginnings of the same traumas. In a gripping *Vanity Fair* article, Donovan Webster searched for and found "the man in the hood" from the macabre Abu Ghraib photos. Haj Ali told Webster of being hooded, stripped, handcuffed to his cell, and bombarded with a looped sample of David Gray's "Babylon." It was so loud, he said, "I thought my head would burst." Webster then cued up "Babylon" on his iPod and played it for Haj Ali to confirm the song. Ali ripped the earphones off his head, and started crying. "He didn't just well up with tears," Webster later told me. "He broke down sobbing."[21]

◆ ◆ ◆

Sounding brass in front of your enemy has always been a part of war, from Joshua's trumpets tumbling walls in the Bible to a mean fife and drum ringing out "Rule, Britannia!" across the Plains of Abraham. When American forces invaded Panama in 1989, Manuel Noriega fled to the papal nunciature, and American forces roared Twisted Sister's "We're Not Gonna Take It," and songs with the word "jungle" in the lyrics in front of His Holiness's house. During the siege of Fallujah in April 2004, American soldiers cranked the volume on their AC/DC. Their preferred song? "Shoot to Thrill."[22]

The calculated use of American music in interrogations is less about rallying the troops than destroying a detainee. The US innovation in the interrogation practice of blaring loud noises is the deliberate use of American culture as an offensive weapon. While culture has long been a rationalization for conquest (consider the "civilizing mission" of European colonialisms), and while much post-Holocaust European thought has viewed contemporary culture as coercive and potentially authoritarian, neither colonialism nor the Frankfurt School witnessed the transformation of culture into the very instrument of torture. For them, culture was more the end than the means of conquest.

But culture as warfare is Pentagon policy. Donald Rumsfeld and Lieut. Gen. Ricardo Sanchez approved its deployment in their lists of harsher interrogation techniques for detainees. Rumsfeld did so in April 2003 and Sanchez in September 2003, and their almost identical memos both specify, along with the use of auditory stimuli or music, that "interrogators be provided reasonable latitude to vary techniques depending on the detainee's culture." The Sanchez memo also allows the presence of military working dogs, which "exploits Arab fear of dogs."[23]

Altering interrogations according to a detainee's culture is not necessarily damaging, but the Pentagon's multiculturalism doesn't run deep, just wild. With the dissemination of the Abu Ghraib photos, Seymour Hersh reported in the *New Yorker* that the "bible" among neoconservatives was *The Arab Mind*, a piece of trash scholarship more than a generation old that claims Arabs understand only force, shame, and humiliation. When the book was reissued in 2002, Norvell De Atkine, director of Middle East studies at the JFK Special Warfare Center and School at Fort Bragg, wrote its foreword. This is "essential reading," writes the man who has "briefed hundreds of military teams being deployed to the Middle East." So essential, in fact, that *The Arab Mind* "forms the basis" of his "cultural" curriculum.[24]

Despite (or maybe because of) the continued use of the book, military professionals' knowledge of other cultures is actually dangerously low. A 2005 article in the military journal *Joint Force*

Quarterly reveals how little American forces understand Iraqi society, using an example of how the US military frequently misunderstands Iraqi hand gestures, leading to tragic consequences and preventable deaths. The article goes on to quote a Special Forces colonel assigned to the under secretary of defense for intelligence. "We literally don't know where to go for information on what makes other societies tick," admits the colonel, "so we use Google to make policy."[25]

What the practice of sounding loud American music at Muslims reveals most is the power American forces associate with American culture. Any prolonged loud noise in the right circumstances stands a good chance of driving you mad. Yet narcissistically, American intelligence seems to believe American music will break you more quickly. "These people haven't heard heavy metal. They can't take it," a psy-ops sergeant told *Newsweek*.[26] And in Guantánamo, they even have a name for it. The Pentagon's Schmidt investigation identifies it as "futility music"—that is to say, screamingly loud and deliberately Western music that will, per the Army field manual, "highlight the futility of the detainee's situation." (On the other hand, "cultural music," Schmidt reports, is "played as an incentive.") Twenty-four thousand interrogations later and after questions about its legality were raised, "futility music," according to Schmidt, remained authorized.[27]

◆ ◆ ◆

Fifty years ago, the great Martinican poet Aimé Césaire wrote that the trouble with colonization was not just that it dehumanizes the colonized but that it also "decivilizes" the colonizer.[28] Torture does the same. While transforming a human being into a thing of pain, it simultaneously strangles human society. Torture threatens to decivilize us today not only because its practices are being normalized within our national imagination but also because civil society is being enlisted to rationalize its demands. In most arenas, this process has elicited at least some vocal opposition. When it was revealed that medical professionals were assisting in abusive interrogations, debates among doctors and psychologists followed about torture, medical ethics, and war. And while administration lawyers have attempted to narrow the definition of torture and to authorize new methods of inflicting pain, other attorneys, including top military lawyers, have challenged interrogation policies on legal, moral, and tactical grounds.

And so the B-side to the torture music issue flips to the music community's response to the practice. While many musicians may not even be aware of this instrumentalized use of their songs, Metallica's James Hetfield did comment on the phenomenon to Terry Gross on NPR's *Fresh Air*. Asked about a BBC report that described his band's music being blared during Iraqi interrogations, he responded with "pride" that his music is "culturally offensive" to Iraqis. Hetfield said that he considers his music "a freedom to express my insanity. . . . If they're not used to freedom," he said, "I'm glad to be a part of the exposure."[29]

But Hetfield's voice must not be the only one. Where do other musicians stand? Will Eminem rage against the torture machine, or will Bruce Springsteen speak out as his music is press-ganged into futility and pain? If American musicians oppose the use of their music in torture, it's time for them to make some noise.

Coda

Since the original publication of this essay, several musicians have indeed protested the use of their music as a weapon of torture and abuse. The British human rights organization Reprieve organized "zero dB—stop music torture," a movement to bring an end to the use of loud music as an interrogation technique. Rage Against the Machine, Pearl Jam, Elbow, R.E.M., Massive Attack, Dizzee Rascal, and others have signed on.[30] Other musicians who have protested the use of their music as an instrument of torture include Nine Inch Nails, David Gray, and Christopher Cert, the composer of the *Sesame Street* theme song. (Stevie Benton of the group Drowning Pool, on the other hand, told *Spin* magazine that it was an "honor to think that perhaps our song could be used to quell another 9/11 attack or something like that.")[31] Early in 2014, the industrial punk band Skinny Puppy invoiced the US government in the amount of $666,000 for the use of their music in Guantánamo, is considering suing the US government for the illegal use of their music, and titled their late-2013 album *Weapon*.[32] On February 2, 2007, the Society for Ethnomusicology passed a statement condemning "the use of music as torture."[33] And while he refuses to prosecute those responsible, President Obama repudiated the use of torture when he assumed office in January 2009.[34] This does not mean that torture or its equivalent at the hands of American forces has ended. The brutal forced feeding of detainees who protest their continued confinement by hunger striking has been labeled "cruel, inhumane, and degrading," by the United Nations Office of the Commissioner for Human Rights.[35] The US military's response to criticisms of its policy was simply to stop reporting hunger strikes.[36] Also, Ramzi bin Al-Sibh, a "high-level detainee" at Guantánamo, alleged in December 2013 that guards were deliberately keeping him awake at night, thereby continuing the technique of sleep deprivation by other means.[37] Finally, despite Obama's 2009 executive order titled "Ensuring Lawful Interrogations," music torture may not be explicitly forbidden. As the *Guardian* reported on January 25, 2014, "President Obama's January 2009 executive order would seem to have halted the use of what the Defense Department called 'gender coercion,' but not 'music futility.' But we don't know because of pervasive secrecy exactly what military or other interrogators do or don't do when they employ the 'Futility' technique."[38] We deserve to know and must continue to demand that this practice end, once and for all.

14

The Race Is On

Muslims and Arabs in the American Imagination

"We are so racially profiled now, as a group," the Arab American comedian Dean Obeidallah says in his routine, "that I heard a correspondent on CNN not too long ago say the expression, 'Arabs are the new blacks.' That Arabs are the new blacks." Obeidallah continues,

> When I heard that—I'm going to be honest—I was excited. I'm like, "Oh my God, we're cool." Before you know it, hot Asian women will stop dating black guys and start dating Arabs. White kids in the suburbs, instead of acting and dressing black to be cool, will now start pretending to be Arab. . . . Pimping their car to look like a taxi cab. Dressing like Arabs, some old-school in traditional Arab headdress. . . . Tilt to the side a bit. Walkin' up to each other, goin', "What up, Moustafa," Sayin', "Where my Arabs at?" "Arab, please!"[1]

It is a funny bit, but Obeidallah is on to something more than a joke, something about the mischievous power of race and representation in contemporary US culture both to incorporate and to reject. By taking an observation—the analogy of Arabness to blackness—to its literal extreme, Obeidallah is playing with general perceptions of blackness and whiteness along the way. And by turning a liability into an asset, he flips the script of social exclusion to one of popular inclusion. What is more American today, after all, than the African American?

But most people mean something else when they talk about Arabs (or Muslims) becoming "the new blacks," a sentiment routinely expressed since the terrorist attacks of September 11, 2001. Perhaps most directly, the idea is meant to evoke the practice of racial profiling. "Black New Yorkers joke among themselves about their own reprieve from racial profiling," explains a *New York Times* article from October 2001. "Even the language of racial grievance has shifted: Overnight, the cries about driving while black have become flying while brown—a phrase referring to reports of Muslim Americans being asked to get off planes." The article continues. "Ever so slightly, the attacks on the trade center have tweaked the city's traditional racial divisions."[2] These oscillations prompted African American novelist Ishmael Reed to write, "Within two weeks after the World Trade Center and Pentagon bombings, my youngest daughter, Tennessee, was called a dirty Arab, twice." America's racial legacy, replete with the "one-drop rule," where a single drop of African blood made a person black in the eyes of Jim Crow law, enabled Reed, after September 11, to ask the question, "Is anyone with dark skin Arab American?"[3]

The reasons are easy to see. Racial profiling was almost universally loathed prior to 2001, so much so that candidate George W. Bush explicitly ran against it. But the practice acquired a new lease on life in 2003 when President Bush's Justice Department ordered a ban on profiling but included exceptions permitting extra scrutiny of racial and ethnic groups when officials had "trustworthy" information that members of these groups were plotting a terrorist attack or a crime.[4] While it could be said that profiling per se was officially un-American, the fine print made it clear that profiling Arabs and Muslims made good national security sense. The program of special registration (officially labeled NSEERS), whereby adult males from twenty-four Muslim-majority countries had to register their whereabouts in the country, is just one example of state-mandated racial profiling. Special registration led to approximately fourteen thousand deportation proceedings.[5] (The UN Committee on the Elimination of Racial Discrimination repeatedly called on Washington to end "racial profiling against Arabs, Muslims and South Asians.")[6] After the London bombings of 2005, conservative critics like the Hoover Institute's Paul Sperry, Representative Peter King (R-NY), and the *Washington Post*'s Charles Krauthammer advocated further profiling, prompting another *Washington Post* columnist, Colbert King, to respond with a column titled "You Can't Fight Terrorism with Racism." Echoing Reed, he wrote, "It appears not to matter to Sperry that his description also includes huge numbers of men of color, including my younger son, a brown-skinned occasional New York subway rider who shaves his head and mustache."[7]

Prior to September 11, popular perceptions of Arabs and Muslims had no significant American component. Invisibility was the word heard most often. In *Food for Our Grandmothers*, a 1994 anthology by Arab American and Arab Canadian feminists, the editor Joanna Kadi labeled Arab Americans "the Most Invisible of the Invisibles."[8] In "Resisting Invisibility," an essay published in a 1999 volume, Therese Saliba noted, "When Arabs are mentioned within the multicultural debate, it is often as a point of political tension between blacks and Jews, or as an afterthought, 'as the other Jewish Americans.'"[9] Through the 1980s, as Edward Said puts it in *Covering Islam*, the "ubiquitous" images of Arabs and Muslims outside the United States were "frequent caricatures of Muslims as oil suppliers, as terrorists and . . . as bloodthirsty mobs."[10] The reliance on Orientalist stereotypes was premised on the idea of an unbridgeable distance between two essentially different parts of the world, the rational Occident and unruly Orient.

No Offense, Sir

But in a present of growing immigration and international terrorism, things have changed (and, of course, also remain depressingly the same). In the domestic arrangement of race and difference, Arabs and Muslims in the United States have been pushed from the shadows into the spotlight, and the associations they carry are often ones of racial differences that can be patrolled with profiling. Such associations surface in small, curious ways. In a 2008 *New York Times* book review, for example, the Harvard sociologist Orlando Patterson, commenting on racial profiling, reaches not for the African American example, but writes that "nearly all of us have a civil liberties threshold: Imagine Pakistani madrassa graduates lining up at airport security; race matters in such cases, and need involve no animus."[11] Spike Lee's film *The Inside Man* has only one significant scene of racial conflict: A Sikh hostage in a bank heist emerges from the building hooded like the perpetrators, who have cleverly dressed in matching coveralls and forced the bank personnel and customers to do the same. The cops yank off his hood, thinking he is a bank robber, then spot his turban and lose their cool. "Oh shit, it's a fucking Arab!" one cop yells, as they back away, guns leveled. The Sikh then has his turban ripped from his head and is beaten. In the next scene, he complains to the detective, played by Denzel Washington. "I'm not saying anything until I get my turban back! I'm sick of this shit, man. Everywhere I go, my civil rights are violated. Go to the airport, and I always get pulled out. Random search, my ass!" (Washington responds, "But you can always get a cab, right?" "It's one of the perks," he admits.)

And in John Updike's silly and thoroughly unconvincing novel *Terrorist*, there is a deep and abiding devotion to America's enduring racial hierarchies mixed with shopworn nostalgia for the Waspy simplicity that has packed up and moved away to the pages of history. Updike's story revolves around Ahmad Malloy, eighteen, half

Irish, half Egyptian, and totally confused. Ahmad, whom Updike repeatedly describes as "dun" of complexion, searches aimlessly for meaning in his failing suburb of New Prospect, New Jersey, finding solace at the feet of Sheikh Rashid, an embittered Yemeni imam who exhorts the neophyte to violence. Meanwhile, Ahmad's high school guidance counselor, Jack Levy, has an affair with his mother. Levy eventually brings the boy back from the brink, saving the nation from a senseless terrorist attack. In the meantime, he tells him that he has "fucked his mother," prompting this ridiculous exchange in the final pages of the novel:

> "No offense, sir, but do understand. . . . I'm not thrilled to think of my mother fornicating with a Jew."
>
> Levy laughs a coarse bark. "Hey, come on, we're all Americans here. That's the idea; didn't they tell you that at Central High? Irish Americans, African Americans, Jewish Americans; there are even Arab Americans."
>
> "Name one."
>
> Levy is taken aback. "Omar Sharif," he says. He knows he could not think of others in a less stressful situation.
>
> "Not American. Try again."
>
> "Uh—what was his name? Lew Alcindor?"
>
> "Kareem Abdul-Jabbar," Ahmad corrects.[12]

The confusion of labeling Abdul-Jabbar, who is African American, as Arab American, is obvious, and appears to indicate Levy's own ignorance, making the character bizarrely more American in his daftness. But Levy stands for more than that. Against the foreignness of Arab Americans, Updike uses Levy's Jewishness as a measure of successful American ethnic assimilation, as opposed to all those who now "occupy the inner city," namely those who are "brown, by and large, in its many shades."[13] ("Jews and Irish," Updike writes, "have been sharing America's cities for generations.")[14] Levy's overweight wife Beth believes that Levy "will never leave her: [out of] his Jewish sense of responsibility and a sentimental loyalty, which must be Jewish, too. If you've been persecuted and reviled for two thousand years, being loyal to your loved ones is just good survival tactics."[15]

If Arab Americans are now frequently coded with a kind of blackness, then being Jewish today is to have earned the status of whiteness, demonstrated by Levy's ascribed loyalty to wife, city and country. Nor is honorary whiteness limited to Jewish characters. Hindus, too, are often endowed with similar respectability. Think of Thomas Friedman's endless exultations about Indian capitalists and Silicon Valley pioneers. Or consider this paragraph from Steven Pinker's 2008 article in the *New York Times Magazine* titled "The Moral Instinct." Pinker writes about ethics and moral foundations held in common across distinct societies in the modern world. His is an effort to promote a family-of-humankind *Weltanschauung*. But in so doing, he divides the world in interesting ways. "Many of the flabbergasting practices in faraway places become more intelligible when you recognize that the same moralizing impulse that Western elites channel toward violations of harm and fairness (our moral obsessions) is channeled elsewhere to violations in the other spheres," he writes. "Think of . . . the holy ablutions and dietary restrictions of Hindus and Orthodox Jews (purity), [and] the outrage at insulting the Prophet among Muslims (authority)."[16] Of course, "holy ablutions and dietary restrictions" could just as easily be attributed to Muslims (and not just the orthodox), but instead Jews and Hindus are lumped together in this benign behavioral mode. Muslims, on the other hand, are assigned rage.

What is going on here? In brief, Arabs and Muslims (who, in the real world, are two overlapping categories, but in the world of American perceptions essentially the same thing) have entered the American imagination with full force, but their entry has been racialized. What this means in the specific inflections of the American vernacular is an association with blackness, for Arabs and Muslims in America are not a part of the immigrant fabric of the nation but a social problem to be dealt with. While Jews and Hindus are today handed ethnicity, Arabs and Muslims are saddled with race. They have become an American dilemma.

The difference between race and ethnicity matters. To be ethnic means to have mores, habits, and rites that do not interfere with being modern. In fact, the rituals often lend to bland modernity the color and richness that it so often seeks. Ethnics make tactical decisions about when and how to reveal or put away those charming, atavistic aspects of themselves when in public. They are, in other words, given agency.

Races, however, have little to no agency. Agencies rather formulate policies about them. Races do not make history. They are history. Social forces pulsate through them. While ethnicities are threads in the tapestries of the nation, races are the elements that make the nation's mix combustible. What James Baldwin wrote about the black man in 1955 is almost as applicable to Arab/Muslim Americans today. "The Negro in America," Baldwin writes, "is a social and not a personal or human problem. To think of him is to think of statistics, slums, rapes, injustices, remote violence."[17] (Consider Pew's 2007 study on Muslim Americans in this light. Is it likely that a flagship survey of any other religious group would be subtitled *Middle Class and Mostly Mainstream*?)[18] Ethnicities get their documentary histories screened during PBS pledge week. Races appear as the subjects of government and police commissions of inquiry, on episodes of PBS *Frontline* with the spooky voiceover, and on the crawl on Fox News.

And political leanings matter little. Liberals view the situation of Muslims and Arabs in America as an example of the limits of the nation and its excesses in maltreating those who are irretrievably "other." Conservatives define them as a minority threat to a perceived majority. Either way, the race is on.

Be All That You Can Be

The irony is that while Arabs and Muslims are increasingly racialized as black (in ways that approximate Cold War images of African Americans), African Americans are emerging in popular culture as leaders of the American nation and empire. Moreover, this depiction revolves fundamentally around the idea of black friendship with Muslims and Arabs, a friendship not among equals but one reflecting a modified projection of American power. This image appears to seek to transform the image of the United States itself.

Consider two different films in this regard: *The Siege* (1998), again starring Denzel Washington, and *The Kingdom* (2007), starring Jamie Foxx. *The Siege* was, of course, made before 2001 and has since been lionized for its prescience in portraying a large-scale Arab terrorist attack on American soil, but it is essentially about how Clinton-era foreign policy failures endangered the nation's institutions. Its story centers on Special Agent Anthony Hubbard, a law-degree-wielding veteran of the Eighty-Second Airborne with a Catholic school upbringing in the Bronx. At one point, Hubbard sarcastically dubs himself "Colin Powell," and the implication is clear. Hub, as he is called, is the embodiment of African American achievement, like the future secretary of state who was then widely thought to be Most Likely to Be Elected President While Black. Upright, industrious, serious but not dour, Hub is the film's moral center. The main spoke on his wheel is Frank Haddad (played by Tony Shalhoub), a Lebanese Shi'i FBI agent (the only American in the film, incidentally, who speaks with a foreign accent) who serves as chauffeur and translator.

After US commandos capture a radical imam modeled after Sheikh Omar Abdul Rahman, a series of terrorist attacks plague New York City. Elise Kraft, a CIA agent of loose morals played by Annette Bening, competes with Hub in investigating the attacks. Her mole is Samir Nazhde, a Brooklyn College professor of Arab studies who appears (and later is confirmed) to be connected to the terrorists. When Hub and the FBI are unable to stop the rash of attacks, the government proclaims martial law in Brooklyn, and Bruce Willis's character, the unsubtle general William Devereaux, who was responsible for the extralegal extraction of the imam, rounds up Arab American males in ways reminiscent of Japanese American internment during World War II. Haddad's son, thirteen, is jailed, leading the FBI agent to a crisis of faith in American righteousness. He rashly surrenders his badge to Hub, saying he will not be the government's "sand nigger" any longer. But Hub eventually gets Haddad's son out. Hub and Haddad, meanwhile, discover that Nazhde is the final terrorist in the country, and follow him to a showdown. Nazhde is killed, Kraft is sacrificed, and Hub stands up to Devereaux's unconstitutional torture and murder of an innocent Arab American man. Martial law is then lifted, and the Constitution is saved.

With its two Arab/Muslim characters, one an FBI agent, the other a terrorist, *The Siege* operates within the logic of "good Muslim, bad Muslim" that Mahmood Mamdani has identified as central to the cultural logic of the War on Terror. "The central message of such discourse," Mamdani explains, "[is that] unless proved to be 'good,' every Muslim [is] presumed to be 'bad.' All Muslims [are] now under an obligation to prove their credentials by joining in a war against 'bad Muslims.'"[19] Melani McAlister astutely names *The Siege* as a film "incorporating the challenge of multiculturalism into the logic of the New World Order."[20] But it is also something else. *The Siege* taps into the paranoia surrounding immigration, which, together with geopolitics, has turned the streets of Brooklyn into the stereotypical "Arab street," redolent with strange smells and teetering on the edge of apocalypse. (The script identifies Brooklyn's Atlantic Avenue as "The Third World. Teeming, roiling. Kinshasa meets Beirut meets Tel Aviv meets Moscow," and Hub says, "America's the place to be if you're a terrorist.") Moreover, this frightening external world that is invading the United States is suffused with an Arab and Muslim proclivity for ancestral feuds. When Nazhde is taken in, he is punched by Haddad, who apologizes to Hub saying, "Sorry, family matter." Later, Haddad is upbraided by Hub, who tells him he will "have his badge" if he "ever hit[s] a prisoner again." "Someday I'll tell you what those people did to my village in 1971," Haddad responds.

But the key message of *The Siege* is that US entanglement in these ancient hatreds has compelled the United States to sell itself, body (the whorish Elise Kraft) and soul (the heartless Gen. Devereaux). In so doing, the national security state is losing the heart of the nation. This betrayal is why Hub's character is so essential. In his enduring commitment to values, Hub is the most American of all the characters. He is uncorrupted by international politics ("I need names," he says to his agents, "I don't need a history lesson") and willing to fight both the racist policy of internment and the brutal violence of the Arabs. Who better than Hub, after all, to show his Arab underling that the United States is not, at bottom, racist, in either its foreign or domestic policy? His own story of uplift illustrates all that "America" can be. Hub is best suited to protect Arab Americans not only from the overreach of the state but also from themselves.

"America's Not Perfect"

If *The Siege* projects the idea that an African American will save the nation, *The Kingdom* does this trope one better. The US empire has a Great Black Hope as well. In *The Kingdom*, terrorists attack an American compound in Riyadh. Back in Washington, the FBI itches to investigate the carnage, particularly since two of their own have been killed. Domestic politics initially holds them back. (This setting is almost certainly inspired by the FBI's inquiry into the 2000 attack on the USS *Cole*, where the lead investigator John O'Neill battled in vain with the US ambassador in Yemen, Barbara Bodine, who refused to let him interrogate Yemeni government officials he thought were in league with al-Qaeda. O'Neill later became chief of security at the World Trade Center and was killed on September 11.) The attorney general is concerned that American boots on Saudi Arabian soil will anger Muslims, but, as in *The Siege*, the FBI is independent of the dirty machinations of the political world and stands for American righteousness. "If you were running the FBI," the attorney general tells Special Agent Ronald Fleury (played by Jamie Foxx), "you might turn it into Patton's Third Army." Fleury takes the initiative by threatening the Saudi royal family, and the FBI is given immediate approval to land in Riyadh. He leads a team of four, himself, a white woman, Agent Mayes, and two men, Agent Leavitt, who is Jewish, and Agent Sykes, a good ol' boy, in the investigation.

Saudi Arabia turns out to be an odd, inverted world. The team is assigned a minder, Col. Faris al-Ghazi, a police officer who lost men at the compound but whose unit is also implicated in the attack. Just as in Washington, the FBI team must negotiate with timid politicians to gain access to the crime scene, and the agents complain constantly of their pusillanimity. More to the point, the Saudi Arabians are totally inept in their investigation. "Do you understand evidence?" Sykes asks al-Ghazi patronizingly. "Little things that are clues? Clues can be very helpful to a fellow trying to solve a crime." In this film, civilization is bestowed upon the natives through forensic science.

Initially, the Saudi Arabians are more concerned with policing morality—taking offense at swearing, uncovered women, and non-Muslims touching dead Muslims—than with solving crime. But al-Ghazi slowly comes around. He is the good Muslim in this drama, a film that turns the capacious boulevards of Saudi Arabia into the dingy avenues of Baghdad. Al-Ghazi has a warm home life, as conveyed by the soft music of the soundtrack while he leads his family in prayer. Fleury and he begin a friendship.

Eventually, the FBI team commences pursuit of Abu Hamza, an Osama bin Laden wannabe who may be the mastermind of the initial attack, and the film's pace quickens as they near their quarry. After killing several junior terrorists in a firefight, the crew is congratulated for their efforts and are headed home when Leavitt is kidnapped on the road to the airport. The agents track the abductors to Suweidi, "a very bad neighborhood," which seems to be a cinematic cross between Fallujah and East LA. There, the final shootout of the film transpires. Leavitt is saved by Mayes, the female FBI agent, who stabs an Arab terrorist in the groin (and head) with her knife. Abu Hamza and his son are killed. Al-Ghazi, too, is tragically cut down, and the film ends with Fleury offering his condolences to the Saudi Arabian cop's family. "Your father was a good friend of mine," he tells al-Ghazi's son.

The Kingdom is a pulpy thriller that relies heavily upon stock car chase sequences and plenteous explosions. But it exhibits a few other traits that might also soon be conventions. It divides its swarthy Arabs by the "good Muslim, bad Muslim" logic. Its white male characters are narrow-minded and borderline racist, and its African American leading man is not just an action hero but also a figure projecting the true compassion of the American state.

The Kingdom only obliquely acknowledges Fleury's race. "America's not perfect," he says to a Saudi prince. "Not at all. I'll be the first to say that." It is this kind of honesty that enables Fleury to achieve a level of human communication with the Saudi Arabians that is not shared by the other characters. When he reaches out to al-Ghazi, he discovers that his Arab counterpart is thoroughly Americanized. "I spent four days in Quantico," al-Ghazi tells Fleury. "I also saw Michael Jordan play for the Washington Wizards." (It takes a real American to know that Jordan played briefly for the Wizards and not just the Chicago Bulls.) The Saudi Arabian continues that he became a police officer because he watched *The Incredible Hulk* on television as a child. And, as in *The Siege*, where one character quips of speaking to Arabs, "Ask a question, get an atlas," *The Kingdom* plays up the virtues of an antipolitical position, this time attributed to the Arab character. "I find myself in a place where I no longer care why we are attacked," al-Ghazi confesses to Fleury. "I only care that 100 people woke up a few mornings ago and had no idea why it was their last. When we catch the men who murdered these people, I don't care to ask even one question. I want to kill them. Do you understand?" "Yes, I do," Fleury responds.

Interestingly, *The Siege* emphasizes the Arabness of Haddad, its Arab American character, while *The Kingdom* highlights the Americanness of its good Arab. Why? Perhaps it is because *The Siege* is about the need for a principled national ethos for resisting the invasion of international politics (and bodies) into the domestic sphere, while *The Kingdom* is about the need for proper American tutelage in a harsh and disordered world. *The Siege*'s imagination is national. *The Kingdom*'s is more imperial.

Despite their differences, *The Siege* and *The Kingdom* both illustrate an emerging subgenre. Other examples include Showtime's TV series *Sleeper Cell* (2005 and 2006) and the 2008 film *Traitor*, starring Don Cheadle. *Sleeper Cell*'s lead character is Special Agent Darwyn Al-Sayeed, played by Michael Ealy, an African American Muslim who is determined to save both his country and his faith from the crazy radicals (more like misfits with anthrax, really). Sporting a constipated squint throughout the series, Al-Sayeed tries hard to swallow the anguish of having to pass, not as a white man, but as a terrorist in the service of his beloved religion. ("Don't African Americans have a long history of trying to pass for white?" asks al-Farik, the lead terrorist, of Al-Sayeed. "I don't," responds the undercover agent.) *Traitor* replicates many of the same conventions. Cheadle plays the role of Samir Horn, formerly a US special forces soldier supporting the Afghan jihad against the Soviets and currently a seller of illicit weapons to unsavory Muslims. Again, the leading man is a devout Muslim, but the film collapses the good Muslim/bad Muslim dichotomy into a single character, since the audience is left guessing for the first half of the film where his loyalties lie. Moreover, the central relationship in the film is the deepening bond between Samir and Omar, an Arab terrorist with doubts, and Samir is almost able to bring him over from the dark side before Omar is killed in a climactic gun battle.

The central idea sustaining this subgenre is the notion of African American leadership of the Arab world, intertwined with friendship with it. Here there is a twist on a tale already told by Benjamin DeMott in *The Trouble with Friendship: Why Americans Can't Think Straight about Race*. DeMott explains how popular culture exploded in the 1980s and 1990s with images of black-and-white comity that served as a kind of "wish fulfillment," of "interracial sameness," in order to discover that people of different races "need or delight in or love each other." The black-and-white friendships of that era, symbolized by the interracial buddy movie (Eddie Murphy and Judge Reinhold, Danny Glover and Mel Gibson, Samuel L. Jackson and John Travolta, Wesley Snipes and Woody Harrelson), illustrated that "race problems belong to the passing moment. Race problems do not involve group interests and conflicts developed over centuries. Race problems are being smoothed into nothingness, gradually, inexorably, by good will, affection, points of light."[21] Interracial amity popped up all over the cinematic spectrum. There was the lowbrow farce *White Men Can't Jump*, the high-minded drama *Driving Miss Daisy*, and the middle-class morality play *Lethal Weapon*, where Danny Glover as the suburban black family man with a badge was a kind of precursor to the character of Hub.

Arab and African American friendship comes similarly loaded but with an international agenda appended. Such representations suggest that African Americans know better than whites how to talk to Arabs (Fleury learns a few Arabic words in *The Kingdom*).

The semiotics of African American leadership roles in film and popular culture today refer to the fact that racial conflict has been made residual and even overcome in the United States, which is why race gets only passing mention. Moreover, African American connections to other people of color seem based on authentic sentiment, as opposed to knee-jerk reaction or bald-faced opportunism. They are more real because of the collective past of suffering. African American leadership of Arab characters illustrates a pilgrim's progress narrative for the twenty-first century, where the promise of America is most clearly exhibited through racial uplift. The sins of slavery, Jim Crow, and Sheriff Clark's water cannons have been redeemed by achievement. Through such representations, the United States is understood as having surmounted its historic deficiencies, and the liberal (and liberating) potential of the American empire is consequently affirmed. Camaraderie, in other words, is connected to the benevolence of American imperialism, for if the face of the United States belongs to an African American, how racist could the empire be? Put another way, what is more American today, after all, than the African American?

A Lot Like Me at Home

But such representations of blacks at the helm, speaking from the liberal heart of American empire, contradict, if not undermine, a long and powerfully expressed tradition of African American opposition to US expansionism. This tradition connects the denial of civil rights at home to the deprivations of overseas conquest. Its history goes back at least to the US-Mexican war of 1848, which Frederick Douglass labeled as "disgraceful, cruel and iniquitous." In a potent editorial opposing the war, Douglass wrote, "Mexico seems a doomed victim to Anglo-Saxon cupidity and love of dominion. . . . We have no preference for parties, regarding this slaveholding crusade. . . . Our nation seems resolved to rush on in her wicked career. . . . We beseech our countrymen to leave off this horrid conflict, abandon their murderous plans and forsake the way of blood."[22]

Fifty years later, the Spanish-American War excited similar outrage among key members of the African American leadership. Thomas Wallace Swan, editor of *Howard's American Magazine*, wrote in 1900, "We recognize in the spirit of Imperialism, inaugurated and fostered by the administration of President McKinley, the same violation of Human Rights, which is being practiced by the Democratic Party in the recently reconstructed States, to wit, the wholesale disenfranchisement of the Negro."[23] Even Booker T. Washington was uncomfortable with the conflict. "My opinion is that the Philippine Islands should be given an opportunity to govern themselves," he wrote. "Until our nation has settled the Negro and Indian problems I do not believe that we have a right to assume more social problems."[24]

African Americans initially greeted the colonial war in the Philippines with mixed feelings. In an age of massive discrimination and frequent lynching, some believed military service to be a civic duty, where participation in overseas adventure would once and for all prove to the white masses that African Americans were entitled to full citizenship rights. Others felt that the war would, as William Gatewood puts it, "divert attention from the racial crisis at home."[25] By the war's end, disillusionment had set in. Segregation had deepened, mob violence against blacks had increased, and black soldiers often felt that they were in fact exporting Jim Crow to the rest of the dark world. (Some black soldiers deserted and joined the Filipino insurgency.) Emigration schemes regained their popularity.

In the first half of the twentieth century, African Americans spoke out against imperial aggression, linking it again to their plight at home. The Italian invasion of Ethiopia, in particular, incensed many black leaders. Paul Robeson led the effort. "The American Blacks have been yearning for freedom from an oppression which has predated fascism," he wrote. "It dates most clearly perhaps from the fascist invasion of Ethiopia in 1935. Since then, the parallel between his own interests and those of oppressed peoples abroad has been impressed upon him daily as he struggles against the forces which bar him from full citizenship, from full participation in American life."[26]

Robeson later helped found the Council on African Affairs, and W.E.B. Du Bois would be vice chair. Du Bois, of course, was similarly driven by a principled anti-imperialism for virtually the duration of his long career as an intellectual. And both Du Bois and Robeson would pay a price for their politics, as both were investigated for subversion by the US government and forbidden to travel abroad during much of the Cold War.

African American anticolonialism ebbed during the Cold War. With the rise of McCarthyism, "civil rights groups had to walk a fine line," according to Mary Dudziak, "making it clear that their reform efforts were meant to fill out the contours of American democracy, and not challenge or undermine it."[27] In this period, the American conversation on race changed from an analysis based largely on economics and politics to one oriented around sociology and psychology. According to Penny Von Eschen, "the embrace of Cold War American foreign policy by many African-American liberals, as well as US government prosecution of Paul Robeson and the Council, fundamentally altered the terms of anti-colonialism and effectively severed the black American struggle for civil rights from the issues of anti-colonialism and racism abroad."[28] (Du Bois, never playing along with the Cold War agenda, would write things like, "We want to rule Russia, and we cannot rule Alabama.")[29] By 1951, St. Clair Drake was writing, "Whether or not espousal of 'civil rights' for Negroes becomes separated, in the popular mind, from

'Communist Agitation' may be a decisive factor" in the success of the civil rights movement.[30] Cedric Robinson has described how during this period "the NAACP bent its efforts to constructing political coalitions with similarly liberal and anti-communist organizations."[31] During this period, black leadership essentially accepted the Cold War on Washington's terms in order to push for achievable civil rights gains.

With the rise of black militancy in the 1960s, anticolonialism and internationalism reasserted themselves, explaining Malcolm X's desire to see the African American struggle as one of "human rights" versus "civil rights." "The American white man has so thoroughly brainwashed the black man to see himself as only a domestic 'civil rights' problem that it will probably take longer than I live before the Negro sees that the struggle of the American black man is international," he observed in the final chapter of his autobiography.[32] And in 1972, James Baldwin wrote, "Any real commitment to black freedom in this country would have the effect of reordering all our priorities, and altering all our commitments, so that, for horrendous example, we would be supporting black freedom fighters in South Africa and Angola, and would not be allied with Portugal, would be closer to Cuba than we are to Spain, would be supporting the Arab nations instead of Israel, and would never have felt compelled to follow the French into Southeast Asia."[33]

The dominant paradigm, then, for more than a century and a half, was African American disapproval of US overseas adventurism, either because such exploits deflated the urgency of the problems at home or because they added to the problems at home and abroad. Either way, these views pointed to a necessary change in the basic structure of American society.

Moreover, the connection between African American international consciousness and the Arab and Muslim worlds is equally rich. This history, though often beset by a conservative cultural politics, is fundamentally concerned with developing alternative structures of allegiance, radical redefinitions of self and community, new universalisms through religion, and a kind of critical consciousness through which to examine the structure of power and race in the US and the West. In 1887, for example, Edward Wilmot Blyden published his magnum opus, *Christianity, Islam and the Negro Race*. Blyden frequently suggested that Islam offers a better option for "the Negro, who under Protestant rule, is kept in a state of . . . tutelage and irresponsibility," and that African emigration to and colonization of parts of America would create a class of "redeemers" of the race from the ravages of slavery.[34] He argued that Islam had brought dignity and advancement to Africa, Christianity only horror. "The Mohammedan Negro is a much better Mohammedan than the Christian Negro is a Christian," he writes, "because the Muslim Negro, as a learner, is a disciple, not an imitator. A disciple . . . may become a producer; an imitator never rises above a mere copyist."[35]

In the early years of the twentieth century, several new urban northern religious movements arose among African Americans, including the Moorish Science Temple, which claimed that black people were not "Negroes" at all, but "Moorish Americans." *The Divine Instructions*, the Temple's holy book, reveals that "through sin and disobedience every nation has suffered slavery, due to the fact that they honored not the creed and principles of their forefathers. That is why the nationality of the Moors was taken away from them in 1774 and the word Negro, black and colored was given to the Asiatics of America who were [of] Moorish descent, because they honored not the principles of their mother and father, and strayed after the gods of Europe whom they knew nothing of." Membership in the Temple brought one a "passport," in whose pages Drew Ali declared the holder "a Moslem under the Divine Laws of the Holy Koran of Mecca—Love, Truth, Peace, Freedom and Justice." The document ended with "I am a citizen of the USA."[36]

The creed of the Moorish Science Temple differed from that of its later competitor, the Nation of Islam, in its acknowledgment of American citizenship for blacks. The Temple opened a door of rejection for African Americans from ascribed identities, while the Nation walked through the passage, teaching African Americans that they must return to their original faith of "Islam." By combining nationalism and religion, the Nation sought to unite African American aspirations for racial uplift and nationhood with promises of return to their "original religion." Malcolm X would become the most famous member of the Nation and later of Sunni Islam in America, rivaled only by the boxer Muhammad Ali, whose Third World identifications also played into his vilification at home and heroism abroad.

But African American affiliation with the Arab and Muslim worlds was not limited to the sacred realm. Culturally and politically, alliances have been repeatedly forged with the idea that Third World oppression and denials of domestic human rights were similar, if not identical, struggles. A 1963 novel by William Gardner Smith, *The Stone Face*, for example, tells the story of Simeon Brown, a Philadelphia journalist and painter, who after suffering repeated racial outrages at home, packs up and moves to Paris. There he discovers the African American expatriate community living well, but the Arabs of France surviving in conditions reminiscent of home. They wear the same "baggy pants, worn shoes and shabby shirts," and have the "sullen, unhappy, angry eyes" that Brown recognizes from the streets of Harlem.[37] Brown is arrested one night with a bunch of Arabs, and after his release, one of the Arabs he passes in the street asks him a question that surprises him. "How does it feel to be a white man?" he asks him.[38] The novel brilliantly brings together the Holocaust, the Algerian War, racial tension in Paris, and the US civil rights struggle to articulate the need for action to transform a debased and race-torn world.

And in 1976, Sam Greenlee published his little-known novel titled *Baghdad Blues*. The story concerns Dave Burrell, an African American US Information Agency man assigned to Baghdad in the 1950s, when 'Abd al-Karim Qasim and his fellow officers overthrew the Iraqi monarchy. As with *The Stone Face*, this novel connects both domestic and international struggles. "More and more I began to understand the Arabs," Burrell reflects, "and not until much later did I realize that all that time I was learning more and more about myself."[39] Later he holds a conversation with Jamil, an Iraqi intellectual and friend (unlike in *The Kingdom*, this is a friendship of equals). "We will make our own mistakes, solve our own problems, create our own nation. To hell with the Americans and the British," Jamil says. Burrell narrates:

> I loved him, envied him, identified with him. To build a nation. . . .
>   "Well, man, you know I'm an American."
>   "Oh, but you are different; you understand."
>   "There are a lot like me at home." As I said it, I wondered if it were true.[40]

Of course, this type of identification persisted in later decades. Andrew Young, US ambassador to the UN, met with the PLO in the late 1970s and lost his post as a result. June Jordan wrote powerfully about the Israeli invasion of Lebanon. "I was born a black woman / and now / I am become a Palestinian," says a stanza in her "Moving Towards Home."[41] Amiri Baraka composed "Somebody Blew Up America."

The point is that there has been a strong and dedicated cultural politics for a very long time within the African American tradition that has sought an alliance with the rest of the world, including its Arab and Muslim corners, and the terms of that alliance were fundamentally about transformation. Connecting with other peoples and their struggles across the planet was not about advancement of the race at home. It was about transforming the very nature of American society—and with it global political culture—in pursuit of a world free of racist oppression and imperial aggression.

A Real Big Promotion

But the idea of African American global leadership as a sign of liberal success is not so novel either. It, too, has a history, dating at least to World War II. Robinson has written of how "during the 'patriotic period' of the [World War II] and for a few short years afterward, Black liberalism was on the ascendancy, achieving point of purchase among America's Black political and economic elite."[42] (This elite would later be excoriated by E. Franklin Frazier in his 1957 book *Black Bourgeoisie*.)[43] During this period, the image of black success, more than true integration, began to signify (white) acceptance of African Americans in the general culture.

Black diplomacy was central to this effort. From World War II onward, African American leaders pushed the government to employ African Americans in the diplomatic corps. It would be seen, they argued, as a sign of racial progress, and both the Truman and Eisenhower administrations were keenly interested in counteracting Soviet propaganda exploiting American racism. A. Philip Randolph told the State Department that it should hire more black personnel for service in Asian countries, arguing, "The American race problem represents the proving ground to the colored peoples of the world as to the sincerity of the United States in the democratic cause. Jim Crow is America's national disgrace. Its existence confuses and embarrasses our foreign policy."[44]

Adam Clayton Powell, Jr. informed Eisenhower that "one dark face from the US is of as much value as millions of dollars in economic aid."[45] And the life and career of civil rights leader and diplomat Ralph Bunche assumed massive public relations proportions.

Bunche, who was also the highest-ranking black OSS officer during World War II, when he composed psy-ops pamphlets for North and West African campaigns, stated that the key to winning over the "elite African" was the "legend of America as a liberalizing force in world affairs."[46] Sounding very much like a character out of the present, Bunche argued that "carefully chosen Negroes could prove more effective than whites [in diplomacy to the dark world], owing to their unique ability to gain more readily the confidence of the Native on the basis of their right to claim a good relationship."[47]

This line of argument accepted the terms of the Cold War to push for civil rights reform at home. By doing so, the larger connections drawn between global justice and domestic oppression were severed, and black participation in various American foreign policy initiatives was understood as a way of advancing the race. (Some, like Louis Armstrong, refused to cooperate; Stokely Carmichael put it another way: "You can't have [Ralph] Bunche for lunch.")[48]

Thus, the argument for black leadership within—rather than transformation of—the United States reappears today, bringing with it the idea that civil rights is yesterday's news and that global leadership represents individual opportunity, the kind of "upward mobility" that, according to Frazier, produced "exaggerated Americans" out of the black bourgeoisie. Rihanna's video for the song "Hard" is a good example. The video is a disturbing celebration of US military exploits somewhere in the Middle East as visual accompaniment to a song glorifying personal achievement. And in *The Kingdom*, the Jamie Foxx character's friendship with al-Ghazi brings the black American to a meeting with a former al-Qaeda operative. "Does he know where bin Laden is?" Fleury asks al-Ghazi breathlessly. "'Cause that'd be a real big promotion for me, if I could get that one." The East is again a career.

Race, nation, and empire. Their mixing, in the end, describes a complicated, if not confused, situation. On the one hand, as they suffer social exclusion, Arabs and Muslims are increasingly racialized. But the same gesture, in a post–civil rights era world, somehow manages to Americanize them. Arab and Muslim Americans signify both the incompleteness and the human triumph of the project of the American nation. African Americans are cast at the same time in sheltering roles, protecting the nation, those vulnerable and good Arabs and Muslims, and the empire. Such representations simultaneously prove that true equality has been won and that there exists an enduring need for civil rights thinking in the United States. What is largely missing is the recognition that black heroism, for it to be truly noble, must not be staged on the backs of another people. What is required is the critical consciousness that would build an alliance among Arabs, Muslims, and African Americans against global and domestic aggression and terrorism. (To be fair, *The Kingdom* hints toward this consciousness at the end.) In the absence of that idea, such representations in fact co-opt the struggle for racial equality into the project of an unequal nation and that of an expanding empire.

Or do they? For is not the analysis offered here ultimately misplaced or, at the very least, out of date? Does not the election of Barack Obama lay bare the naked truth that all Americans live in a postracial age? The country has its first African American president, and he is an ex–community organizer, not a retired general. Does not the presidency of Obama prove—despite his expansion of drone attacks in Pakistan and Afghanistan or his backtracking on Israeli settlements or his failure to call for accountability for US torture or his use of Bagram Airfield as a legal no-man's land— despite all of this and more, does not the presidency of Barack Obama prove that the United States is prepared to engage in a dialogue with the rest of the world based not on conquest but on mutual respect, shared interests, and basic human dignity? Is not a positive transformation of the United States away from empire and toward the community of nations what we should expect from an African American president who publicly cites his debt to the profound sacrifices of the long civil rights struggle and who writes intelligently and sensitively about anticolonial struggle in his own memoir? In other words, is not Obama himself the culmination of the oppositional agitation in the face of injustice that makes up the enormous depth and richness of African American history?

To this question, there is but one answer: "Arab, please!"

15

Men Behaving Badly

The Innocence of Muslims is an amateurish fourteen-minute video with the production quality of a cable-access show from the 1980s. A preposterous provocation, this ridiculous film easily managed to ignite fevered protests in Muslim-majority countries around the world, and once again everyone was worse off as a result. The episode played like a sequel to the 2005 Danish cartoon controversy, but with bigger and better explosions than the original.

The film—a schlocky piece of derision that resembles a pornographic version of *The Ten Commandments* spliced together with reruns of *The A-Team*—does not even make much sense. The lead actor playing Muhammad, the Prophet of Islam, looks as if Colin Farrell and Forrest Gump had a baby and groomed him to look like Jesus. The whole fourteen minutes, which is in fact the trailer for a longer film, is so painfully bad and so archly stupid that watching it ought to qualify as an enhanced interrogation technique.

And if the video itself is not strange enough, the story surrounding it is weirder. The director may or may not be Alan Roberts, who directed such memorable classics as *The Happy Hooker Goes Hollywood*, and the actors claim to have been duped. Now distancing themselves from the project, they explained in a press release that they simply responded to a casting call on Craigslist, that highwater mark of the Hollywood acting establishment (and the "casual encounters" genre), which said they were to act in an innocuous trifle called *Desert Warriors*, produced by the production company Media for Christ. The most blasphemous lines were clumsily dubbed in afterward. The producer of the video, a Coptic Egyptian American named Nakoula Basseley Nakoula, initially claimed to be "an Israeli American" named Sam Bacile who said he had secured five million dollars of funding for a full-length film from "100 Jewish donors," throwing some good old anti-Semitism into the Islamophobic fire. Nakoula, it turns out, is not just an Islamophobe and anti-Semite but also a felon, convicted of bank fraud in 2009 and placed on probation for five years. Before that, he had been arrested on charges of making PCP, otherwise known as angel dust. The video, posted months ago on YouTube, drew attention only when the Islamophobic Coptic American activist Morris Sadek emailed hundreds of journalists and associates a link to the video (and posted it on his website) in connection to an "International Judge Muhammad Day" organized by Pastor Terry Jones, of burn-a-copy-of-the-Qur'an infamy. This nexus should come as no surprise. The Islamophobic right in the United States is closely tied to the far-right fringes of the evangelical Christian community. Jones's event, incidentally, was scheduled for September 11, 2012.

The rest of the story is equally stupid, but more tragic. Demonstrators in Cairo scaled the US embassy walls and replaced the flag with their own, and violence in Libya claimed the life of the American ambassador and three others. Protests escalated, in about twenty countries around the world, and more lives were lost. In the United States, where protests did not erupt, the events were nonetheless framed as one would expect, within a narrative about politically immature Muslims who are forever intolerant of solemn Western values. "Such intolerance," writes ex-Muslim Ayaan Hirsi Ali in her *Newsweek* cover story, "is the defining characteristic of Islam."[1] And so we come full circle. Islamophobes provoke. Too many Muslims respond. Non-Muslims believe Muslims are crazy. Muslims are told the West hates them, and the Islamophobic right sleeps well at night with their cozy dreams of a mission accomplished.

But before we jump, as the pundits would have us do, to conclusions about the inexorability of the clash of civilizations, before we breezily proclaim the end of the Arab awakening (a generational shift that will take years to settle into stability), and before we decide that Arabs prefer or deserve death over liberty, we should pause to think about the idiotic nature of this entire fiasco and decide if we want really want right-wing lunacy, from West and East, to determine the direction of global politics.

In fact, the better lens through which to view the tumult over this doltish movie is not the Danish cartoon conflagration but the manufactured controversy over the "Ground Zero Mosque," an Islamic cultural center originally slated to be built two blocks from the former site of the World Trade Center in Lower Manhattan. Back in 2010, and months after plans for the center had been announced, the anti-Muslim blogger Pamela Geller stoked enough outrage on the fringes of the right wing to push the story onto the airwaves of Fox News. In its typical fashion, Fox News lent legitimacy to bogus claims—in this case, that the proposed cultural center would be a mosque and would be at Ground Zero, neither of which was true—and trampled on the rest of the media for not picking up the story. Soon enough, the rest of the media followed suit. Imam Feisal Abdul Rauf, the man behind the proposed center, was quickly transformed into a covert cultural jihadist. The center itself was seen as a symbol of Islamic domination, and Newt Gingrich dutifully equated Muslims to Nazis.[2]

The degree to which the far right can set the news agenda and establish the political tenor of domestic debates is frightening. This phenomenon has a name: "the Fox effect," a term coined by David Brock and Ari Rabin-Havt in their book *The Fox Effect: How Roger Ailes Turned a Network Into a Propaganda Machine*.[3] But in the case of *The Innocence of Muslims*, the role of Fox News is not played by Ailes's cable outlet. That distinction belongs instead to an Egyptian television channel called al-Nas (The People), which caters to the archconservative, literal-minded current in Islam known as the

Salafi trend. The inflammatory right wing in this story is not just American, but international.

The video first made it onto Egyptian airwaves on September 8, 2012, when Sheikh Khalid 'Abdallah, known for whipping up sectarian tensions, screened parts of it on his al-Nas program and called for protests. On September 11, thousands showed up at the US embassy, including a strong representation of Salafis and bunches of Ultras, hard-core sports fans who are politically far away from the Salafis but who carry a sharpened grudge against Egyptian security forces after seventy-four fans were killed at the Port Said Stadium in February 2012. (All of this of course occurred when Muhammad Mursi was Egypt's president and well before the military-backed coup in Egypt on July 3, 2013.) One of 'Abdallah's recurrent themes is that Coptic Christians, diaspora Copts in particular, goad the West into prying open the Egyptian Muslim body politic for intervention. *The Innocence of Muslims* offered him Exhibit A for his argument with an opening scene that depicts bearded Salafis ransacking a Coptic clinic and a Coptic father explaining the assault to his daughter by harkening back to the earliest days of Islam. Cue the stream of insults to Muhammad in the "historical" scenes that follow. The implication is not only that Muslims bear collective guilt for the church burnings and other sectarian attacks that occur in Egypt, but also that they are innately bigoted and violent. It is precisely what the likes of 'Abdallah want their followers to think Westerners (and Copts) believe about Islam. The demonstrations in Egypt, in other words, may have spoken the words of civilizational conflict, but what they really reflected were the complicated dynamics of national politics. The same thing can be said of Libya, Yemen, Lebanon, and Syria, in fact, of every place where protests emerged.

Yet, unlike the "Ground Zero Mosque" controversy, *The Innocence of Muslims* conflagration combines the fulminations of the

American far right with the Salafi news media that takes their bait. In this case, the two may be doctrinal and political opposites, but their attraction to each other is nonetheless magnetic. Both are interested in fanning the civilizational fires that have been burning at least since the terrorist attacks of September 11 and smoldering for much longer. And with today's technology, it has become child's play—and will only get easier—to produce and distribute bilious speech that can and will have deadly consequences. The Islamophobes in the United States and the ultra-religious right in Muslim-majority countries need each other to survive. Each side confirms to the other the need for its own existence. To the Islamophobes, all Muslims are extremists. The provocations Islamophobes produce are designed to elicit the very images we see. To the Muslim far right, all Westerners harbor a deep-seated anti-Islamic sentiment and the anti-Muslim provocations supply ample evidence of the inner, hateful workings of the Western mind.

Left out is the vast middle, hundreds of millions of people who neither seek out nor desire a clash of civilizations. And to those who ask where are the Muslims demonstrating in the tens of thousands against this anti-American delirium, one could also ask where are the demonstrations among Christian evangelical circles against these hate-filled productions. In fact, we need desperately to move beyond such feeble-minded "where are the [fill in the blank]" sloganeering. What we need to understand instead are the distinctions that make up politics. When then–Egyptian President Muhammad Mursi called upon the US political establishment to prosecute the filmmaker, he was doing so to outflank his own right wing on this front of the Egyptian culture wars. And culture wars, in Egypt or the United States, are largely diversions from the real and difficult issues of the day, by which Egypt is beset on many sides. Similarly, when President Barack Obama claimed that Egypt is not "an ally, but we don't consider them an enemy,"[4] he was not only scolding, in typical imperial fashion, his Egyptian counterpart the way a parent scolds a child. He was also signaling to the American public that he can outdo his campaign rival Mitt Romney, in the lead-up to the 2012 election, in talking down to ungrateful vassals.

There are, of course, plenty of legitimate grievances in the Middle East with regard to US foreign policy, and Obama's statement that "there is never any justification for violence"[5] rings hollow, particularly when one recalls that, according to administration officials, Obama's policy for drone attacks in the War on Terror is that "all military-age males in a strike zone [count] as combatants unless there is explicit intelligence posthumously proving them innocent," as reported by the *New York Times* on May 29, 2012.[6] Moreover, the fact that there have been ongoing revolutions and reformations in several key Arab countries does not simply erase decades of US complicity with dictators and the continued US support for other repressive regimes in the region. And anti-Muslim sentiment continues to rise around the world and is largely ignored by political leaders in the West, leading many Muslims across the globe to conclude that their lives and issues are considered less worthy by Westerners and that "Western values" are, in practice, ways to delegitimize Muslims concerns. But even if that were the case, Muslim leaders everywhere would do their causes no favors when they seethe at every brickbat thrown their way.

What is true is that publics in Muslim-majority countries around the world would be well served to learn more about how American civil society operates. And it would be in the interest of Western publics to understand the many complexities and contradictions of Muslim-majority societies around the world so they can understand who exactly is protesting and why. In other words, what is really driving the current explosion is not wounded religious sensibilities, or cultures of complaint, or atavistic Islamic rage. It is politics. And it is often a local politics of jockeying for power through mobilization of a religious base, whether in the United States or in Muslim-majority counties. The problem is that if you do not know the politics of the Muslim-majority countries involved, all you see are the screaming beards.

In the meantime, the only award for this terrible show goes to Alan Roberts, who, as the putative director of this insipid little video, has managed to direct not just his own actors but thousands of people around the world to act, and to act very badly indeed.

16

Chaos and Procedure

The timid man, the lazy man, the man who distrusts his country, the over-civilized man, who has lost the great fighting, masterful virtues, the ignorant man, and the man of dull mind, whose soul is incapable of feeling the mighty lift that thrills "stern men with empires in their brains"—all these, of course, shrink from seeing the nation undertake its new duties; shrink from seeing us build a navy and an army adequate to our needs; shrink from seeing us do our share of the world's work, by bringing order out of chaos in the great, fair tropic islands from which the valor of our soldiers and sailors has driven the Spanish flag. These are the men who fear the strenuous life, who fear the only national life which is really worth leading.
—Theodore Roosevelt, "The Strenuous Life"

In Season 4 of *24*, the Fox network's ticking-time-bomb terror drama, Kiefer Sutherland is, once again, in a bind. Sutherland plays Jack Bauer, a driven and talented agent of CTU, the Counter Terrorism Unit, a fictional division of the national security state apparatus that operates like a domestic version of the CIA (although in Season 4, for reasons that need not bother us now, he officially works for the Defense Department). Following the show's established format, the season covers twenty-four hours in the life of Bauer as he battles terrorists and bureaucrats, mostly from a slate-gray bunker in Los Angeles that looks like a SoHo nightclub with computers, and keeps the country safe from the looming evils and jealous monsters of the world. The arch villain in Season 4 is the handsome but malevolent Habib Marwan, a computer analyst by day and Middle Eastern terrorist by night, who attempts to execute the Secretary of Defense and force the meltdown of nuclear power plants across the country before stealing a stealth fighter and shooting down Air Force One, nearly killing the president and thereby placing a weak-chinned Richard Nixon lookalike vice president in the role of commander in chief. Marwan's minions then abscond with the "nuclear football" from the downed Air Force One and proceed to shoot a nuclear warhead into Los Angeles. Their plans are ultimately foiled when CTU intercepts the missile in midair. (Phew!) If it's not clear yet, realism is, well, not one of the show's strengths.

The program was hugely successful—its fans reportedly included Vice President Dick Cheney[1]—and it became the definitive representation for the American public of the War on Terror's early years, so much so that in 2006 the dean of West Point, US Army Brigadier General Patrick Finnegan, and other members of the military and the FBI met with 24's producers because they feared the show and its brazen and breezy endorsement of torture was influencing students to a dangerous degree. Its fourth season, which aired in the first half of 2005—less than a year after the revelations of torture and abuse of detainees by Americans in Iraq, Afghanistan, and beyond—portrayed some of the most extreme examples of torture on TV, which as Jane Mayer notes in the *New Yorker*, became far more common on TV screens after September 11, 2001, than before. Mayer writes,

> Before the attacks, fewer than four acts of torture appeared on prime-time television each year, according to Human Rights First, a nonprofit organization. Now there are more than a hundred, and, as David Danzig, a project director at Human Rights First, noted, "the torturers have changed. It used to be almost exclusively the villains

who tortured. Today, torture is often perpetrated by the heroes." The Parents' Television Council, a nonpartisan watchdog group, has counted what it says are sixty-seven torture scenes during the first five seasons of *24*—more than one every other show.[2]

The worst offender on television, the council notes, is *24*.

In the make-believe world of *24*, torture works. Suspects talk and information is actionable. In the real world, scholars of torture repeatedly tell us, torture rarely if ever works. Putting aside the fact that torture is universally condemned as immoral and considered to be criminal, it is also of questionable utility. When being tortured, a person will say anything to stop the torture, even admitting to things that are blatantly untrue. One man, Shafik Rasul, confessed to attending a meeting between Osama bin Laden and September 11 leader Mohammed Atta in Afghanistan in January 2000 when he was in fact working at a Currys store in the West Midlands, a fact later confirmed by Britain's MI5.[3] Another well-known case from Apartheid South Africa involves a man, who due to a confusion in the use of code names, ultimately confessed to murdering himself.[4] Even the CIA, in January 1989, informed the Senate Subcommittee on Intelligence that "inhumane physical or psychological techniques are counterproductive because they do not produce intelligence and will probably result in false answers."[5] By November 2001, the CIA had changed its position.[6]

But to view *24*'s depiction of torture only as an argument in favor of enhanced interrogation techniques—to use the Bush administration's euphemism—is to miss its larger, aesthetic dimension. Torture does not stand alone in the show; it is part of a panoply of depictions of determination against all odds, of the need to break the rules, even occasionally the rules of physics, in order to reestablish a just and righteous ordering of the world. Frequently, Bauer has to bend the rules to fit the situation, primarily because the evil-doers and nefarious traitors are bound only to their own success and freely break all the rules in their favor, and this fight-against-everything style is an integral dimension of the (romantic) action movie genre.

The Bush years of the War on Terror were also defined by this sense of rule breaking. Perhaps the most obvious example is when the United States wanted to go to war in Iraq. First, the administration sought the approval of the Security Council, and when that was withheld, they ignored the rules of the UN and went to war anyway. Much of this sense of rule breaking was rationalized by the belief that weak-kneed liberal policies had enabled the terrorist attacks of September 11 in the first place, and that what had held the United States back from asserting its proper position in the world was its commitment to principles that its enemies didn't hold sacred (all of which is questionable, of course). "There was before 9/11 and after 9/11," testified Cofer Black, director of the CIA's Counterterrorism Center from 1999 until 2002, to Congress in 2002. "After 9/11, the gloves come off."[7] On September 16, 2001, Dick Cheney told Tim Russert on NBC something similar. "We . . . have to work . . . sort of the dark side, if you will," Cheney said. "We've got to spend time in the shadows in the intelligence world. A lot of what needs to be done here will have to be done quietly, without any discussion, using sources and methods that are available to our intelligence agencies, if we're going to be successful. That's the world these folks operate in, and so it's going to be vital for us to use any means at our disposal, basically, to achieve our objective."[8]

The dark side brings us back to the bind Jack Bauer is in. A suspect has been brought to CTU but cannot be properly questioned because Habib Marwan, having learned of the arrest, has called "Amnesty Global," which quickly finds a federal judge to issue an injunction against any harsh interrogation of the suspect and dispatches an attorney to represent the suspect. Bauer and his superior call the president to override the injunction. "Am I correct in assuming this suspect is unlikely to respond to the kind of Q&A his lawyer would admit," asks Mike Novick, a hawkish presidential advisor who resembles a younger, thinner Dick Cheney without the hunting rifle. "That's correct, Mike," Bauer responds. "If we want to procure any information from this suspect, we're going to have to do it behind closed doors." The neophyte president looks aghast. "You're talking about torturing this man?" he asks. "I'm talking about doing what is necessary to stop this warhead from being used against us," Bauer, the veteran agent, explains. "Give us a moment," the president says, unwilling to authorize torture.

Moments earlier, Bauer had attempted to reason with David Weiss, the Amnesty Global attorney. "All my client wants is due process," Weiss explains to a frustrated Bauer, who responds, "Now, I don't want to bypass the Constitution, but there are extraordinary circumstances." "The Constitution was born out of extraordinary circumstances, Mr. Bauer, not in a back room with a rubber hose," Weiss lectures, and Bauer tenses up. "I hope you can live with that," Bauer says. By the end of the episode, Jack Bauer has solved his dilemma of dealing with an indecisive president and inflexible civil libertarians. He resigns his post and, as a private citizen, is somehow now free to torture the suspect. The gloves then come off, and Bauer breaks the man's fingers until he talks.

What is noteworthy about these scenes is not just the depiction of righteous physical torture by a putatively ex-agent of the government, but the manner in which torture is painted as necessary in a world where evil can manipulate the color of law. What makes the terrorists wily is not just that they operate in the shadows but that they know our weaknesses—here, the American justice system and its procedures. Ours is a system that invites pusillanimity and abuse, 24 seems to be saying, and theirs is a cunning malfeasance. In a world drawn in primary colors, good too must resort to thinking and acting like terrorists. Bauer stands as the righteous rebel, and we cheer his dark intelligence and rogue sensibilities.

He is willing to sacrifice his body and his soul to save the heart and heartland of America, and because he's a covert agent, no one will ever know. In a celebrity-driven culture, this is true heroism.

The rogue quality of the show *24*, combined with its obsession with technology and its need to uncover moles in the highest echelons of government, is what makes CTU resemble the CIA, and also what defines CTU, or really the CIA, as the branch of the national security apparatus best suited to fight the War on Terror, even if the real CIA failed miserably in predicting the September 11 attacks and in its intelligence assessments of Iraq's weapons of mass destruction. As Tim Weiner has shown in his book *Legacy of Ashes*, the entire history of the CIA is far from a sophisticated story of secret operatives righting the world for democracy and more closely resembles a catastrophic history of escalating blunders, profound failures, and dangerous hubris that increasingly threatens the foundations of the country.[9] Yet, none of that matters for *24*. Why? Because *24* is not really a TV show. It's a love letter to a fantasy CIA.

It should really come as little surprise then that the moral universe of *24* closely matched the moral universe of the Bush administration and its staunchest ideologues. In the years immediately following the September 11 attacks, the War on Terror was often presented by them in near messianic terms, an epic battle between good and evil, where the idea of "managing" the conflict, as if it were a conventional war, was the equivalent of stabbing oneself in the side and crying defeat. Richard Perle and David Frum describe the post-9/11 world in precisely such Manichean terms in their 2004 book *An End to Evil: How to Win the War on Terror*. "For us, terrorism remains the great evil of our time and the war against this evil, our generation's great cause," they write. "We do not believe that Americans are fighting this evil to minimize it or to manage it. We believe they are fighting to win—to end this evil before it kills again and on a genocidal scale. There is no middle way for Americans. It is victory or holocaust."[10] (Note that they manage to use the word "evil" four times in this short passage.)

Such end-of-days pontificating over the War on Terror has abated since then. The aesthetics of the War on Terror, by which I mean the ways that the War on Terror gets represented and the structures of feeling that these representations produce, have likewise shifted over time, as has the representation of the CIA in film and television. In fact, 2012 seemed like a banner year for the CIA in film and television. Kathryn Bigelow's *Zero Dark Thirty* and Ben Affleck's *Argo* were blockbuster hits and Oscar winners, and Showtime's *Homeland* continued to enthrall audiences and win awards. The CIA is all over our screens, and these representations have quickly become the standards by which the current phase of the War on Terror is represented and judged. (A recent literary example would be Henry A. Crumpton's memoir *The Art of Intelligence*, a strange—and not very good—book for an agency that protects its secrecy above all else.)[11] But this CIA notably operates differently from *24*'s CTU.

Zero Dark Thirty and *Homeland*, with their emphases on torture and on searching for moles, respectively, would seem to replicate significant elements of *24*, but the differences between the first two and *24* are more important than any similarities. Gone is the heavy reliance on rule breaking to defeat evil. What replaces it is *procedure*—a close, meticulous, and near-obsessive regard for following the rules, the rules of evidence, the rules of human conduct, the rules of procedure itself, even if and especially when bureaucracy gets in the way. This difference matters. What *24* is telling us is that the world is beset by evil and that only by temporarily becoming the very enemy the United States needs to defeat will American rectitude prevail. Victory alone restores righteousness. Meanwhile, such stark moralism, which is of course quite deliberately immoral, is largely, though not completely, absent from *Zero Dark Thirty*. (Revenge, on the other hand, is a plainly evident structure of feeling in the film.) In the late aesthetics of the War on Terror, these representations—in *Zero Dark Thirty*, *Argo*, and *Homeland*—seem to be reassuring us that procedure replaces transgression as the means to ruling and running a successful empire. The world of *24* is like Milton's *Paradise Lost*, where Satan's charm is equal and opposite to God's grace. With his intelligence and good looks, the evil Marwan has a cartoonish and larger than life presence in the show. But, by the time we reach 2012, the black-and-white universe of the early stage of the War on Terror has been replaced by a world not so much evil as chaotic and unpredictable. And through the devoted use of procedure, the agents of American imperialism who are the most successful—those stern women and men with empire in their brains—are those with the means to bring order out of chaos.

The police procedural has replaced the action movie as the genre of the War on Terror. *Zero Dark Thirty*, a film about killing Osama bin Laden, is far less a tale about the Navy SEALs and their raid on the Abbottabad compound than a bloodthirsty detective story featuring a lonesome and driven female CIA analyst. *Homeland*, too, emphasizes suspicion and desire over blood and gore, and *Argo*, though a historical tale, features a story where success is premised on acting your way out of chaos rather than bombing your way into victory. The promise of triumph in all three is achieved by following the rules, not by breaking them.

In *Zero Dark Thirty*, Maya's ability to remember details and to focus on leads—she can tune out the noise to focus on the signal—is what makes her the central character in the film. Maya quickly learns to accept that torture is part of the procedures needed for the war and relies on it and willingly participates in torture to gain actionable intelligence. Torture, in other words, has transitioned from extrajudicial but necessary in *24* to being routine and procedural. But the film's emphasis on procedures doesn't end there, since it also warns us of the errors that occur when procedures are not properly followed.

In a central scene, Maya's colleague Jessica has uncovered a big lead in the hunt for bin Laden. A Jordanian doctor in al-Qaeda is willing to turn into a mole for the CIA, and Jessica sets up a meeting with him at Camp Chapman in Afghanistan. She couldn't go meet him in the mountains of Pakistan because, as the film tells us, "You're white. You'll get kidnapped there." So excited is she to meet her new recruit, Jessica bakes him a birthday cake, to which Maya informs Jessica, "Muslims don't celebrate with cake." This, I must add here, is news to me! I took great pride in the birthday cakes my mother made me when I was growing up in Canada, and there are bakeries and cake shops all over the Middle East. But this bit of gender coding—and we're told that Jessica is a mother of three—is a bit of foreshadowing for the tragedy to come.

At Camp Champman, Jessica is excited to see the doctor's car approach but becomes agitated when observing the security. "Why are there gate guards there? We talked about this. No one is supposed to be there when my source arrives. You might have spooked him already," she says, to Whiplash, the soldier in charge of security. "Procedures only work if we follow them every time," he says. "This is different," Jessica responds, continuing with "I'm sorry. I can't explain, but it's for a good cause." "Look, I'm responsible for everybody's safety, okay? It's not just about you," Whiplash says, to which Jessica answers, "I just need them to go away for a minute. You can search him as soon as he gets here." He leans into his radio on his shoulder. "All stations. This is Whiplash. Go ahead and stand down." Moments after he arrives, the good doctor detonates a bomb and seven CIA agents are killed.[12] Without proper procedure, chaos ensues.

Following Jessica's death, Maya becomes hardened to kill bin Laden, and Debbie, another female CIA operative in crisp Ann Taylor–like suit—and not khakis, in which many of the CIA men are dressed during the movie—comes to her with news. "I've painstakingly combed through everything in the system and found this."

(Why does she say "painstakingly"? In a film that venerates its own true-life quality, it's a strange utterance, though it highlights a kind of devotion to procedure. But really, wouldn't most people simply say "I've combed through everything"?) What Debbie found was evidence that Maya ultimately uses to confirm the existence of bin Laden's courier, and this discovery eventually leads to the Navy SEALs' raid on bin Laden's compound. After delivering the folder, Debbie tells Maya that she's been an inspiration to her. "Maybe you'd let me buy you a kebab sometime," Debbie asks. "Don't eat out," Maya says to her. "It's too dangerous."

The world is too chaotic for these women of the CIA, but that's okay because the real work of the War on Terror is in crunching data, following paper, and torturing prisoners in secure black sites. Maya and Debbie are the perfect agents for this data war. Women, the representations seem to be telling us, are better suited (in both senses of the word) for this kind of close detail work. Jessica, on the other hand—a mother of three, a birthday cake baker, and thus a nurturer—had tapped into the wrong side of her female talents.

In Season 1 of *Homeland*, Carrie Mathison is likewise information-obsessed, and this compulsion is what accounts in large part for the success of the series. The internal bedlam of her obsessive-compulsive mind trying to array itself plays out externally in the need to discover the motivations of Nicholas Brody. Both her interior and exterior life are about bringing rational order out of the chaos. We witness this directly when Carrie has a manic episode and is visited by Saul, her avuncular superior. Carrie has spread documents all over the floor, since she intuits that the missing piece of information on a terrorist cell is waiting to be found. Over the course of one night, Saul assembles the documents, which are as jumbled as Carrie's mind, into a rational timeline. In this case, Saul and Carrie work together to order the chaos and the result is propitious. When rules are occasionally broken in *Homeland*, they are most often transgressed because of Carrie's own mental instability.

Homeland and *Zero Dark Thirty* are advertisements for women in the CIA. While it relies more typically on male leadership, *Argo* is equally concerned with making and following rules if success is to be achieved in the exfiltration mission of bringing out six Americans as if they were a Canadian film crew in revolutionary Iran. "What's your name," Mendez quizzes Joe Stafford about his alias. When Stafford hesitates, Mendez responds, "He's an American spy. Shoot him," and then says, "Let's go again." Learning your lines is equivalent to learning the rules of survival and success.

Unsurprisingly, all three of these representations rely on a stock Islamophobic and Orientalist imagination. Iran is peopled only by angry men with ZZ Top beards and one potentially sympathetic Iranian housekeeper. The order of the Canadian ambassador's house is also shown in visual opposition of the chaos of the bazaar. (Incidentally, the scene where the six Americans and Mendez visit the bazaar never happened, at least as far as the account by Tony Mendez posted on the CIA's own website states that the group stayed in the ambassador's house the entire time.)[13]

Zero Dark Thirty is more sinister, repeatedly showing the violence of terrorism but never the violence of war, except for the film's final sequence. Even there, the Navy SEALs exhibit plenty of regret for killing noncombatants. The terror of war, in other words, is unidirectional in the film, and the Pakistanis—who, bizarrely, speak Arabic more often than Urdu in the film—are always suspicious looking, unless they work for the Americans. The good Muslim/bad Muslim dichotomy is plainly evident here, as it is in *Argo* and *Homeland*.[14] Only if you are on the side of the Americans can you begin to qualify as a good Muslim, and they are few and far between.

Homeland is clearly the most Islamophobic of them all, and also gets many details wrong, showing the Muslim Brody praying with his shoes on, for example. And Brody's Arabic sounds more like Hebrew than Arabic. (The credits to *Homeland* tell us it is based on the Israeli show *Hatufim*.) The message of *Homeland* is insidious, for virtually all of the Muslims in the show have a connection to the terrorists, and like Don Cheadle's film *Traitor* and Showtime's previous show *Sleeper Cell*, *Homeland* suggests that all Muslims in the United States are potential terrorists, terrorist sympathizers, or associates of terrorists. A casual viewer will watch the show and believe the equivalence between being Muslim and being a terrorist and that the only way to break this wicked connection would be to volunteer your talents to the Americans. There is no third way.

These are generally old tropes of Hollywood, and who is really surprised by them anymore? Perhaps what is novel is not the use of these tropes but the fact that the producers of culture in our multicultural age won't even bother to get the details right. In the end, it doesn't really matter much, for the focus in all three is not Muslim life but American life—specifically white American life—in chaos, a chaos produced by a dark other. When Jessica is told she will be kidnapped because of her white skin and that Muslims don't celebrate with cake—the two points are said within sentences of each other in *Zero Dark Thirty*—the effect is to highlight how different, and completely un-American, these terrorist/Muslims are and the point is made without needing to be enunciated.

The shift in genre is more surprising than the continued use of simplistic stereotypes. Why did the representations of the War on Terror transform from the moralizing action adventures of the early years to the virtually amoral procedural realism of today? We could speculate that the change speaks to a public that was promised quick victory, while the wars in Afghanistan and Iraq have dragged on, expanded to other geographies like Pakistan and Yemen, and became messier and morally questionable as news of American atrocities during the campaigns have trickled out. Perhaps the films reflect the moods of the American public. Heroes were needed immediately following 9/11, even cartoon heroes of superhuman strength, whereas the mood now, as the War on Terror continues with no conceivable end in sight, is one precisely of management—poor Richard Perle—as the War on Terror is institutionalized into the government and military structure of the United States. And perhaps even more to the point, if *24* reflects a Bush-era (im)moralism, *Zero Dark Thirty*, *Homeland*, and *Argo* illustrate in their focus on procedure an Obama doctrine of prosecuting the War on Terror in a fashion dangerously similar to that of George W. Bush but with a seemingly lighter rhetoric and a (falsely) progressive face. Speaking about targeted killings by predator drones, Obama told CNN in September 2012 that he "struggled" with his decisions. "If you don't, then it's very easy to slip into a situation in which you end up bending rules thinking that the ends always justify the means," Obama said. "That's not who we are as a country."[15]

But there may be an even more direct answer to this question, one that speaks more of the CIA specifically than it does of our cultural moment writ large. In her important book, *The CIA in Hollywood*, Tricia Jenkins reminds us that, since 1996, the CIA has forged an explicit connection with the film and television industries.[16] Initially led by Chase Brandon, the first cousin of Tommy Lee Jones and a twenty-five-year veteran of the agency, the CIA's entertainment liaison office has helped "to shape the finished product's tone and content," as Jenkins puts it, of such movies and television shows as *JAG*, *Enemy of the State*, *Alias*, *The Sum of All Fears*, *The Recruit*, and *Covert Affairs*.[17] The office has also been directly involved with *24*, *Argo*, *Zero Dark Thirty*, and *Homeland*.

What Jenkins analyzes is significantly different from, although certainly related to, the relationship that the CIA established during the Cold War to global cultural production. This line of inquiry is perhaps best exemplified by Frances Stonor Saunders's book *The Cultural Cold War: The CIA and the World of Arts and Letters*.[18] In it, Saunders offers a comprehensive account of how the CIA, through the Congress for Cultural Freedom, first led by Sidney Hook, covertly advanced what it perceived to be American interests (and anticommunism) throughout Western Europe and the rest of the world via the promulgation of key cultural forms and financial support for specific artists. Magazines such as *Partisan Review*, art movements such as Abstract Expressionism, and theologians such as Reinhold Niebuhr all benefited from CIA largesse. Saunders's excavation lays bare the dependence of highly successful American art on the American state in a Kulturkampf that defined itself as autonomous when compared to Soviet artistic slavishness. Hugh Wilford refined and disputed elements of Saunders's thesis in his book *The Mighty Wurlitzer: How the CIA Played America*, arguing that many of the artists who benefited from CIA funds did their own thing anyway or were motivated by a liberal idealism that easily aligned with CIA interests.[19] Nevertheless, the desire of the CIA to infiltrate itself into the realms of culture is irrefutable. It also keeps surfacing. In a 2014 article published by the *Chronicle Review*, titled "How Iowa Flattened Literature," Eric Bennett illustrates how Paul Engle, the director of the Iowa Writers' Workshop, took money from a CIA front organization and developed an approach to fiction writing, also promoted by his successor Frank Conroy, that pushed an antiabstraction aesthetic that, in its sensuous particularity, was "doing ideological combat" with the Soviet Union.[20]

What Jenkins analyzes is different. Rather than concentrating on how the CIA attempted to direct the idea of culture from the sidelines, Jenkins focuses on how the CIA promotes, controls, and manipulates the representations of the CIA itself. Reviewing the history of the agency on film and television, Jenkins tells us that Langley began appearing in popular culture in any significant way only in the 1960s and that, prior to the Bay of Pigs fiasco, the American public had little regard for or interest in the agency. The representations that followed often showed CIA agents as rogues (*The Amateur*), assassins (*Three Days of the Condor*), or buffoons (remember *Get Smart*?). Frustrated by these projections, the CIA decided in 1996 to reverse its nonparticipation policy with Hollywood and began consulting with the entertainment industry directly because, in the words of Chase Brandon, the agency was "tired of being depicted on screen as a nefarious organization full of rogue operatives."[21] This policy though came with an imperative: that the CIA be presented in a positive light. The agency has complained that this charge has been an uphill battle due to historic hostility from Hollywood for the agency. Jenkins explains, "Bill Harlow, former [CIA] Director of Public Affairs, stated that most difficult task for the public affairs staff was to get people to make a movie in which the Agency's officers were the heroes or viewed in a positive light precisely because of the politics guiding the entertainment community," and Paul Berry, Chase Brandon's successor, stated that the "'challenges facing the public image of the CIA [were] more daunting' [in 2008] than right after 9/11, in part because of strong opposition to Bush's policies from the Hollywood community."[22]

There is not much evidence, however, for this difficulty that the agency much protests. Langley's work with the entertainment industry is explicit and intimate. The Public Affairs Office's website outright suggests possible story lines to producers and writers to explore. ("Looking for inspiration for a new film or book? Our Entertainment Industry Liaison offers recommendations here. Check back often for his new picks," the website says.[23] They also have a "Kid's Page.")[24] The office directly contacts writers and directors to whom it pitches ideas, supplies stock footage, explains procedures and protocols, offers tours of its facilities, and more. The website reads,

> If you are part of the entertainment industry, and are working on a project that deals with the CIA, the Agency may be able to help you. We are in a position to give greater authenticity to scripts, stories, and other products in development. That can mean answering

questions, debunking myths, or arranging visits to the CIA to meet the people who know intelligence—its past, present, and future. In some cases, we permit filming on our headquarters compound. (Please visit our Headquarters Virtual Tour.) We can also provide stock footage of locations within and around our main building.

Intelligence is challenging, exciting, and essential. To better convey that reality, the CIA is ready for a constructive dialogue with a broad range of creative talents.

For further information, please contact our Entertainment Industry Liaison.[25]

The CIA reportedly gets between forty and sixty requests a month from domestic and international filmmakers for assistance.[26]

Paul Berry has said that "Hollywood is the only way that the public learns about the Agency,[27]" but what they learn is of course a very-slanted CIA version of the agency. The image that the CIA projects of itself also fulfills several functions. For one, it aids in recruitment to the agency, which jealously saw *Top Gun* as the "single best recruiting tool of the navy" and, in creating its liaison with the entertainment industry, sought to replicate that success.[28] This was key, particularly in the late 1990s, when the fall of the Berlin Wall meant that applications to the CIA were down by 20 percent and the very existence of the agency, which had failed to predict the demise of the Soviet Unison, was being questioned at high levels of the government. The terrorist attacks of September 11 reversed the CIA's recruitment worries, which were averaging six hundred a week prior to the attacks and jumped to nearly three thousand in the week immediately following. The television show *Alias*, featuring Jennifer Garner as a graduate student of English by day and CIA operative by night, also "helped distance the CIA from its long-standing image as an old boys' network," according to Jenkins.[29] One can't help but conclude that *Zero Dark Thirty* and *Homeland* are also a kind of targeted marketing to would-be female analysts.

To gain access to CIA assistance, projects must also represent the CIA favorably, which was also important for the agency following the bad news in 1994 that Aldrich Ames, a CIA counterintelligence officer and analyst, had been spying for the Soviet Union and Russian intelligence for the better part of a decade. Ames, incidentally, has stated that there is no "rational need for thousands of case officers and tens of thousands of agents working around the world, . . . as the information our vast espionage network acquires is generally insignificant or irrelevant to our policy makers' needs."[30] His arrest was embarrassing to the agency, and two years later Langley opened its entertainment liaison office.

The agency modeled their program on the Pentagon's own media outreach, which, according to Jenkins, "often provides military personnel and equipment, including fighter jets, submarines, and aircraft carriers at little to no cost to film and television creators as long as they seek to make movies that depict the military in a positive light."[31] Moreover, the CIA is forthright about the audiences it reaches via Hollywood, noting that "terrorists watch TV, too."[32] The torture scenes of *Zero Dark Thirty*, in particular, may begin to resonate as more than controversial documentary realism if we take this into account. As the Bush administration threatened sending people to Guantánamo Bay as a means to achieve dominance in the War on Terror, the CIA during the Obama administration may very well be attempting to send a message to its opponents about their possible fate through *Zero Dark Thirty*.

In fact, when it comes to *Zero Dark Thirty*, the cooperation between Hollywood and the government is even clearer. The filmmakers behind *Zero Dark Thirty* benefited directly from high-level leaks of classified information about the raid on Osama bin Laden's compound that came not from the CIA's liaison office but from

Leon Panetta, the director of the CIA, and from Michael Vickers, the Defense Department's top intelligence official.[33]

As Jenkins points out, the activities of the liaison office of the CIA raise significant constitutional questions. Because the CIA is a government agency, First Amendment issues are germane to its activities. Since the agency assists only some projects—namely those that project a favorable image of the agency—and not others, it is in fact limiting the free speech of cultural producers. The CIA, for example, declined to work with producers of *The Bourne Identity*. Brandon called the script "ugly" and an "egregious misrepresentation of the Agency's work," and that he "lost track of how many rogue operatives had assassinated people" by page 25 of the script and "chucked the thing in the burn bag."[34] Brandon himself did however contribute an interview to the extended DVD edition of the movie.[35]

Perhaps more important is the fundamental question of propaganda, which is specifically outlawed within the United States. Yet the truth is that the CIA routinely uses public resources to direct the message of films and television shows to burnish its positive image, usually without attribution, to a public that has virtually no knowledge of its involvement in the process. As Jenkins writes, "In 2004, [Brandon] claimed that the CIA's involvement in motion pictures is primarily a function of 'wanting to inform and educate the public that their tax money that keeps our front door open is money well-spent.' In other words, the CIA is interested in 'educating' the public about its successes to keep public support up, but the Agency may ignore and even hide its failures."[36] Robert Baer is another former CIA case officer who has worked with Hollywood, independent of the agency; he has voiced criticisms of the work of the liaison office. "I know the movies the CIA has cooperated on," Baer says, "and they are pro-CIA movies that aren't realistic."[37]

In short, the CIA and Hollywood are selling us a message of how to quell a chaotic world through imperial proceduralism. Their representations have shifted from Sir Walter Scott to Sherlock Holmes. This is a rational empire, we are told, where military adventurism is the consequence and not the cause of the projection of American power. This message is simultaneously more or less overt (in that the films and shows promulgate the message) and more or less covert (in that the CIA's participation is relatively unacknowledged or underappreciated). When it is recognized today, the facts of CIA participation are routinely used to support an argument not only for the torture of detainees in the War on Terror but also for the documentary realism of the representation. *Zero Dark Thirty* begins with the line, "The following motion picture is based on first hand [*sic*] accounts of actual events." *Argo* is well known as a CIA success story. Howard Gordon, *Homeland*'s executive producer (who worked on *24* and is the son of a CIA agent), describes the series as "fiction that should feel real." In an article in *Men's Journal*, Gavin Edwards reports that the "the CIA cooperates with the show, providing a liaison to answer questions about CIA culture and practices—though she won't divulge details of specific operations (or talk to journalists) [note the "she"]. Often, the writers will invent a story element and run it by the CIA, to ensure it isn't laughable to those in the know."[38] President Obama has publicly praised the show. And of course First Lady Michelle Obama, in the White House and flanked by members of the military, awarded the Best Picture Oscar in February 2013 to *Argo*.

This nexus of power and representation ought to trouble those concerned with role of media in our democracy, where their concentration into fewer hands continues alongside the militarization of American foreign policy, a development that clearly concerns the historian and retired military officer Andrew Bacevich. "The citizens of the United States have essentially forfeited any capacity to ask first-order questions about the fundamentals of national security policy," writes Bacevich. "To cast doubts on the principles of [America's] global presence, as Ron Paul and Dennis Kucinich did during the 2008 presidential campaign, is to make oneself as an oddball or eccentric, either badly informed or less than fully reliable; certainly not someone suitable for holding national office."[39] Bacevich calls the condition plaguing the United States the rise of semiwar—a permanent military readiness to act that dangerously distorts our national priorities—and labels the actors in this tragedy "semiwarriors," those who plan, spend, and orchestrate the nation's semiwars with little accountability. Ours has become a spectator rather than participatory democracy, as the covert military assumes more (secret) power to drive an imperial agenda in an age of permanent war while selling a propagandized public image. "Semiwarriors . . . get away with perpetuating the Washington rules [of massive military spending and military adventurism] because those rules draw upon, sustain, and help conceal the implications, moral as well as practical, of contemporary America's impoverished and attenuated conception of citizenship,"[40] writes Bacevich, thus "allow[ing] Washington wide latitude in employing US military power. Unnecessary and misguided wars are but one deleterious result."[41]

The current crop of CIA representations furthers the agenda of the semiwarriors generally and the CIA specifically, which demands the utmost secrecy for its actions but whose actions resemble more and more a private army of the executive. In 2004, the CIA feared legal challenges to the widespread torture and abuse taking place in its vast network of secret prisons established in the wake of 9/11 (on display in *Zero Dark Thirty*; a 2013 Open Society Report implicates fifty-four nations in the program; the Senate report on torture confirms many of them).[42] Their answer, according to a 2013 *New York Times* report, was to develop a program of assassination by predator drone. "Killing by remote control was the antithesis of the dirty, intimate work of interrogation," the *Times* article states. "Before long, the CIA would go from being the long-term jailer of America's enemies to a military organization that erased them."[43] The drone program, of course, "erases" not just America's enemies but plenty of civilians as well and has killed seven American citizens, all under the cover of secrecy. As the CIA expands its military efforts and demands a greater share and role of the lucrative national security pie—the intelligence budget has basically tripled and the workforce of the CIA has grown by about 25 percent since 2001[44]—and as the Obama administration's global wars rely increasingly on covert and special ops, secrecy becomes more integral to the semiwarrior class in its trail of destruction. Hollywood's CIA is an alibi and not an answer to the public's right and need to know about what actions are undertaken in its name.

Premised on the rational use of information and the fetish of procedure, the alibi is as dishonest as was the run-up to the war in Iraq. The procedures of the CIA, rather than stemming the chaos the world, help in producing it. In Pakistan alone, the Bureau of Investigative Journalism has estimated that drone strikes by the CIA and JSOC (Joint Special Operations Command) from 2003 to 2013 have resulted in the deaths of 2,537 to 3,646 people, including 416 to 951 civilians (168 to 200 of whom were children), and injured an additional 1,228 to 1,557 people.[45] Moreover, a recent report from Columbia Law School points out that "while the terms [militant and civilian] seem intuitive, they are in fact ambiguous, controversial, and susceptible to manipulation."[46] James Traub of the Center on International Cooperation explains that public anger in Pakistan over drone strikes has "made it almost impossible for the United States to achieve its long-term goals of helping Pakistan become a stable, civilian-run state."[47] Nor is this limited to Pakistan, of course. A Yemeni friend of mine has described to me the constant sound of drones flying overhead when he last visited Yemen, and the psychological toll of perpetual anxiety in the population as a result. Homes are turned into rubble. Children are orphaned. Property is lost. And anger and resentment are stoked. A Yemeni lawyer tweeted this in May 2012: "Dear Obama, when a US drone missile kills a child in Yemen, the father will go to war with you, guaranteed. Nothing to do with al-Qaeda."[48] The idea that drone warfare is clean, surgical, and less dangerous is a myth and betrays the fact that those making such statements view conflict only from the point of view of the powerful.

In the light of day and away from the cover of darkness, the actual procedures of the War on Terror, promulgated by the CIA and extended to other agencies of the military and including the New York Police Department (see the introduction to this book), begin to look more dubious, absurd, and suspicious in conception and execution—and I use this last term deliberately. The logic of the Age of Bush and Obama has been extraordinary secrecy, and the secrecy hides the failures, costs, and consequences of these programs. In its place, is propaganda—puffery—where Hollywood plays the role cast for it by the CIA and the public sits in a dark theater as a docile audience ready to cheer when the credits roll. *Zero Dark Thirty* gives the American public its visual truth of the killing of Osama bin Laden. It's a postmodern game, where the real world is hidden, a fake one is generated to be venerated through the genre of realism, and the result is chaos.

In 1958, the sociologist C. Wright Mills wrote an angry short book called *The Causes of World War Three*. In it, he describes the continued concentration of power into the hands of fewer and fewer men who are so enamored of and beholden to the bureaucracy that produced them that they can no longer see the real dangers to world peace that their decisions produce. Mills is equally fed up with intellectuals. "Every time intellectuals have the chance to speak yet do not speak, they join the forces that train men not to be able to think and imagine and feel in morally and politically adequate ways," he writes. "When they do not demand that the secrecy that makes elite decisions absolute and unchallengeable be removed, they too are part of the passive conspiracy to kill off public scrutiny."[49] Mills argues in the book that "necessity" and "re-

alism" have become ways for "politicians and journalists, intellectuals and generals, businessmen and preachers" to hide their own
lack of moral and political imagination.

> Among the led and among the leaders moral insensibility to vio-
> lence is as evident as is the readiness to practice violence. The ethos
> of war is now pervasive. All social and personal life is being orga-
> nized in its terms. . . . It shapes their scientific endeavor, limits their
> intellectual effort, increases their national budgets, and has replaced
> what was once diplomacy. The drive toward war is massive, subtle,
> official, and self-directed. War is no longer an interruption of piece;
> in fact, peace itself has become an uneasy interlude between wars;
> peace has become a perilous balance of mutual terror and mutual
> fright.[50]

This is not political realism, Mills argues. It is "crackpot realism."
Translate the term from political science to art and you will have
the appropriate label for the late aesthetics of the War on Terror.
Here, the true-story function of the CIA's role in our current affairs is meant to comfort and assuage a public that America's hidden warriors are succeeding in ordering the mess of the world
out there. Such representations may be presented as virtually real
events, but we should not be duped by the message or the messenger. This isn't cinematic, social, or documentary realism. It's the
crackpot realism of our era, the era of the War on Terror.

Coexistence

I was made aware of Mustafa Bayoumi exactly three months ago when, in a fit of egomania, I Googled myself. I do this only rarely, which is to say only a few times during the day and when I'm at my computer but never at night or when I'm out with friends, because that would be rude and also self-centered. Yet through this limited experience, I've learned that it's useful to type alternative spellings to my name—such as Mostapha Bayoumi, Moustapha Bayoumi, or even Moustafa Bayoumy—into the search engine's inviting rectangle. Like everyone else (or so I imagine), I feel a kind of ontological concordance between the arrangement of letters that make up my name and the person I believe myself to be. But since my name is of Arabic origin, all romanizations are approximations. What this means is that, perhaps unlike people who have always existed first in the Roman alphabet, I see myself equally in the alternatives. It's simply a question of transliteration. Spell me however you want, in other words, because all versions somehow revert back to their Arabic ancestor. As with most things, Google confirms my suspicions, since I invariably find listings about me in surrogate spellings. There are multiple versions of me out there, but they are still me.

Google further corroborates another one of my pet theories, by now a belief held by many people but no less significant because of its nearly universal acceptance. I refer to the idea that existence today is predicated on the algorithms of a company based in Mountain View, California. If it's not on the Internet, it's not really real, or at least not real in any "real" sense, which means sharing it across time and space. Being present in the world is no longer enough. Being able to re-present something to others provides its "proof of life," which is a phrase I learned from watching a movie starring Russell Crowe and Meg Ryan. Speaking personally, this is why finding myself on the Internet is existentially comforting. It makes me feel not just present but alive. I would be lying, though, if I didn't admit that this feeling comes with a twinge of anxiety attached. What if, for some odd reason, I no longer showed up on Google searches? What if all of those electronic traces of me simply vanished one day? If that were to happen, I'm quite sure I would also disappear.

Forgive me. I'm being hyperbolic. But this anxiety of disappearance isn't new and stems, I think, from growing up with a strange-sounding name. When I was a kid in a very Waspy town in Canada, my teachers always seemed to breathe in deeply and pause in discomfort before calling my name on the first day of school. It felt to me as if they were deciding whether I really belonged on their list at all. I later learned to anticipate the silence and preempt them, pronouncing myself for them before they tried to purse their lips into some kind of non-Anglo pucker. Or there was the school trip to Niagara Falls, where my classmates were thrilled to find little tin license plates with their names on them. Naturally mine was nowhere to be found, which my friends thought was hilarious and I pretended was, too. And then there was Easter. Even though I was raised in a Muslim family, I always enjoyed Easter as a kid. Every year, my father would come home with three chocolate Easter eggs for my sister, brother, and me, each inscribed in white icing with our names written in cursive script. Fortunately, you don't have to believe in the crucifixion and resurrection of Our Lord Jesus Christ to enjoy a chocolate Easter egg. Since I have the longest name of us three, I thought I had triumphed by scoring the most icing on this holiday that we weren't celebrating. At first, the eggs seemed like confirmation of belonging. Then one year, when I was in tow with my parents while they were shopping, I saw that Kmart had simply hired someone to personalize the eggs. All I could imagine now was my father spelling out my name, letter by letter, to the woman as she squeezed out the icing from a tube, and I became convinced that she must have thought my bizarre sounding name was either too long or too peculiar, or both, for Easter in Canada. What a fussy, skittish, neurotic little shit of a kid I must have been.

But confusion over my name hasn't stopped as I've gotten older. For years, the most common response to me after pronouncing my name clearly to new acquaintances has been, "Gustav?" I think I look nothing like a "Gustav," with my dark eyes and hairy toes, but now I'm being reductive, if not racialist, in my own assumptions. On two separate occasions in recent years, people learning Arabic thought my name was Mustashfa, which means "hospital" in Arabic. And for some reason, people often think my name is Mohammad after I say "Moustafa." I suppose it would be worse if they thought my name was Osama.

While all of these mistakes are forgivable, there is one that irritates me to an irrational degree, the one that has now become teeth-grindingly familiar to me. After I pronounce my name, the person with whom I am speaking pauses, smiles broadly in recognition, and says, "Oh, Mufasa! Like the Lion King!" "No. Not like the Lion King," I want to say. "I wasn't named after Simba's father. I wasn't trampled to death by wildebeests. I haven't even seen that insipidly multicultural, saccharine-scored sentimental monstrosity supposedly about 'Africa.' My name is centuries old and doesn't refer to some kente clothed-up lion-actor in Broadway feathers and Day-Glo war paint but to the Messenger of God, for Christ's sake! (Moustafa means 'the chosen one,' and was a name used to refer to Prophet Mohammed.) If anything Mufasa got his name from Moustafa, and not the other way around. No, my name is not like Lion King, not at all, so bugger off." But I don't usually say that. To be honest, I've never said that. Instead, I smile like Andy Cohen from *The Real Housewives* franchise and say, "No, I'm Moustafa. Not Mufasa. Close!"

Still, I've never felt the urge to alter my name to suit the general culture around me. That always seemed to me as if I would be performing some kind of violence on myself. And over the years I've become more attached to my name's relatively unique sounds, unique at least to this side of Istanbul. I now live in New York City, which, as Wikipedia confirms to me, is "the most populous city in the United States," and even here I've never met anyone with both my first and last name. Incidentally, in the Canada I grew up in, your first name was sometimes called your Christian name.

So imagine my surprise when, on that day three months ago, as I was egosurfing—which is a term I learned after Googling "googling your name"—I came across a reference to a novel that included a character named Mustafa Bayoumi. At first, I was incredulous. It would be less remarkable to stumble across a character named Mustafa in a novel. Tayeb Salih's *Season of Migration the North* features one very sexual but seriously messed up Mustafa Saeed, or there's Aldous Huxley's *Brave New World*, where Mustapha Mond holds the estimable job of Resident World Controller for Western Europe. I've even read a novel with a character named Bayoumi, a villainous creature of misogyny found in Nawal El Saadawi's *Woman at Point Zero*. But this time was different. Unlike those examples, the name I was reading on the page, which in this case was a screen, was not simply Mustafa or just Bayoumi but the unity of both, the yoking of the first to the last: Mustafa Bayoumi. This, I thought, is kinda weird.

The website where I first found Mustafa Bayoumi looked amateurish, and since I wanted to find out if the book was real, I naturally went to Amazon.com. There I discovered the novel, titled *Thou Shalt Kill*. It's a detective story set in Pittsburgh, published in 2011 by an imprint of Simon & Schuster, and written by one "Daniel Blake," which Amazon informed me was a pseudonym. The mystery was deepening. Google Books kindly allowed me to read a few pages from the novel, and from what I could gather, the plot included a murder at a church that followed an earlier killing of someone named Redwine. Two detectives, Beradino and Patrese, were considering if the murders were related. That's when Patrese says,

"There's no guarantee this is even related to Redwine."

"True. Could be copycat. Could be coincidence. Method's the same, location's completely different. Only a few people had access to where Redwine was killed. Here, anyone could have come in off the street, literally. Few buildings more public than a cathedral."

"And why the smashing of the crucifix? The icon, the windows? None of that with Redwine, was there?" Patrese pointed out.

"Someone who hates religion. Someone who hates Christianity, certainly."

"Someone like Mustafa Bayoumi."

Beradino glanced across at Patrese. "He seemed pretty hostile to it, for sure."

"So we look at Bayoumi first."[1]

Two things immediately became clear to me. First, the prose was bewilderingly awesome. Second, I had to know more, more about this book, more about "Daniel Blake" and more about Mustafa Bayoumi. Who is this "Mustafa Bayoumi," and is he at all related to me, Moustafa Bayoumi? I've written a book, published a bunch of articles, and even won a couple of awards. I have no quarrels with Christianity (some of my best friends are Christians) and, by Google, I know who I am. But now I discover that Christianity-hating Mustafa Bayoumi is suspected of murder? Perhaps "Daniel Blake" had it in for me. Or was this some sort of backhanded compliment, a sign of arrival, as it were? Should I feel insulted or proud? I began questioning my responses. Did I want fame or infamy? It was hard to choose.

What I knew I wanted was my own copy of *Thou Shalt Kill*. I could have downloaded an eBook version right away, but a used copy was available for one cent (plus three ninety-nine shipping and handling), so I placed the order for four dollars, wondering if Mustafa Bayoumi was as cheap as I am.

◆ ◆ ◆

There were resemblances. Mustafa Bayoumi is of Egyptian origin and so am I. Both of our fathers were professors. Mustafa and I are both educated. He's a chemistry student at Pitt; I'm a professor of English at CUNY. But there were differences, too. Mustafa is younger than I am, he had "cheekbones you could cut your wrists on, hair blacker than Reagan's when he'd been hard at the Grecian 2000, and a neatly trimmed beard."[2] He also "looked substantially more black than Arab,"[3] whereas I shave my graying beard to look younger, have nonsuicidal facial architecture, and appear more Arab than black. His father, who died due to a doctor's malpractice, was named Abdul. This confused me, because Abdul is not really a name in Arabic. It's only a part of one. Abdul, which means "servant of," is the first section of a compound name and is always followed by one of the ninety-nine attributes of God in Arabic. Abdul-Jabbar, for example, means servant of the Almighty. Mustafa must know this, so why was he letting "Daniel Blake" represent his family this way?

Mustafa was also angry. Really angry. He thinks that we Muslims "must fight and kill the infidels wherever we find them. We must capture them. We must lie in wait for them in every place. Fight against them till there is no more oppression and all worship is devoted to Allah alone."[4] I've seen Muslims like Mustafa before, on TV, so I know they are out there, but I like to think of myself as a little more levelheaded than Mr. Bayoumi. Luckily, "Daniel Blake" has provided a counterpart to Mustafa, an attractive female

Lebanese American assistant DA (and love interest of Detective Patrese) named Amberin Zerhouni, who wears a hijab but loves the pork in her Cuban sandwich, which confirms not only her lack of Islamic zealotry but also her liberal attitudes regarding communist food.

To be honest, Mustafa Bayoumi was starting to irritate me. I've spent a lot time trying to explain the ways Muslims are stereotyped and caricatured in the media, and here he was acting like a common terrorist. This, I thought, could complicate all my well-meaning efforts at coexistence. I tried to contain my anger, however, because, after reading about how Mustafa Bayoumi manages his rage, I became worried about my own.

I decided to seek out advice about what to do if your doppelgänger was threatening your own reputation, so I called up Phillip Roth, who once had a man impersonate him all over Jerusalem, and he agreed to meet me on the Upper West Side of Manhattan. By the way, Phillip Roth is not the famous writer—that's Philip Roth—but a character I made up who coincidentally looks remarkably like Philip Roth. It was a cold December day, and he was sitting on a bench in Riverside Park, *Operation Shylock* on his lap and his cell phone in his hands.

He nodded as I introduced myself, and then I went on a rather long-winded explanation about who Mustafa Bayoumi is and how his extremist ideas threatened to undermine my own reputation.

"Do you know I haven't read a single book since I got this iPhone?" Phillip Roth said, after I finished.

"I'm sorry Mr. Roth, but did you hear what I said?"

"If you have one, it's just impossible not to play with it."

"Mr. Roth. What if people think I'm Mustafa Bayoumi?" My voice had too much emotion in it. I regretted that immediately.

"Calm dawn and stop complaining," he said, still staring into his phone. He finally looked up. "I would tell you to find out if he has a girlfriend and then sleep with her, but here's your only problem," he said. "He's not real. He's a character in a book, so chances are his girlfriend, if he has one, isn't real either."

I protested that I knew Mustafa Bayoumi wasn't real, but that he was "real" enough to cause me problems, because in this world the representation is more important than the thing itself. The representation *becomes* the thing, I tried to explain, realizing I was beginning to speak in italics. "Did you know that *two-thirds* of the American public has never met a Muslim?" I said.

> But then they watch *Homeland*, or *Argo*, or *24* or *The Hurt Locker* or they read Updike or Amis or "Daniel Blake" and they know Muslims are scary and should be bombed, which truth be told aligns with our foreign policy. It's not that there aren't violent Muslims out there, but there are a lot of other ways of being Muslim. Since the violent Muslim is the only type we are ever exposed to, that's the only one that a lot of the public accepts as true! And that leads to other terrible consequences. Take Sikhs and Hindus, who are also harmed, *as Muslims*, today. Why? Because they are *representationally* Muslim, you see? When the representation becomes more real than the people being represented, it's dangerous. Art cedes its autonomy, and representation gets subcontracted out to shape and support public opinion instead of informing criticism. You said something like that in *Operation Shylock*: "The representations of 'it' *are* 'it.' They're everything."[5]

Phillip Roth stared at me for what felt like a full minute, and then pivoted his head back like a cock about to crow. His mouth opened wide enough for me to stare at the pink at the back of his throat shivering. He started laughing so uncontrollably that I couldn't decide if I ought to be insulted or concerned for him. He is rather advanced in age. "What's so funny?" I asked. He tried to catch a breath. "You don't see it?" he asked me. I shook my head while keeping my eyes on him. He swallowed hard but I could tell he was about to laugh again. "It's just so ridiculous," he said, tears in the corners of both eyes. "You think you're Jewish!"

◆ ◆ ◆

I left Phillip Roth on his bench and was disappointed that he hadn't been more helpful. I headed toward the subway when someone who looked very familiar walked quickly up to me. After a split second, I recognized him.

"Mustafa?" I said.

"Moustafa?" he said.

We hugged. I felt like I had known him my entire life. I had so many questions for him, including why he was on the streets of New York, but before I could say anything, he spoke.

"Listen, Moustafa. I've been looking for you, and I don't have much time left. I have something for you."

He took out an envelope and placed it in my hand.

"I want you to take this and make sure you get it published. Do you understand? I'm just a chemistry student, but you're a writer. You know how to get things published. And make sure it's online. So not *Harper's*. And not behind one of those shitty paywalls either. I hate those. Everyone does."

"What is it?"

"I stole it from 'Daniel Blake's' desk. 'Daniel Blake,' by the way, is some dude named Boris Starling. He's not even American. He's a friggin' Brit trying to pass himself off as today's Raymond Chandler or something. But he's no Walter Mosley and for sure no Chester Himes. I mean, we're all just so *predictable*. But that's all you get today because of The Rules."

I was trying to keep up.

"Wait. So what are you giving me?"

"The Rules! I swiped it from his desk."

I looked at him without saying anything.

"Don't tell me you don't know about The Rules. The Eleven Rules for Writing Muslim Characters? You've heard about them, at least." I shook my head. "Jesus, Moustafa. How useless are you? Really, why were you born? As a joke by your Creator? I thought *you* at least would know about The Rules. *The Rules*!"

Mustafa Bayoumi was starting to creep me out.

"Just make sure they get published. Everyone should know they exist. We'll blow Hollywood's secret wide open! And it's not just Hollywood. It's writers, too. And TV. Especially TV. They're all told just to follow The Rules, and they do! That's the saddest part of the whole fiasco. They just do as they're told! Don't tell me you haven't wondered why there's this incredible consistency in representation. Ha! That sounds like a phrase *you* would use." He took a breath, but before I could say anything, he started speaking again. "Anyway, I gotta go. I won't be around much longer. And remember, no paywall!"

He gave me another quick hug and then disappeared up Broadway. I stood for a minute thinking of what to do and, after deciding I had no idea, I took the stairs down to the Seventy-Second Street subway station. I boarded the 2 train for Brooklyn, which thankfully wasn't too crowded, so I was able to sit down. I took out the envelope Mustafa had given me. Inside was just one sheet of paper, which I am reproducing here for you, as per Mustafa's instructions:

THE ELEVEN RULES FOR WRITING MUSLIM CHARACTERS—BY ABDUL

1. Be very careful. Palestine is not Pakistan, Iraq is not Iran, and Hamas is not Hizbullah. Iranians are not Arabs. Turks are Turks. Farsi is Persian which is not Arabic. Shia is the same as Shi'ite, and Sunnis and Shias are not ethnic groups, like Kurds, who are both Sunni and Shia (or Shi'ite). I know it's confusing. Sorry about that.

Before 9/11, you could get away with simply describing this mess as "ancient hatreds," but in this age of the Internet "ancient hatreds" now sounds like amateur hour. If you're still confused, hire a consultant, preferably ex-CIA.

2. Muslim men with beards should never be shown smiling.

3. You will probably have an older male Jewish character. Make him wise. (That he is sad, or "inconsolable" if this is a book, goes without saying.) Don't bother showing Arab Christians. No one will believe you. Same goes for Indonesian Muslims.

4. Always have someone, preferably the wise Jewish character, say that not all Muslims are terrorists. That way, the association between Muslims and terrorists will be cemented. Very useful.

5. Be sure to have at least one good Muslim character, preferably one good one for each bad one. People will then say your film or book is "balanced" (when in fact, as you know, its function is more akin to an alibi). Besides, fifty-fifty are pretty good odds that half of all Muslims are terrorists (see above).

6. Black Muslim characters—excellent idea. Also valuable in film because African American men look angrier when wearing kufis and African American women are photogenic in white hijabs (appearing like Florence Nightingales, but not). However, and this goes for both books and films, be careful not to have too many of them in major roles. This will only confuse the viewer/reader if the Muslim character's rage derives from race or religion.

7. When establishing the Muslim character's motivation for the deplorable act to come, make sure the US government is responsible for some reprehensible action in the past, either at home or abroad. Strive for moral ambiguity. The only thing better than moral ambiguity is contrived moral ambiguity.

8. When you have good American Muslim characters, make sure to exaggerate their Americanness. Playing sports like football or basketball (less good, too black) and consuming bubble-gum pop culture are good for this.

9. When you have bad American Muslim characters, make sure to exaggerate their foreignness. Spicy cuisine and suicide vests are good tools for this.

10. There will be sex. Muslim men are very charming and very sexy until they kill you (or someone else). Then they must become less charming and sexy. If a Muslim woman is sexy, she must have a domineering father from which she seeks to escape, often though not necessarily with help from her infidel boyfriend. Such Muslim women should wear hijabs only in family situations and always awkwardly.

11. White converts hate their families. And America.

What kind of list was this, I thought. Was this for real? Had Mustafa, in his own Muslim paranoia, just made it up? Or had someone else written this list and passed it off to him as authentic and he fell for it? Who the hell was "Abdul"? Had "Daniel Blake" written this, too?

I was getting nowhere thinking about "The Rules," so instead I pulled out *Thou Shalt Kill* from my backpack and began reading where I had last left off. Detectives Beradino and Patrese were again on the case, and Mustafa Bayoumi was already back in Pittsburgh. He had gone to a Steelers game at Heinz Field wearing a suicide vest. Amazingly, Detective Beradino had figured out Mustafa's evil plot just in time and was frantically calling Patrese, who coincidentally was at the stadium. Beradino finally got through to Patrese on his cell phone. "Mustafa Bayoumi. He's there at Heinz Field. He's going to blow himself up," Beradino told Patrese.[6]

As I was reading, I found myself hoping Beradino was wrong, but I knew he wasn't. The mood was tense. Would Patrese find Mustafa and stop the terrorist attack that could kill hundreds of people? I would be lying if I said that my heart was not pounding. Patrese went to the control room first to talk to the stadium staff. "'We've already checked the ticket sales roster,' said one of the stadium staff. 'There's no record of a Mustafa Bayoumi.'"[7] He then used the security cameras to scan the crowd. "He ran his eyes from screen to screen, skimming the sea of faces. Bayoumi's skin tone alone wouldn't be enough to mark him out. Bayoumi looked more black than Arab [again!], and plenty of Steelers fans were black."[8] But Patrese finally spotted Mustafa in the bleachers. And that's when it became clear that the young detective has no choice. I understood, even sympathizing with Patrese's position. And yet, somehow I felt sorry for Mustafa, though I knew I shouldn't.

"Two minutes to go, three points between the teams. The Steelers on offense, second-and-10, thirty-two yards out. Patrese looked through the crowd and got a fix on Mustafa. *There*. Mustafa, his mouth working furiously. Talking to himself. Praying."[9]

Patrese ran to Mustafa's row of seats, pulling out his gun and frightening the crowd. I continued reading:

"Mustafa turned toward the commotion at the end of his row and saw Patrese, Ruger Blackhawk held in two hands front and center, bead drawn on Mustafa." I knew what would happen next: "Patrese squeezed the trigger, faster than thought, and Mustafa's head exploded. Not all of him. Just his head. Split like a watermelon and gone in puffs of blood."[10]

I had to reread those last sentences.

"Patrese squeezed the trigger, faster than thought, and Mustafa's head exploded. Not all of him. Just his head. Split like a watermelon and gone in puffs of blood."

Oh.

His head exploded.

A powerful feeling of melancholy started to tremor through me, like a moving subway car shaking on the tracks. There were still a hundred-odd pages left in the book, but instead of soldiering on, I found myself staring straight ahead, my mind as empty and sad as a blank sheet of paper. I closed the covers and sat in silence.

Mustafa Bayoumi is dead. Long live Mustafa Bayoumi.

Conclusion

Our Muslim American Lives

In his short story "The Problem of Our Laws," Franz Kafka describes a society that, since ancient times, has been ruled by nobles who govern over others by keeping the laws of the land a secret, so secret in fact that the very existence of these laws could be doubted. "It is an extremely painful thing," our nameless narrator writes, "to be ruled by laws that one does not know." We are told that some in this society believe that interpreting the actions of the nobles over time will finally reveal the laws, but they speculate this will take centuries, and so they blame themselves—and not the nobles—for their ignorance and powerlessness. A dangerous few, however, suspect the nobles really have no laws, that "the Law is whatever the nobles do." This creates a paradox. "Any party that would repudiate not only all belief in the laws, but the nobility as well, would have the whole people behind it," the narrator explains. "Yet no such party can come into existence, for nobody would dare repudiate the nobility. We live on this razor's edge. . . . The sole visible and indisputable law that is imposed upon us is the nobility, and must we ourselves deprive ourselves of that one law?"[1] In his own inimitable way, Kafka is simultaneously describing both the architecture and the comfort of those who rule and those who are ruled. Power can often be self-serving and self-justifying, Kafka is telling us, but shattering the fictions or exaggerations of those in power can be deleterious, if not downright petrifying. It's often easier simply not to ask questions.

But we must ask questions about the direction American society has been taking since the terrorist attacks of 2001 and the inauguration of the War on Terror, a war that could possibly never end and that can also be self-serving and self-justifying. While preventing terrorism is a legitimate goal for a government to perform, the War on Terror has also enabled a massive national security state that has come to overwhelm many aspects of our lives. It has furthermore created its own War on Terror culture, one that exploits people's fears and traffics liberally in stereotypes of others. Muslim Americans understand this well, perhaps better than others, because, in the United States at least, we are the ones cast most directly into its net. As *This Muslim American Life* has shown, War on Terror culture has meant that we are now regularly seen as dangerous outsiders, that our daily actions are constantly viewed with suspicion, that our complex histories in this country are neglected or occluded, and that our very presence and our houses of worship have become issues of local, regional, and national politics. While it is socially unacceptable to be outwardly racist in the United States today, the same simply isn't true when it comes to Muslims. In the revised edition of *Covering Islam*, Edward Said writes in his introduction, "Malicious generalizations about Islam have become the last acceptable form of denigration of foreign culture in the West; what is said about the Muslim mind, or character, or religion, or culture as a whole cannot now be said in mainstream discussion about Africans, Jews, other Orientals, or Asians."[2] He composed those lines in October 1996. Since September 2001, these same malicious generalizations have only grown in both volume and influence. In fact, considering the cult of anti-Muslim terrorism "experts" hired by law enforcement agencies around the country for training or the success of anti-Muslim demagogues such as Robert Spencer and Pamela Geller or the frequency with which Muslims are vilified on conservative media outlets, to be bombastically anti-Muslim is not just to scream one's bigoted opinions from the rooftops. It can also be the path to a very lucrative career, indeed.[3]

War on Terror culture has had profound effects far beyond conservative politics. Writing in the *Harvard National Security Journal*, Naz Modirzadeh argues that the very practice of both international humanitarian law and human rights law has changed since September 11, as US-based international law and human rights lawyers have exchanged their strict allegiance to the principles of international law for the (unrealized) potential to influence the decisions made by the president. As Modirzadeh puts it, "the positions many US-based lawyers in the disciplines of international humanitarian law and human rights law took in 2013 on issues of lethal force and framing of armed conflict vis-à-vis the Obama Administration would have been surprising and disappointing to those same professionals back in 2002, when they began their battle against the Bush Administration's formulations of the 'Global War on Terror.'"[4] Her article warns that the practice and possibilities of international law have effectively been diluted and weakened during the course of the War on Terror.

Other results of the War on Terror have been equally corrosive, not just to the legal profession but also to the national psyche. As a nation, we had previously considered illegal (even if we condoned) such things as targeted killings, indefinite detention without trial, and torture. Now these actions are not only condoned but generally accepted as necessary and prudent, and they are frequently portrayed as such on television and in the movies.

These consequences of War on Terror culture lead to a mindset that fundamentally undermines many key components of international law and threatens the idea of forging a common global destiny based on shared values. In fact, War on Terror culture is no longer solely an American phenomenon. Dozens of countries around the world, many of them run by repressive governments, have adopted antiterror laws modeled on the Patriot Act. The

United States often encourages the passing of such legislation, laws that limit civil liberties and expand the powers of law enforcement in the name of national security.[5] Moreover, War on Terror culture is happily taken up by some of the most autocratic regimes around the world. In Egypt or Saudi Arabia or Russia or China, to name only a few, governments freely, uncritically, and opportunistically adopt the rhetoric of fighting terrorism as a way of excluding their opposition not just from their national political systems but really from humanity itself.

In other words, the Global War on Terror has produced its own Global War on Terror culture, not just in the United States but internationally. This is a culture that too often rationalizes away unnecessary killing while supporting authoritarian-leaning practices. It thrives on secrecy and militarism. War on Terror culture furthermore is obsessed with exploiting fear and with shaping the realms of politics, the law, and representation in its own image, and it feeds on the dubious and paranoid logic of scapegoating others. In this book I have sketched how some of this is currently working in the United States, but much more about how War on Terror culture ticks, in the United States and abroad, could be probed and investigated. New approaches to solving our common problems are clearly necessary.

In the meantime, we Muslim Americans, the most ethnically diverse religious community in the United States,[6] will continue to live our lives with countless varieties of religious experiences and political opinions. Whether our differences from the rest of the nation will also continue to be exaggerated and exploited remains to be seen. The challenge today for all, and not just Muslim Americans, is to understand the connections between domestic racism and foreign policy, to recognize the link between curbing civil liberties at home and rising authoritarian structures abroad, and to repudiate all forms of politics that rely on the shock and awe of killing innocent people, whether through the evils of terrorism or the cynical prosecution of the War on Terror.

The Palestinian filmmaker Hany Abu-Assad was recently asked if he believed in nationalism, and his answer is instructive beyond the particularities of the Palestinian struggle and can be generalized to suggest a way of escaping the violent gridlock of the War on Terror. "Nationalism is about having or wanting a country, with its own national identity," he said. "Right now, I don't care about 'country.' I care about civil rights, human rights, equal opportunity, justice; I don't care about whether you are Palestinian or Christian or Muslim or Jewish. These are individual identities that are not necessary to share with others. What you share with others is your values, rather than your identity. You can do what you want, believe in whatever god you want, have different opinions about everything, but our values should still be about respecting each other's equality and civil rights."[7] What we share with others is our values rather than our identities, and our values must be about respecting each other's equality. That's something worth striving for, not just in the United States but across the globe. This is precisely the kind of idea that can—and should—have the whole people behind it.

Notes

Introduction

1 Matt Apuzzo and Adam Goldman, "With CIA Help, NYPD Moves Covertly in Muslim Areas," Associated Press, August 23, 2011.

2 Ibid.

3 Len Levitt, "The NYPD: Spies, Spooks and Lies," *NYPD Confidential*, September 5, 2011, http://nypdconfidential.com/columns/2011/110905.html; Len Levitt, "The NYPD: Spies, Spooks, and Lies," *Huffington Post*, September 7, 2011, http://www.huffingtonpost.com/len-levitt/the-nypd-spies-spooks-and_b_950448.html.

4 Matt Apuzzo and Adam Goldman, *Enemies Within: Inside the NYPD's Secret Spying Unit and Bin Laden's Final Plot Against America* (New York: Touchstone, 2013), 193–94.

5 NYPD Technical Operations Unit, "Surveillance Request: Mohammad Elshinawy," February 2, 2009, 5.

6 Ibid., 5.

7 Ibid., 6.

8 Ibid., 6.

9 The Demographics Unit was renamed the "Zone Assessment Unit" in 2010 out of concern for how the former would sound to the public if discovered. See Apuzzo and Goldman, *Enemies Within*, 282. The CIA paid Sanchez's salary from 2002 to 2004, despite the fact that the CIA is forbidden from having "any police, subpoena or law enforcement powers or internal security functions." See the National Security Act of 1947 (P.L. 80–235, 61 Stat. 496, July 26, 1947). Sanchez remained in his post until 2010, and the NYPD paid his salary after 2004. After 2010, a former CIA clandestine officer, Lance Hamilton, replaced Sanchez until his identity became known, after which he was recalled. See ibid., 283. Working out of an office in the Brooklyn Army Terminal, the Intelligence Division divided the community into what they called "Ancestries of Interest," twenty-eight countries mostly from the Middle East and South Asia as well as former Soviet states with large Muslim populations. They also included "American Black Muslim" on the list, as if being Muslim and black meant your ancestry belonged to another nation. See ibid., 75.

10 Sam Harris, "Police Demographics Unit Casts Shadows from Past," *City Room: The New York Times*, January 3, 2012, http://cityroom.blogs.nytimes.com/2012/01/03/police-demographics-unit-casts-shadows-from-past/.

11 J. R. Minkel, "Confirmed: The U.S. Census Bureau Gave Up Names of Japanese-Americans in WW II," *Scientific American*, March 30, 2007; William Seltzer and Margo Anderson, "After Pearl Harbor: The Proper Role of Population Statistics in Time of War" (paper, Population Association of America annual meeting, Los Angeles, March 2000), http://www.uwm.edu/~margo/govstat/integrity.htm.

12 Lynette Clemetson, "Homeland Security Given Data on Arab-Americans," *New York Times*, July 30, 2004.

13 Apuzzo and Goldman, *Enemies Within*, 72.

14 Here's an example of the kind of hard-hitting investigative work the NYPD was involved in. The Intelligence Division produced a thirty-eight-page memo called the "Sports Venue Report," pinpointing fifty-five locations in the five boroughs where Muslims gather to play or watch sports. The report begins by stating that "the Demographics Unit identified the sports of cricket, soccer and billiards as the primary sports within the communities," and concludes that "there are distinct differences between the South Asian and Arab communities with regard to the sports played and the general level of sporting interest," noting that South Asians play a lot of cricket and Arabs play pool. "Billiards serves a dual purpose in the Arab community," the report says. "People play Billiards for the sport in it as well as the opportunity to socialize with their friends in a friendly atmosphere." See NYPD Intelligence Division: Demographics Unit, "Sports Venues Report," n.d., 2.

15 Another study produced by the NYPD was the "Internet Café Report," which used open-source research to identify Internet cafés located near "communities of concern." The report states that "locations, public or private that only offer a wireless access point for your computer (i.e., . . . Starbucks, Bryant Park etc) are not included in this report," which naturally calls into question its usefulness, not only due to the limited technical overview of the report but also since cafés and stores change so frequently in New York. (And if you think nothing evil can happen in a Starbucks, you clearly have never used one of their restrooms.) NYPD Intelligence Division: Demographics Unit, "Internet Cafe Report," June 15, 2007.

16 NYPD Intelligence Division: Demographics Unit, "Egyptian Locations of Interest Report," July 7, 2006, 14.

17 NYPD Intelligence Division: Demographics Unit, "Pakistani Travel Agency Report," n.d.

18 Apuzzo and Goldman, *Enemies Within*, 87, 147. NYPD Intelligence Division, "Egyptian Locations of Interest Report," 2.

19 Apuzzo and Goldman, *Enemies Within*, 180.

20 Ibid., 181.

21 While testifying in a deposition on June 28, 2012, Assistant Chief Thomas Galati, commanding officer of the Intelligence Division, revealed that no leads had been discovered or investigations begun as a result of the Demographics Unit's work. Galati also revealed that the NYPD was suspicious of foreign languages. The department was concerned about "Islamics [*sic*] radicalized towards violence," and

so it kept surveillance records on two Pakistani men who in a conversation in Urdu had complained about the mistreatment they felt Muslims received at the hands of airport security in the United States. When Galati was shown the document, he responded, "I'm seeing Urdu. I'm seeing them [the officers] identify the individuals involved in that [conversation] are Pakistani. I'm using that information for me to determine that this would be a kind of place that a terrorist would be comfortable in," adding that "most Urdu speakers from that region would be of concern, so that's why it's important to me." He says essentially the same thing about Bengali speakers later in the deposition. As the AP notes, "About 15 million Pakistanis and 60 million Indians speak Urdu. Along with English, it is one of the national languages of Pakistan." See Matt Apuzzo and Adam Goldman, "NYPD: Muslim Spying Led to No Leads, Terror Cases," Associated Press, August 21, 2012. Also see Galati Deposition, June 28, 2012, 29, 85–86, 92.

22 Noa Yachot, "NYPD Shutters Muslim Mapping Unit—But What about Other Tactics?," ACLU.org, April 15, 2014, https://www.aclu.org/blog/national-security-religion-belief/nypd-shutters-muslim-spying-unit-what-about-its-tactics.

23 Matt Apuzzo and Adam Goldman, "Informant: NYPD Paid Me to 'Bait' Muslims," Associated Press, October 23, 2012.

24 Ibid.

25 Joseph Goldstein, "New York Police Recruit Muslims to Be Informers," *New York Times*, May 10, 2014.

26 US Senate, Committee on Homeland Security and Governmental Affairs, "The Role of Local Law Enforcement in Countering Violent Islamist Extremism" (hearing, Washington, DC, October 30, 2007), http://www.gpo.gov/fdsys/pkg/CHRG-110shrg34411/html/CHRG-110shrg34411.htm, emphasis added.

27 Ibid. In his testimony, Sanchez was drawing directly from the highly problematic NYPD study "Radicalization in the West: The Homegrown Threat." See Mitchell Silber and Arvin Bhatt, "Radicalization in the West: The Homegrown Threat" (New York: New York City Police Department, 2007). Also see Aziz Huq, "Concerns with Mitchell D. Silber & Arvin Bhatt, N.Y. Police Dep't, *Radicalization in the West: The Homegrown Threat* (August 2007)" (New York: Brennan Center for Justice, NYU, August 30, 2007), http://www.brennancenter.org/sites/default/files/legacy/Justice/Aziz%20Memo%20NYPD.pdf. Sanchez says this in his testimony: "The key to [preventing radicalization] was first to understand it and to start appreciating what most people would say would be non-criminal, would be innocuous, looking at behaviors that could easily be argued in a Western democracy, especially in the United States, to be protected by First and Fourth Amendment rights, but not to look at them in a vacuum, but to look across to them as potential precursors to terrorism. . . . I said before that part of our mission drives the way we do business, and part of our mission is to protect New York City citizens from becoming the terrorists. The Federal Government does not have that mission, so automatically, by definition, their threshold is higher. So they are going

to have a lot harder time having to deal with behaviors that run the gamut on First and Fourth Amendment rights and to be able to even look and scrutinize them without having even reached a standard of criminality that you need if your prime objective is you are going to lock them up." See http://www.gpo.gov/fdsys/pkg/CHRG-110shrg34411/html/CHRG-110shrg34411.htm.

28   Spencer Ackerman, "FBI Teaches Agents: 'Mainstream' Muslims Are 'Violent, Radical,'" *Wired*, September 14, 2011, http://www.wired.com/2011/09/fbi-muslims-radical/all/1; Spencer Ackerman, "Al-Qaeda Expert Philip Mudd Retires from FBI," *Washington Independent*, April 21, 2010, http://washingtonindependent.com/82879/al-qaeda-expert-philip-mudd-retires-from-fbi; Spencer Ackerman, "Exclusive: Senior US General Orders Top-to-Bottom Review of Military's Islam Training," *Wired*, April 24, 2012, http://www.wired.com/2012/04/military-islam-training/.

29   Elizabeth Bumiller, "Later Terror Link Cited for 1 in 7 Freed Detainees," *New York Times*, May 20, 2009, http://www.nytimes.com/2009/05/21/us/politics/21gitmo.html; Peter Bergen and Bailey Cahall, "How Many Guantanamo Detainees 'Return to the Battlefield'?," May 7, 2013, http://newamerica.net/sites/newamerica.net/files/profiles/attachments/GTMO_Appendix_5–7–2013.pdf. Cliff Sloan, a former State Department special envoy tasked with closing Guantánamo, stated in an op-ed that Vice President Cheney has claimed a 30 percent recidivism rate among former detainees. Sloan puts the number at 6.8 percent for those released during the Obama administration. Cliff Sloan, "The Path to Closing Guantánamo," *New York Times*, January 6, 2015, http://www.nytimes.com/2015/01/06/opinion/the-path-to-closing-guantanamo.html. Although the situations between state prisons and Guantánamo are very different, around 40 percent of inmates released from state prisons return to prison within three years. Pew Center on the States, *State of Recidivism: The Revolving Door of America's Prisons* (Washington, DC: Pew Charitable Trusts, April 2011).

30   Jo Becker and Scott Shane, "Secret 'Kill List' Proves a Test of Obama's Principles and Will," *New York Times*, May 29, 2012.

31   Ibid.

32   "Remarks by the President at the National Defense University" (National Defense University, May 23, 2012), http://www.whitehouse.gov/photos-and-video/video/2013/05/23/president-obama-speaks-us-counterterrorism-strategy#transcript.

33   Nick Turse, "America's Lethal Profiling of Afghan Men," *Nation*, September 18, 2013, http://www.thenation.com/article/176253/americas-lethal-profiling-afghan-men.

34   "Controversies over Mosques and Islamic Centers across the U.S." (Pew Research Center's Forum on Religion & Public Life, September 27, 2012). http://features.pewforum.org/muslim/2012Mosque-Map.pdf. Either because of or despite the opposition, mosque construction has grown significantly across the country. Nevertheless, no other religious community has faced such sustained hostility in

recent years in establishing their religious centers as Muslim Americans have. See Cathy Lynn Grossman, "Number of US Mosques Up 74% since 2000," *USA Today*, February 29, 2012.

35 James Baldwin, "Open Letter to the Born Again," *Nation*, September 29, 1979.

36 Charles Kurzman, "Muslim-American Terrorism: Declining Further" (Triangle Center on Terrorism and Homeland Security, February 1, 2013), 1; Charles Kurzman, "Muslim-American Terrorism in 2013" (Triangle Center on Terrorism and Homeland Security, February 5, 2014), 2.

37 Arie Perliger, *Challengers from the Sidelines: Understanding America's Violent Far Right* (West Point, NY: Combating Terrorism Center at West Point, 2012).

38 Gallup, *Muslim Americans: Faith, Freedom, and the Future* (Abu Dhabi: Gallup Center, 2011), 6.

39 Trevor Aaronson, *The Terror Factory: Inside the FBI's Manufactured War on Terrorism* (Brooklyn, NY: lg Publishing, 2013); Daniel Schwartz, "Q&A: The FBI's Role in 'Manufacturing' Terrorism," *CBC News*, May 2, 2013, http://www.cbc.ca/news/world/q-a-the-fbi-s-role-in-manufacturing-terrorism-1.1337748.

40 Arun Kundnani, *The Muslims Are Coming! Islamophobia, Extremism, and the Domestic War on Terror* (New York: Verso, 2014), 10.

41 Conor Friedersdorf, "If the Law Vegas Killers Were Muslims, We'd Call Them Terrorists. But Should We?," *Atlantic*, June 10, 2014, http://www.theatlantic.com/politics/archive/2014/06/if-these-killers-were-muslims-wed-call-them-terrorists/372472/.

42 Paul Farhi, "In the News Media, Are Muslims the Only Terrorists?," *Washington Post*, June 10, 2014.

43 Tom Breen, "Great Resume, Too Bad about Your Religion," *UConnToday.com*, June 16, 2014, http://today.uconn.edu/blog/2014/06/great-resume-too-bad-about-your-religion/; Bradley R. E. Wright, Michael Wallace, John Bailey, and Allen Hyde, "Religious Affiliation and Hiring Discrimination in New England: A Field Experiment," *Research in Social Stratification and Mobility* 34 (December 2013): 111–26; Michael Wallace, Bradley R. E. Wright, and Allen Hyde, "Religious Affiliation and Hiring Discrimination in the American South: A Field Experiment," *Social Currents* 1 (June 2014): 189–207.

44 Anna Lekas Miller, "Forgetting 'Little Syria' at the 9/11 Memorial," *Al Jazeera*, August 2, 2013, http://www.aljazeera.com/indepth/features/2013/07/2013730135344232174.html; Chris Fielder, "9/11 Memorial Insults Arabic Speakers," *Kansas City Star*, May 27, 2014, http://www.kansascity.com/opinion/readers-opinion/as-i-see-it/article419268/911-memorial-insults-Arabic-speakers.html; Sharon Otterman, "Visitors Fault Sept. 11 Museum's Portrayal of Islam," *New York Times*, June 1, 2014.

45 George W. Bush, "Address to a Joint Session of Congress and the American People," September 20, 2001, http://georgewbush-whitehouse.archives.gov/news/releases/2001/09/20010920-8.html.

46 Mohja Kahf, *The Girl in the Tangerine Scarf* (New York: Public Affairs, 2006); Randa Jarrar, *A Map of Home* (New York: Penguin, 2009); Mohsin Hamid, *The Reluctant Fundamentalist* (New York: Harcourt, 2007); Amy Waldman, *The Submission* (New York: Farrar, Straus and Giroux, 2011); *The New Muslim Cool*, directed by Jennifer Maytorena Taylor (2009); *The Muslims Are Coming!*, directed by Dean Obeidallah and Negin Farsad (2013). The Poets House program can be found here: http://www.poetshouse.org/programs-and-events/poetry-in-the-world/bridging-cultures. The NEH program is here: http://bridgingcultures.neh. gov/muslimjourneys/. I can personally testify to the amazing efforts of many people trying to educate their publics about Muslims and Muslim Americans as I've been invited dozens of times and across the country to participate in such programs.

47 Hisham Aidi, *Rebel Music: Race, Empire, and the New Muslim Youth Culture* (New York: Pantheon, 2014); Evelyn Alsultany, *Arabs and Muslims in the Media: Race and Representation after 9/11* (New York: NYU Press, 2012); Louise Cainkar, *Homeland Insecurity: The Arab American and Muslim American Experience after 9/11* (New York: Russell Sage Foundation, 2011); Sohail Daulatzai, *Black Star, Crescent Moon: The Muslim International and Black Freedom beyond America* (Minneapolis: University of Minnesota Press, 2012); Kambiz Ghaneabassiri, *A History of Islam in America: From the New World to the New World Order* (New York: Cambridge University Press, 2010); Zareena Grewal, *Islam Is a Foreign Country* (New York: NYU Press, 2013); Deepa Kumar, *Islamophobia and the Politics of Empire* (Chicago: Haymarket, 2012); Sunaina Maira, *Missing: Youth, Citizenship, and Empire after 9/11* (Durham, NC: Duke University Press, 2009); Timothy Marr, *The Cultural Roots of American Islamicism* (New York: Cambridge University Press, 2006); Junaid Rana, *Terrifying Muslims: Race and Labor in the South Asian Diaspora* (Durham, NC: Duke University Press, 2011); Steven Salaita, *Anti-Arab Racism* (London: Pluto, 2006); Denise Spellberg, *Thomas Jefferson's Qur'an: Islam and the Founders* (New York: Knopf, 2013).

48 Quinnipiac University, "New Yorkers Say 2–1 Cops Treat Muslims Fairly," March 13, 2012, http://www.quinnipiac.edu/institutes-and-centers/polling-institute/new-york-city/release-detail?ReleaseID=1716.

49 Elaine Scarry, "Resolving to Resist," *Boston Review*, February 1, 2004, http://bostonreview.net/us/resolving-resist-elaine-scarry.

Chapter 1. Letter to a G-Man

1 Abraham Mitrie Rihbany, *A Far Journey* (Boston: Houghton Mifflin, 1914), 202–3.
2 "A Picturesque Colony," *New York Daily Tribune*, October 2, 1892.
3 William Waller Hening, ed., *The Statutes at Large: Being a Collection of All the Laws of Virginia*, vol. 2 (New York: R & W & G Bartow, 1823), 490.
4 Allen D. Austin, ed., *African Muslims in Ante-bellum America: A Sourcebook* (New York: Garland, 1984), 160.

5 Somini Sengupta, "Ill-Fated Path to America, Jail, and Death," *New York Times*, November 5, 2001.

6 James Madison, "Federalist 51," in *The Federalist Papers*, by James Madison, Alexander Hamilton, and John Jay, edited by Charles R. Kessler (New York: Penguin, 1999), 321.

Chapter 2. East of the Sun (West of the Moon)

1 C. Eric Lincoln, *The Black Muslims of America* (Grand Rapids, MI: Eerdmans, 1994), 49.

2 *Moslem Sunrise*, July 1921, 3.

3 Quoted in Yvonne Haddad and Jane Smith, *Mission to America: Five Islamic Sectarian Communities in North America* (Gainesville: University Press of Florida, 1993), 55.

4 Hazrat Mirza Ghulam Ahmad, *Message of Peace* (1908; repr., Columbus, OH: Ahmadiyya Anjuman Isha'at Islam Lahore, 1993), 23.

5 Quoted in Richard Brent Turner, *Islam in the African American Experience* (Bloomington: Indiana University Press, 1997), 112.

6 Ibid., 115.

7 "If Jesus Comes to America," *Moslem Sunrise*, April 1922, 55–56.

8 Roger Didier, "Those Who're Missionaries to Christians: Prophet Sadiq Brings Allah's Message into Chicago and Makes Proselytes," reprinted in *Moslem Sunrise*, October 1922, 139.

9 Aminah McCloud reports that eventually dissension arose among Ahmadis over the fact that more African Americans were not appointed to leadership positions and that the Indian customs of the missionaries and the immigrant Muslims eventually clashed with the African American desires to apply the faith to domestic situations. See Aminah McCloud, *African American Islam* (New York: Routledge, 1995), 21. However, in the early years, the community was certainly highly multiracial in many ways, including in its leadership roles. *Moslem Sunrise* contains many such photographs and examples, including highlighting the role of one early "zealous worker for Islam, appointed a Sheikh to work among his people in the district of St. Louis and vicinity," named Sheikh Ahmad Din (formerly P. Nathaniel Johnson). See, for example, *Moslem Sunrise*, July 1922, 119.

10 J. A. Rogers, "Bilal Ibn Rahab—Warrior Priest," *Messenger* 9 (July 1927): 213–14. Rogers states, "When the Christian Negro points with pride to St. Augustine, the Numidian Negro, and tells what he did to advance Christianity, the Mohammedan one can point to Bilal, and tell what he did for Christianity's greatest rival. The Mohammedan Negro is, however, hardly likely to do as Islam not only in theory, but in actuality, knows no color line. This probably accounts for its success in Africa." Also see A. T. Hoffert, "Moslem Propaganda: The Hand of Islam stretches out to Aframerica," *Messenger* 9 (May 1927): 141, 160. Hoffert describes, "A woman convert who had belonged to various churches spoke of her previous life like that of a dog or cat before its eyes are opened; they are going to have their share of good

things and stand on their own feet. She spoke of the universality of Islam, its way of life, one God, one aim, one destiny." Blanche Watson, "The First Muezzin," *Opportunity*, September 1930, 275.

11 "True Salvation of the American Negroes: The Real Solution to the Negro Question," *Moslem Sunrise*, April–July 1923, 184.

12 It should be stressed that the dichotomy I am establishing here, between the particularism of the Nation and the ecumenicalism of the Ahmadis, is obviously more complicated in many circumstances and that the Nation has at its heart the ability to see itself as a universal theology in certain respects, just as the Ahmadi creed can be (and is often, by the mainstream Muslim community) understood as a narrower and more particular vision, especially since the Ahmadis themselves are marginalized by the mainstream Muslim establishment. The Nation also often employed Sunni Muslims as advisors and teachers, such as Abdul Basit Naeem, editor of a couple of small publications (*Moslem World & the USA* and the *African-Asian World*) and author of the introduction to Elijah Muhammad's *The Supreme Wisdom*, vol. 2 (Atlanta: Messenger Elijah Muhammad Propagation Society, n.d.), 3. These advisors and, later, Elijah Muhammad himself recognized the radical differences between the Nation of Islam creed and mainstream Sunni beliefs yet justified the Nation's theology as the best way to bring African Americans to Islam. At the very end of his life, it appears that even Elijah Muhammad believed in mainstream Islam. Similarly, Louis Farrakhan, now facing his mortality as he battles cancer, has made significant gestures by way of reforming Nation of Islam creeds toward an acceptable form of mainstream Islam.

13 Louis DeCaro, *On the Side of My People: A Religious Life of Malcolm X* (New York: NYU Press, 1996), 136.

14 Ibid., 97–98.

15 *The Autobiography of Malcolm X* (New York: Grove Press, 1964), 247.

16 Malcolm X, *Malcolm X Speaks*, ed. George Breitman (New York: Grove Press, 1965), 72–87; Alex Lubin, *Geographies of Liberation: The Making of an Afro-Arab Political Imaginary* (Chapel Hill: University of North Carolina Press, 2014).

17 "Moslem Musicians Take Firm Stand Against Racism," *Ebony*, April 1953, 111.

18 Charley Gerard, *Jazz in Black and White: Race, Culture, and Identity in the Jazz Community* (Westport, CT: Praeger, 1998), 75.

19 C. O. Simpkins, *Coltrane: A Biography* (Baltimore: Black Classic Press, 1975), 118.

20 Ibid., 84.

21 Ibid., 151.

22 John Coltrane, liner notes, *A Love Supreme* (Impulse! Records, 1964).

Chapter 3. Racing Religion

1 *In re Hassan*, 48 F. Supp. 843 (E.D. Mich. 1942), 844.

2 Alien Act, 1798, http://avalon.law.yale.edu/18th_century/alien.asp; Immigration and Nationality Act of 1952, § 311, chap. 2, 66 Stat. 239 (codified and amended at 8 USC § 1422 [1988]).

3 Ian Haney Lopez, *White by Law* (New York: NYU Press, 1996).

4 Act of July 14, 1870, sec. 7, 16 Stat. 254, 256.

5 Nationality Act of October 14, 1940, 54 Stat. 1137.

6 Haney Lopez, *White by Law*, 42–45.

7 Gabriel Chin, "Segregation's Last Stronghold: Race Discrimination and the Constitutional Law of Immigration," *UCLA Law Review* 46, no. 1 (1998): 15.

8 Haney Lopez, *White by Law*, 67–77.

9 *In re Hassan*, 844.

10 Ibid., 846.

11 Ibid., 847.

12 Ibid., 845. One should note that, according to the judge, Arabs have a culture while Americans have a civilization.

13 Ex parte *Mohriez*, 54 F. Supp. 941 (D. Mass. 1944), 942, 943.

14 Ibid., 943.

15 Established in September, NSEERS did not begin to be implemented until October 2002.

16 Miriam Jordan, "Controversial Surveillance Program Launched after 9/11 Ends," *Wall Street Journal*, April 27, 2011.

17 In a draft memo proposing special registration, Assistant Attorney General Viet Dinh reminds the attorney general of his ability to require registration for aliens who are "fourteen years of age or older." Viet Dinh, "Registration of Aliens from Countries Sponsoring Terrorism and Other High Risk Countries, November 15, 2001" (unpublished draft memorandum for the attorney general, on file with the author). The age of fourteen dates to the Alien Act of 1798 (also called the Act Respecting Enemy Aliens). This act provides the executive branch with the authority to deport any enemy alien over the age of fourteen without judicial review (and was controversial in its day, but is still lawful). Of course, those who are subject to special registration are, overwhelmingly, not enemy aliens. Alien Act, 1798, http://avalon.law.yale.edu/18th_century/alien.asp (accessed December 30, 2013).

18 A January 21, 2003, advisory note from the Department of Justice came with the following information: "Registrants will be asked questions 'under oath.' The INS agent will 'record' the answers. The registrant will be fingerprinted and photographed. The officer may ask to see travel documents, including passport and I-94; any other government-issued identification; proof of residence, including leases or proof of titles; proof of school matriculation; and proof of employment. The officer may ask many other, unrelated questions, including questions related to national security and law enforcement" (Revised Questions and Answers 2003; Special Call-in Registration 2002). Also see AILA InfoNet doc. no. 02121642 (posted February 24, 2003), http://www.aila.org/content/default.aspx?bc=1016%7C6715%7C6721%7C8815%7C10207%7C8018.

19 Two friends of mine, unknown to each other and having different countries of origin, went through the procedure, including the requirement of American citizen guarantors and personal questions about their political beliefs.

20 "U.S. Detains Nearly 1,200 during Registry," *Washington Post*, January 16, 2003.

21 "Hundreds of Muslim Immigrants Rounded Up in Southern California," Reuters, December 19, 2002.

22 Chisun Lee, "Detainees Protest Mass Arrests," *Village Voice*, December 25–31, 2002.

23 Department of Homeland Security, "Changes to National Security Entry/Exit Registration System" (December 1, 2003) (on file with the author).

24 The Pakistani newspaper *Dawn* termed this the "largest deportation in [American] history" (see "Thirty-Five Percent of Deportees from US Are from Pakistan," *Karachi Dawn*, July 29, 2003).

25 Cam Simpson, Flynn McRoberts, and Liz Sly, "Immigration Crackdown Shatters Lives," *Chicago Tribune*, November 16, 2003.

26 Department of Justice, "Special Call-In Registration Procedures for Certain Non-immigrants," November 26, 2002, http://www.ice.gov/doclib/nseers/CALL_IN_ALL.pdf.

27 Simpson, McRoberts, and Sly, "Immigration Crackdown."

28 There is a legal tradition in European law for deporting enemy aliens, and it likely derives from the work of Emmerich de Vattel, who in 1758 wrote, "The sovereign who declares war has not the right to detain the subjects of the enemy who are found within his state, nor their effects. They have come to his country in public faith; in permitting them to enter and live in the territory, he has tacitly promised them all liberty and surety for their return. A suitable time should be given them to withdraw their goods; and if they stay beyond the time prescribed, it is lawful that they should be treated as enemies, though as disarmed enemies" (quoted in James W. Garner, "Treatment of Enemy Aliens," *American Journal of International Law* 12, no. 1 [1918]: 27–55).

29 Chin, "Segregation's Last Stronghold," 1–74; Meredith K. Olafson, "The Concept of Limited Sovereignty and the Immigration Law Plenary Power Doctrine," *Georgetown Immigration Law Review* 13, no. 2 (1999): 433–53.

30 Chin, "Segregation's Last Stronghold," 3–4.

31 *Federal Register* 67, no. 155 (August 12, 2002): 52584–93.

32 Ibid., 52585. The Department of Justice cites, among other cases, *Fiallo v. Bell* (1977), quoting the Supreme Court decision: "Over no conceivable subject is the legislative power of Congress more complete than it is over the admission of aliens. . . . The power to expel or exclude aliens is a fundamental sovereign attribute exercised by the Government's political departments largely immune from judicial control" (ibid., 52585).

33 All except for North Korea, which approximates a null category since the number of visitors from North Korea to the United States must be zero or very close to it.

34 *Federal Register* 67, no. 114 (June 13, 2002): 40581–86.

35 George Fredrickson, *Racism: A Short History* (Princeton: Princeton University Press, 2002), 170.

36 Ibid., 19.

37 Although he acknowledges it, Fredrickson fails to fully appreciate the persecution of Muslims during the Spanish Inquisition. For Muslim persecution during this period, see Henry Kamen, *The Spanish Inquisition: A Historical Revision* (New Haven: Yale University Press, 1998).

38 Kamen, *Spanish Inquisition*, 62.

39 Ibid., 223.

40 Etienne Balibar, "Is There a Neo-Racism?," in *Race, Nation, Class*, ed. E. Balibar and E. Wallerstein (New York: Verso, 1991), 22.

41 Fredrickson, *Racism*, 9.

42 Michael Omi and Howard Winant, *Racial Formation in the United States* (New York: Routledge, 1986), 1.

43 *Federal Register* 67, no. 155 (August 12, 2002): 52592.

44 Memorandum for Regional Directors, September 30, 2002 (on file with the author).

45 "One Religion, 12 Voices," *Toronto Star*, September 11, 2003.

46 *In re Najour*, 174 F. 735 (N.D. Ga. 1909), 735.

47 *In re Halladjian*, 174 F. 834 (C.C.D. Mass. 1909), 835.

48 *United States v. Dolla*, 177 F. 101 (5th Cir. 1910).

49 Ibid., 102.

50 *In re Ellis*, 179 F. 1002 (D. Or. 1910), 1003.

51 Ex parte *Shahid*, 205 F. 812 (E.D. S.C. 1913), 813.

52 Ibid., 814.

53 Ibid., 816.

54 Ibid., 817.

55 Ex parte *Dow*, 211 F. 486 (E.D. S.C. 1914).

56 Ibid., 487.

57 Ibid., 489.

58 Ibid., 489.

59 *In re Dow*, 213 F. 355 (E.D. S.C. 1914), 362.

60 *Dow v. United States*, 226 F. 145 (4th Cir. 1915).

61 Alixa Naff, *Becoming American: The Early Arab Immigrant Experience* (Carbondale: Southern Illinois University Press, 1985), 256.

62 *United States v. Thind*, 261 U.S. 204 (1923).

63 *In re Ellis*, 1002.

64 *In re Halladjian*, 840.

65 Ibid., 841.

66 Ibid., 841.

67 Ibid., 841.

68 Ibid., 841.

69 Ex parte *Shahid*, 812.

70 *In re Dow*, 362.

71 *United States v. Cartozian*, 6 F. 2d 919 (D. Or. 1925), 919.

72 Ibid., 921.

73 *Wadia v. United States*, 101 F. 2d 7 (2nd Cir. 1939), 7.

74 In fact, one could logically argue that Christian Arabs were admitted as white people not because they are intrinsically white but because of their religious difference from Muslim Arabs. Thus, the race of Muslims was, in fact, first negatively determined with Najour's petition in 1909 and first positively determined with Hassan's in 1942.

75 John Tehranian, "Performing Whiteness: Naturalization Litigation and the Construction of Racial Identity in America," *Yale Law Journal* 4, no. 109 (January 2000): 817–49.

76 Ibid., 839.

77 Ibid., 820.

78 Ibid., 821.

79 Haney Lopez, *White by Law*, 46.

80 Ibid., 56.

81 Ibid., 202.

82 Rogers Smith, *Civic Ideals: Conflicting Ideas of Citizenship in US History* (New Haven: Yale University Press, 1999), 6.

83 The others were ineligible for citizenship, of course, owing to the naturalization laws that excluded Japanese from citizenship.

84 On March 9, 1942, criminal sanctions were added to relocation, making this date perhaps more significant than Roosevelt's executive order. General Dewitt's orders read, "[A]ll persons of Japanese ancestry, both alien and non-alien, will be evacuated from the above areas by 12 o'clock noon, P.W.T., Saturday, May 9, 1942" (see Peter Irons, *Justice at War: The Story of the Japanese American Internment Cases* [Berkeley: University of California Press, 1983], 48–74). To understand the political nature of racialization even better, one need only compare the fate of people of Japanese descent in Hawaii to those on the West Coast. While West Coast Japanese were rounded up as enemy aliens, Hawaiian Japanese—the dominant ethnic group (with larger numbers than whites, Filipinos, or Native Hawaiians)—were not interned en masse, despite the fact, of course, that Pearl Harbor is on Oahu. In California, the Japanese were politically vulnerable and thus imminently "racializable" (to coin an ugly word) by the state, whereas in Hawaii, mass evacuation of the Japanese descendent population would have crippled the islands.

85 *INS Monthly Review* 1, no. 1 (1943): 16.

86 Ibid., 17.

87 Ex parte *Mohriez*, 942, emphasis added.

88 Hannah Arendt, *On Violence* (New York: Harcourt, 1969), 81.

89 One ominous remembrance of things past is the revelation that the Census Bureau provided specially indexed and extremely detailed population statistics on Arab Americans to the DHS (and will continue to do so under high-level approval). Japanese internment was facilitated by similar Census Department work. See Lynette Clemetson, "Homeland Security Given Data on Arab-Americans," *New York Times*, July 30, 2004, and "Census Now Limiting Arab Data Sharing," Associated Press, August 30, 2004.

90 *In re Hassan*, 846.

91 Alan Cooperman, "Armenians in U.S. Not on INS List," *Washington Post*, December 18, 2002.

92 "Three Star Bigotry" (editorial), *Los Angeles Times*, August 25, 2004; "Holding the Pentagon Accountable for Religious Bigotry" (editorial), *New York Times*, August 26, 2004.

93 Arendt, *On Violence*, 82.

Chapter 4. Sects and the City

1 Joseph Conrad, *Heart of Darkness* (New York: Dover, 1990), 5.

Chapter 5. A Bloody Stupid War

1 Marvin Opler and F. Obayashi, "Senryu Poetry as Folk Expression," *Journal of American Folklore* 58 (January–March 1945): 1, 4.

2 Ibid., 9.

3 "Guantanamo Bay Naval Base," *New York Times*, last updated January 6, 2015, http://projects.nytimes.com/guantanamo (accessed January 19, 2015).

4 Nicholas Horrock and Anwar Iqbal, "Waiting for Gitmo," *Mother Jones*, January–February 2004; Ted Conover, "In the Land of Guantánamo," *New York Times Magazine*, June 29, 2003; David Rose, "How We Survived Jail Hell," *Observer*, March 14, 2004; Max Fisher, "US Could Save Millions by Paying Each Gitmo Prisoner $2 Million Annual Salary to Do Nothing," *Washington Post (blog)*, July 31, 2013.

5 Neil A. Lewis and Eric Schmitt, "Cuba Detentions May Last Years," *New York Times*, February 13, 2004.

6 "Excerpts from Appeals Court Rulings on Detention Policy," *New York Times*, December 19, 2003.

7 Matthew Purdy and Lowell Bergman, "Inside the Lackawanna Terror Case," *New York Times Magazine*, October 12, 2003; Marc Kaufman, "Afghan Figure Sent to U.S. Facility in Cuba," *Washington Post*, March 29, 2003; Dana Priest and Barton Gellman, "U.S. Decries Abuse but Defends Interrogations," *Washington Post*, December 26, 2002; Luke Harding, "US Military 'Brutalised' Journalists," *Guardian*, January 13, 2004. See also Amnesty International, "United States of America: The Threat of a Bad Example, Undermining International Standards as 'War on Terror' Detentions Continue" (August 19, 2003). Amnesty says, "The legal

black hole that is Camp Delta has gained such notoriety that US and other authorities have reportedly used it as a threat during interrogation, including US soldiers in Iraq. Amnesty International has been told by relatives of detainees in Yemen, for example, that as the problem of arbitrary detentions increased in the context of Yemen-US security co-operation following 11 September 2001, the Yemeni security police began frequently to threaten detainees that they would be handed over to US agents to take them to Guantánamo. An Afghan prisoner released from the US Air Base in Bagram, where he was reportedly held for 18 days in what he described as a regime of 24-hour illumination and sleep deprivation, also alleged that he was threatened with transfer to Guantánamo to try to force cooperation during interrogation. Another released Afghan prisoner said that during interrogation he was threatened with transfer to Guantánamo. He said: 'One of them brought me 50 small stones and said "count these stones." When I finished he said, "We will send you there for 50 years."' He was not transferred to Cuba." http://www.amnesty.org/en/library/asset/AMR51/114/2003/en/404244e8-d6a7–11dd-ab95-a13b602c0642/amr511142003en.html.

8   Edward W. Said, *The Question of Palestine* (New York: Vintage, 1980), 59.

9   Roy Gutman et al., "Guantanamo Justice," *Newsweek*, July 8, 2002, 34.

10 Morris Davis, "Where Is Justice for the Men Still Abandoned in Guantánamo Bay?," *Guardian*, January 16, 2015, http://www.theguardian.com/commentis-free/2015/jan/16/justice-abandoned-guantanamo-bay.

11 Council on American Islamic Relations (CAIR), *The Status of Muslim Civil Rights in the United States 2002: Stereotypes and Civil Liberties* (Washington, DC: CAIR, 2002), 1.

12 Ibid., 38. Shirley Wentworth, "Muslims Struggle amid Security Concerns in U.S.," *Tri-City (WA) Herald*, July 21, 2003; Hilary Russ, "Leave Home without It: Credit Card Companies Cancel on Muslim New Yorkers," *City Limits Monthly*, May 2003.

13 Peter Irons, *Justice at War: The Story of the Japanese American Internment Cases* (Berkeley: University of California Press, 1983).

14 *Hirabayashi v. United States*, 320 U.S. 81 (1943).

15 Irons, *Justice at War*, 219–52.

16 *Hirabayashi v. United States*.

17 Elaine Povich, "L[ong] I[sland] Muslims Fume over King's Remarks," *Newsday*, February 12, 2004.

18 Niraj Warikoo, "Arabs in U.S. Could Be Held, Official Warns," *Detroit Free Press*, July 20, 2002.

19 Tom Segev, "A Black Flags Hangs over the Idea of Transfer," *Ha'aretz*, April 5, 2002.

20 Tom Hays, "Post-9/11 Detainee Returns to His Life," Associated Press, August 17, 2006, http://www.washingtonpost.com/wp-dyn/content/article/2006/08/17/AR2006081700831.html.

21 David Cole, *Enemy Aliens* (New York: Free Press, 2003); Office of the Inspector General, *The September 11 Detainees: A Review of the Treatment of Aliens Held on*

Immigration Charges in Connection with the Investigation of the September 11 Attacks (Washington, DC: U.S. Department of Justice, June 2003). Also see Office of the Inspector General, *Supplemental Report on September 11 Detainees' Allegations of Abuse at the Metropolitan Detention Center in Brooklyn, NY* (Washington, DC: U.S. Department of Justice, September 2003).

22 Cam Simpson, Flynn McRoberts, and Liz Sly, "Immigration Crackdown Shatters Lives," *Chicago Tribune*, November 16, 2003. Also see Deborah Charles, "U.S. Changes Post–9/11 Foreign Registration Rule," Reuters, December 1, 2003.

23 Clifford Krauss, "On Border Ire, Canada Says: Blame U.S.," *New York Times*, November 8, 2002.

24 Hicham Safieddine, "One Religion, Twelve Voices: Interviews (with Omar Alghabra)," *Toronto Star*, September 11, 2003.

25 "Canadian Sues U.S. Officials; Terror Suspect Was Deported to Syria, Jailed and Tortured," *Washington Post*, January 23, 2004; Monia Mazigh, *Hope and Despair: My Struggle to Free My Husband, Maher Arar* (Toronto: McClelland and Stewart, 2008).

26 Hannah Arendt, *The Origins of Totalitarianism* (New York: Harcourt, 1968), 296–97.

27 Neil A. Lewis, "Guantánamo Detainees Deliver Intelligence Gains," *New York Times*, March 21, 2004.

28 Arendt, *Origins of Totalitarianism*, 145.

29 David Rose, "How We Survived Jail Hell," *Observer*, March 14, 2004.

30 "Senate Select Committee on Intelligence—Committee Study of the Central Intelligence Agency's Detention and Interrogation Program, Executive Summary" (approved December 13, 2012, updated for release April 3, 2014, declassification revisions December 3, 2014).

31 Giorgio Agamben, *Homo Sacer: Sovereign Power and Bare Life*, trans. D. Heller-Roazen (Stanford: Stanford University Press, 1998), 32.

32 Edward W. Said, *Orientalism* (New York: Vintage, 1978), 27, 12.

33 Edward W. Said, *Covering Islam* (1981; repr., New York: Vintage, 1997), 150.

34 Michel Foucault, *Discipline and Punish*, trans. Alan Sheridan (New York: Vintage, 1979), 27.

35 Said, *Orientalism*, 266–67.

36 John V. Whitbeck, "'Terrorism': A World Ensnared by a Word," *International Herald Tribune*, February 17, 2004.

37 Toby Dodge, "Inventing Iraq: A Failed Experiment in Nation Building" (speech, Los Angeles World Affairs Council, November 13, 2003); Brian Whitaker, "Iraq's Fresh Start May Be Another False Dawn," *Guardian*, September 5, 2003.

38 Moustafa Bayoumi, "Must Knowledge Serve Power?," *Clarion*, February 2004, 10.

39 Daniel Golden, "Colleges Object to New Wording in Ford Grants," *Wall Street Journal*, May 4, 2004. The Ford Foundation Grant Application Guide now states, "As we pursue the foundation's goals, we take all reasonable measures to fulfill our

responsibilities as a tax-exempt charitable organization. We want to make sure that our funds are used for their intended charitable purposes and do not support any activities that violate the U.S. tax code or anti-terrorism laws. Because we appreciate the important work that our grantees do around the world, some in extremely difficult environments, we strive to fulfill our oversight responsibilities without creating undue burdens for them or being overly intrusive." http://www.fordfoundation.org/pdfs/grants/grant-application-guide.pdf.

40 Robin Wright, "U.S. Readies Push for Mideast Democracy Plan," *Washington Post*, February 28, 2004.

41 Nicholas Blanford, "Arabs Debate Political Reforms," *Christian Science Monitor*, April 5, 2004.

42 Kareem Fahim, "The Middle East, Still Dark in Bush's Gaze," *Village Voice*, March 17–23, 2004.

43 Zbigniew Brzezinski, "The Wrong Way to Sell Democracy to the Arab World," *New York Times*, March 8, 2004.

Chapter 6. The God That Failed

1 Edward W. Said, *Orientalism* (New York: Vintage, 1978), 12.

2 Ibid., 3.

3 Ibid., 7.

4 Ibid., 222.

5 Quoted in Said, *Orientalism*, 277.

6 Edward W. Said, *Covering Islam* (1981; repr., New York: Vintage, 1997), xvi.

7 Ibid., xvi.

8 See Robert F. Worth, "The Reporter's Arab Library," *New York Times Book Review*, October 30, 2005.

9 Michael R. Gordon, "The Former-Insurgent Counterinsurgency," *New York Times Magazine*, September 2, 2007.

10 Adam Shatz, "The Native Informant," *Nation*, April 28, 2003, 15.

11 Reza Aslan, *No god but God: The Origins, Evolution, and Future of Islam* (New York: Random House, 2005), 165.

12 Irshad Manji, *The Trouble with Islam: A Muslim's Call for Reform in Her Faith* (New York: St. Martin's, 2003), 59.

13 Wael B. Hallaq, "Was the Gate of Ijtihad Closed?," *International Journal of Middle East Studies* 16, no. 1 (1984): 4.

14 Ayan Hirsi Ali, *Infidel* (New York: Free Press, 2007), 350.

15 Sayyid Qutb, *Islam: The Religion of the Future* (Riyadh, Saudi Arabia: International Islamic Federation of Student Organizations, 1984), 63.

16 Hirsi Ali, *Infidel*, 229.

17 Ibid., 239.

18 Ibid., 239.

19 Ibid., 243.

20 Ibid., 279.

21 Ibid., 272.

22 Manji, *Trouble with Islam*, 1.

23 Ibid., 11.

24 Ibid., 5.

25 Ibid., 158.

26 Ibid., 149.

27 Ibid., 59.

28 Ibid., 85.

29 Ibid., 33, 31.

30 Ibid., 21.

31 Ibid., 3.

32 Aslan, *No god but God*, 139.

33 Ibid., 140.

34 Ibid., 146.

35 Ibid., 215.

36 Ibid., 218–19.

37 Ibid., 222–23.

38 Ibid., 248.

39 Ibid., 248.

40 Richard Crossman, ed., *The God That Failed* (New York: Bantam Books, 1949), 58.

41 Ibid., 89.

42 Ibid., 6.

Chapter 7. The Rites and Rights of Citizenship

 1 Joseph Goldstein, "Documents Show Extent of FBI's Role in Terror Case," *New York Times*, November 13, 2012; Christopher Robbins, "Is The NYPD's Terrorist 'Lone Wolf' More Like a 'Stoned Squirrel?,'" *Gothamist*, November 22, 2011, http://gothamist.com/2011/11/22/is_the_nypds_terrorist_lone_wolf_mo.php.

 2 Daniel Cox, E. J. Dionne, Jr., William A. Galston, and Robert P. Jones, *What It Means to Be an American: Attitudes in an Increasingly Diverse America Ten Years after 9/11* (Washington, DC: Brookings Institution and Public Religion Research Institute, 2011), 11.

 3 Pew Forum on Religion and Public Life, "Muslims Widely Seen as Facing Discrimination" (Washington, DC: Pew Forum on Religion and Public Life, 2009), 9–12.

 4 Center for Human Rights and Global Justice, Asian American Legal Defense and Education Fund, "Under the Radar: Muslims Deported, Detained, and Denied on Unsubstantiated Terrorism Allegations" (New York: NYU School of Law, 2011).

 5 Rogers Smith, *Civic Ideals: Conflicting Ideas of Citizenship in US History* (New Haven: Yale University Press, 1999), 15.

Chapter 8. Between Acceptance and Rejection

1 "Dueling Demonstrations Held in NYC after 9/11 Memorial," *CBS New York*, September 11, 2010, http://newyork.cbslocal.com/2010/09/11/dueling-demonstrations-begin-after-911-memorial/.

2 Sylviane Diouf, *Servants of Allah: African Muslims Enslaved in the Americas* (New York: NYU Press, 1998).

3 For Internet links to many of these condemnations, see http://www.muhajabah.com/otherscondemn.php.

4 "Washington Post-ABC News Poll," *Washington Post*, http://www.washingtonpost.com/wp-srv/politics/polls/postpoll_09072010.html?sid=ST2010090806236.

5 R. M., "Mosque Building and Its Discontents," *Economist*, August 19, 2010, http://www.economist.com/blogs/democracyinamerica/2010/08/islamic_cultural_centre_sorta_near_ground_zero. The 55 percent figure comprises the 27.7 percent "somewhat unfavorable" and the 27.7 percent "very unfavorable."

6 David Cole, *Enemy Aliens* (New York: New Press, 2003), 25.

7 Ibid., 31.

8 Anushka Asthana, "Domestic Detainee Released," *Washington Post*, July 21, 2006, A09.

9 See U.S. Department of Justice Office of the Inspector General, *The September 11 Detainees: A Review of the Treatment of Aliens Held on Immigration Charges in Connection with the Investigation of the September 11 Attacks* (Washington, DC: U.S. Department of Justice, June 2003), http://www.justice.gov/oig/special/0306/index.htm, and a supplemental report on allegations of abuse while in detention published in December 2003.

10 Eric Lichtblau, *Bush's Law* (New York: Anchor Books, 2009), 6.

11 See, for example, "US: Misuse of the Material Witness Statute," *Human Rights Watch*, January 29, 2011, http://www.hrw.org/en/news/2011/01/28/us-misuse-material-witness-statute. This is an amicus brief for *Ashcroft v. Al-Kidd*, a case before the U.S. Supreme Court regarding the use of the Material Witness Statute.

12 Nicole J. Henderson et al., executive summary for *Law Enforcement & Arab American Community Relations after September 11, 2001: Engagement in a Time of Uncertainty* (New York: Vera Institute of Justice, 2006), 4–5, http://www.vera.org/sites/default/files/resources/downloads/Arab_American_community_relations.pdf.

13 Gayle Fee et al., "Bill Cosby Down with Plan for Muslim 'Cosby Show,'" *Boston Herald*, February 11, 2011, http://www.bostonherald.com/track/inside_track/view/2011_0211bill_down_with_muslim_cosbys/.

14 Evelyn Alsultany, *Arabs and Muslims in the Media: Race and Representation after 9/11* (New York: NYU Press, 2012), 12.

15 Pew Research Center, *Muslim Americans: Middle Class and Mostly Mainstream* (Washington, DC: Pew Research Center, May 22, 2007).

16 James McKinley, Jr., "Judge Blocks Oklahoma's Ban on Using Sharia Law in Court," *New York Times*, November 29, 2010.

17 "Controversies over Mosques and Islamic Centers across the U.S." (Washington, DC: Pew Forum on Religion, September 24, 2010), http://features.pewforum.org/muslim/assets/mosque-map-all-text-10–5.pdf.

18 Phil Whillon, "Islamic Group Denounces Planned Temecula Mosque Protest," *Los Angeles Times*, July 28, 2010.

19 Peter Catapano, "Freedom to Inflame," *New York Times*, April 8, 2011.

20 Justin Elliot, "Tea Party Leader: Defeat Ellison Because He's Muslim," *Salon*, October 26, 2010, http://www.salon.com/news/politics/war_room/2010/10/26/tea_party_nation_phillips_ellison_muslim.

21 David Schanzer, Charles Kurzman, and Ebrahim Moosa, "Anti-Terror Lessons of Muslim Americans" (Durham, NC: Triangle Center on Terrorism and Homeland Security, January 6, 2010), 1.

22 Charles Kurzman, "Muslim-American Terrorism since 9/11: An Accounting" (Durham, NC: *Triangle Center on Terrorism and Homeland Security*, February 2, 2011).

23 Laurie Goodstein, "Muslims to Be Congressional Hearings Main Focus," *New York Times*, February 7, 2011.

24 Greg Sargent, "Pete King: No Law Enforcement Officials Will Substantiate My Claims about Muslims," *Plum Line*, February 8, 2011, http://voices.washington-post.com/plum-line/2011/02/what_if_pete_king_holds_a_hear.html.

25 John Higham, *Strangers in the Land: Patterns in American Nativism, 1860–1925*, 2nd ed. (New York: Antheum, 1977), ii.

26 Richard Hofstadter, *"The Paranoid Style in American Politics" and Other Essays* (New York: Vintage, 2008), 3.

27 Ibid., 27.

28 Ibid., 39.

29 Alex Altman, "TIME Poll: Majority Oppose Mosque, Many Distrust Muslims," *Time*, August 19, 2010; Josh Gerstein, "Poll: 46% of GOP Thinks Obama's Muslim," *Politico*, August 19, 2010, http://www.politico.com/blogs/joshgerstein/0810/Poll_46_of_GOP_thinks_Obamas_Muslim.html.

30 Hofstadter, *"Paranoid Style,"* 24–25.

Chapter 9. Fear and Loathing of Islam

1 Mitchell Silber and Arvin Bhatt, "Radicalization in the West: The Homegrown Threat" (New York: New York City Police Department, 2007).

2 Brian Michael Jenkins, "Would-Be-Warriors: Incidents of Jihadist Terrorist Radicalization in the United States since September 11, 2001" (Santa Monica, CA: RAND, 2010), vii.

3 Charles Kurzman, "Muslim-American Terrorism in the Decade since 9/11" (Durham, NC: Triangle Center on Terrorism and Homeland Security, 2012), 7.

4 Gallup, *Muslim Americans: Faith, Freedom, and the Future* (Abu Dhabi: Gallup Center, 2011), 6.

5 Sharon Otterman, "Sheepshead Bay Journal: A Planned Mosque Inches Along, but Critics Remain," *New York Times*, September 7, 2012; Kim Severson, "Judge Allows Muslims to Use Tennessee Mosque," *New York Times*, July 18, 2012; Julie Bosman, "Plans for Arabic School in Brooklyn Spurs Protests," *New York Times*, May 4, 2007; Robert Steinback, "Report Aiming to Prove 'Creeping Shariah' Theory Proves the Opposite" (Montgomery, AL: Southern Poverty Law Center, June 14, 2011); Joe Coscarelli, "Halal Turkeys Are Tainting Thanksgiving, Says Pamela Geller," *New York Magazine*, November 23, 2011.

6 Spencer Ackerman, "FBI Teaches Agents: 'Mainstream' Muslims Are 'Violent, Radical,'" *Wired*, September 14, 2011, http://www.wired.com/danger-room/2011/09/fbi-muslims-radical/; Michael Schmidt and Charlie Savage, "Language Deemed Offensive Is Removed from FBI Training Materials," *New York Times*, March 28, 2012.

7 Michael Powell, "In Police Training, a Dark Film on US Muslims," *New York Times*, January 23, 2012.

8 Noah Shachtman and Spencer Ackerman, "US Military Taught Officers: Use 'Hiroshima' Tactics for 'Total War' on Islam," *Wired*, May 10, 2012, http://www.wired.com/dangerroom/2012/05/total-war-islam/; Spencer Ackerman, "Army Sticks 'War on Islam' Teaching in Bureaucratic Depths," *Wired*, November 26, 2012, http://www.wired.com/dangerroom/2012/11/dooley/.

9 Judy Keen, "Mosque Projects Face Resistance in Some US Communities," *USA Today*, May 29, 2012; also see https://www.aclu.org/maps/map-nationwide-anti-mosque-activity.

10 "Religion-Based Charges Filed from 10/01/2000 through 9/30/2011 Showing Percentage Filed on the Basis of Religion-Muslim," http://www.eeoc.gov/eeoc/events/9–11–11_religion_charges.cfm.

11 Peter Finn, "Documents Provide Rare Insight into FBI's Terrorism Stings," *Washington Post*, April 12, 2012; Graham Rayman, "Newburgh 4 Terror Case: Judge Sentences Three to 25 Years in Prison, U.S. Constitution Shivers," *Village Voice*, June 29, 2011; Chris Dolmetsch and Bob Van Voris, "New York Synagogue-Bomb Plotter Laguerre Payen Sentenced to 25 Years," *Bloomberg News*, September 7, 2011.

12 Alex Altman, "Time Poll: Majority Oppose Mosque, Many Distrust Muslims," *Time*, August 19, 2010.

13 Jon Cohen and Jennifer Agiesta, "Americans Support Goal of Improved Relations with Muslim World," *Washington Post*, April 6, 2009.

14 Conor Friedersdorf, "Herman Cain's Anti-Muslim Prejudice Returns," *Atlantic*, November 14, 2011, http://www.theatlantic.com/politics/archive/2011/11/herman-cains-anti-muslim-prejudice-returns/248471/; Ali Ghraib, "Rick Santorum's Islamophobia Problem," *ThinkProgress*, January 5, 2012, http://thinkprogress.org/security/2012/01/05/398688/santorum-islam-eradicate/; Matt DeLong, "Newt Gingrich Compares 'Ground Zero Mosque' Backers to Nazis,"

Washington Post, August 16, 2010; Jonathan Stein, "No Muslims in My Cabinet," *Mother Jones*, November 27, 2007.

15 David Jackson, "Many Southern Republicans Say Obama Is Muslim," *USA Today*, March 12, 2012.

16 Samuel G. Freedman, "Waging a One-Man War on American Muslims," *New York Times*, December 16, 2011; John Esposito, "The Madness over All-American Muslim," *Washington Post*, December 16, 2011.

17 "Syrian Locations of Concern Report" (New York: New York Police Department Demographics Unit, n.d.), 15.

18 Cathy Lynn Grossman, "Number of US Mosques Up 74% since 2000," *USA Today*, February 20, 2012.

19 Gallup, *Muslim Americans: Faith, Freedom, and the Future* (Abu Dhabi: Gallup Center, 2011), 39.

20 Rick Perlstein, "How FBI Entrapment Is Inventing 'Terrorists'—and Letting Bad Guys Off the Hook," *Rolling Stone*, May 15, 2012.

21 "A New Attack on the Constitution" (editorial), *New York Times*, May 18, 2012.

Chapter 10. The Oak Creek Massacre

1 Andrew Kaczynski, "CNN: Sikhs 'Unfairly' Mistaken for Muslims," *BuzzFeed*, August 5, 2012, http://www.buzzfeed.com/andrewkaczynski/ cnn-sikhs-unfairly-mistaken-for-muslims.

2 "As Election Season Heats Up, Extremist Groups at Record Levels" (Montgomery, AL: Southern Poverty Law Center, March 8, 2012), http://www.splcenter.org/ get-informed/news/ southern-poverty-law-center-report-as-election-season-heats-up-extremist-groups-at.

3 Marilyn Elias, "Sikh Temple Killer Wade Michael Page Radicalized in the Army," *Southern Poverty Law Center Intelligence Report* 148 (Winter 2012), http://www. splcenter.org/get-informed/intelligence-report/browse-all-issues/2012/winter/ massacre-in-wisconsin.

4 Robert Steinback, "Jihad Against Islam," *Southern Poverty Law Center Intelligence Report* 142 (Summer 2011), http://www.splcenter.org/get-informed/intelligence-report/browse-all-issues/2011/summer/jihad-against-islam.

5 Laila Lalami, "Islamophobia and Its Discontents," *Nation*, July 2–9, 2012.

6 Erica Goode and Serge F. Kovaleski, "Wisconsin Killer Fed and Was Fueled by Hate-Driven Music," *New York Times*, August 6, 2012.

7 Wajahat Ali, Eli Clifton, Matthew Duss, Lee Fang, Scott Keyes, and Faiz Shakir, *Fear Inc.: The Roots of the Islamophobia Network in America* (Washington, DC: Center for American Progress, August 2011); Tara Culp-Ressler, "Federal Judge Orders Tennessee to Stop Blocking Muslims from Worshiping in New Mosque," *ThinkProgress*, July 19, 2012, http://thinkprogress.org/justice/2012/07/19/546861/

federal-judge-orders-tennessee-to-stop-blocking-muslims-from-worshiping-in-new-mosque/.

8 Jeff Lehr, "Arson Suspect Linked to Mosque Fire in Court Document," *Joplin Globe*, October 21, 2013.

9 Liz Goodwin, "Was the Sikh Temple Shooting Domestic Terrorism?," *Yahoo News*, August 6, 2012, http://news.yahoo.com/blogs/lookout/sikh-temple-shooting-domestic-terrorism-201724889.html.

10 Jarad Vary, "Meet Mitt Romney's Radical, Right-Wing, Sharia-Phobe Foreign Policy Advisor," *New Republic*. October 24, 2011.

11 Chris Lisee, "Rep. Michele Bachmann's Muslim Brotherhood Claims Draw Fierce Fire," *Washington Post*, July 19, 2012.

12 Moustafa Bayoumi, "Peter King's 'Islamic Radicalization' Hearings Fan Paranoid Fantasies," *Nation*, March 10, 2011.

13 Amy Bingham, "Half of Americans Do Not Know the President's Religion," *ABC News*, July 28, 2012.

14 Mackenzie Peterson, "Frozen justice: Top ICE Official Sends Islamaphobic Email without Facing Repercussion," *People's Constitution*, August 4, 2012, http://www.constitutioncampaign.org/blog/?p=9257#.UuFt_RA0600.

15 Erin Durkin, "Mayor Bloomberg and NYPD Commissioner Raymond Kelly Visit Queens Sikh Temple and Say City Has 'No Tolerance for Intolerance,'" *New York Daily News*, August 6, 2012.

Chapter 11. White with Rage

1 George W. Bush, "Islam Is Peace: Remarks by the President at Islamic Center of Washington D.C." (September 17, 2001), http://georgewbush-whitehouse.archives.gov/news/releases/2001/09/20010917–11.html.

2 John Ashcroft, "Attorney General Remarks: FBI Headquarters," September 18, 2001, http://www.justice.gov/archive/ag/speeches/2001/0918pressbriefing.htm.

3 John Ashcroft, "Prepared Remarks for the US Mayors Conference," October 25, 2001, http://www.justice.gov/archive/ag/speeches/2001/agcrisisremarks10_25.htm.

4 Nat Hentoff, "Ashcroft's Master Plan to Spy on US," *Village Voice*, August 6, 2002.

5 Eric Lichtblau, *Bush's Law: The Remaking of American Justice* (New York: Anchor, 2009), 81.

6 Peter Galbraith, *The End of Iraq: How American Incompetence Created a War without End* (New York: Simon & Schuster, 2007), 83.

7 "Transcript: Illinois Senator Candidate Barack Obama," *Washington Post*, July 27, 2004.

8 Ed Henry and Ed Hornick, "Rage Rising on McCain Campaign Trail," *CNN*, October 11, 2008, http://www.cnn.com/2008/POLITICS/10/10/mccain.crowd/.

9 Alex Seitz-Wald, "Her Muslim Witch Hunt," *Salon*, July 13, 2012, http://www.salon.com/2012/07/13/bachmann%E2%80%99s_muslim_witch_hunt/.

10 Wajahat Ali, Eli Clifton, Matthew Duss, Lee Fang, Scott Keyes, and Faiz Shakir, *Fear Inc.: The Roots of the Islamophobia Network in America* (Washington, DC: Center for American Progress, August 2011).

11 Carol Morello and Ted Mellnik, "Census: Minority Babies Are Now Majority in United States," *Washington Post*, May 17, 2002.

12 "Most Children Younger Than Age 1 Are Minorities, Census Bureau Reports" (Washington, DC: U.S. Census Bureau, May 17, 2002), http://www.census.gov/newsroom/releases/archives/population/cb12–90.html.

13 Laurie Goodstein, "Percentage of Protestant Americans Is in Steep Decline, Study Finds," *New York Times*, October 9, 2012.

14 John Del Signore, "Staten Island Mosque Voted Down," *Gothamist*, July 22, 2010, http://gothamist.com/2010/07/22/staten_island_mosque_voted_down.php.

15 Hua Hsu, "The End of White America?," *Atlantic*, January/February 2009, http://www.theatlantic.com/magazine/archive/2009/01/the-end-of-white-america/307208/.

16 Daniel Cox, E. J. Dionne, Jr., William A. Galston, and Robert P. Jones, *What It Means to Be an American: Attitudes in an Increasingly Diverse America Ten Years after 9/11* (Washington, DC: Brookings Institution and Public Religion Research Institute, 2011).

Chapter 12. My Arab Problem

1 Bruce Kesler, "I Just Disinherited My Alma-Mater," *Maggie's Farm* (blog), August 27, 2010, http://maggiesfarm.anotherdotcom.com/archives/15284-I-Just-Disinherited-My-Alma-Mater.html.

2 Abigail Rosenthal, "Brooklyn College-Stan: Letter from a Faculty Member," *Jerusalem Central* (blog of Todd Warnick), August 24, 2010, http://www.jerusalemcentral.com/2010/08/brooklyn-college-stan-letter-from.html.

3 Corky Siemaszko, "Alum to Cut Brooklyn College Out of Will over Required Freshman Reading by 'Radical' Prof," *New York Daily News*, August 31, 2010; Stewart Ain, "Palestinian Propaganda Required Reading at Brooklyn College?," *Jewish Week*, August 31, 2010; Java Sexena, "Brooklyn College Alum 'Disinherits' School over Assignment," *Gothamist*, August 30, 2010; Java Sexana, "Brooklyn College Defends Controversial Book Choice," *Gothamist*, August 31, 2010; Josh Duboff, "Brooklyn College Required Reading Proves Controversial," *New York*, September 1, 2010; "Brooklyn College Alum Cuts School Out of Will over Reading Assignment," *Huffington Post*, August 31, 2010; "Academically Incorrect: Brooklyn College Book Choice Makes a Mockery of Education," *New York Daily News* (editorial), September 7, 2010; Ron Radosh, "Misshaping Minds at Brooklyn College," *New York Post*, September 1, 2010.

4 Elissa Gootman, "Students' Assigned Reading Stirs Debate," *New York Times*, September 2, 2010; Elizabeth Minkel, "How It Feels to Be a Problem," *New Yorker*, September 1, 2010; Warner Todd Huston, "U.S. College Pushes Anti-American,

Pro-Islam Book," *RightWingNews*, September 8, 2010, http://www.rightwingnews.com/democrats/u-s-college-pushes-anti-american-pro-islam-book.

5 "Texas Ed Board Adopts Resolution Limiting Islam in Textbooks," Associated Press, September 25, 2010.

6 "Attacking Religious Freedom: The Anti-Islam Resolution" (Texas Freedom Network, n.d.), http://www.tfn.org/site/PageServer?pagename=issues_sboe_islam_resolution.

7 James C. McKinley, Jr., "A Claim of Pro-Islam Bias in Textbooks," *New York Times*, September 22, 2010.

8 Karen Tumulty, "Some Republican Figures Urge Candidates Not to Focus on NYC Mosque Issue," *Washington Post*, August 18, 2010.

9 Daniel Pipes, "A Madrassa Grows in Brooklyn," *New York Sun*, April 24, 2007.

10 R. M., "Mosque Building and Its Discontents," *Economist*, August 19, 2010, http://www.economist.com/blogs/democracyinamerica/2010/08/islamic_cultural_centre_sorta_near_ground_zero. The 55 percent figure comprises the 27.7 percent "somewhat unfavorable" and the 27.7 percent "very unfavorable." Alex Altman, "TIME Poll: Majority Oppose Mosque, Many Distrust Muslims," *Time*, August 19, 2010.

Chapter 13. Disco Inferno

1 Richard Norton-Taylor, "US Troops Face New Torture Claims," *Guardian*, September 14, 2004.

2 Adam Piore, "Pysops: Cruel and Unusual," *Newsweek*, May 19, 2003.

3 Greg Mitchell, "Exclusive: Shocking Details on Abuse of Reuters Staffers in Iraq," *Editor and Publisher*, May 19, 2004, http://www.editorandpublisher.com/Article/Exclusive-Shocking-Details-on-Abuse-of-Reuters-Staffers-in-Iraq.

4 Richard Norton-Taylor, "US Troops Face New Torture Claims," *Guardian*, September 14, 2004.

5 Carlotta Gall and David Rohde, "New Charges Raise Questions on Abuse at Afghan Prisons," *New York Times*, September 17, 2004.

6 Shafiq Rasul, Asif Iqbal, and Rhuhel Ahmed, "Composite Statement: Detention in Afghanistan and Guantánamo Bay" (Center for Constitutional Rights, July 26, 2004); David Luban, "Torture American Style; This Debate Comes Down to Words vs. Deeds," *Washington Post*, November 27, 2005; Laura Peek and Steve Bird, "Beatings Not as Bad as Psychological Torture, Says freed Briton," *London Times*, March 13, 2004; Neil Lewis, "Broad Use of Harsh Tactics Is Described at Cuba Base," *New York Times*, October 17, 2004; "Army Regulation 15–6: Final Report—Investigation into FBI Allegations of Detainee Abuse at Guantanamo Bay, Cuba Detention Facility" (Schmidt-Furlow Report), April 1, 2005, amended June 9, 2005.

7 Rory McCarthy, "'They Abused Me and Stole My Dignity': Iraqi Was Bound, Beaten and Forced to Spend 18 Days Naked in Cell," *Guardian*, May 13, 2004.

8 "Sesame Street Breaks Iraqi POWs," *BBC*, May 20, 2003.

9 Adam Zagorin and Michael Duffy, "Inside the Interrogation of Detainee 063," *Time*, June 20, 2005; Jon Kass, "On Serious Note, Gitmo Tactics Far from Torture," *Chicago Tribune*, June 17, 2005; Mark Steyn, "Facing the Music," *New York Sun*, June 20, 2005; Dean C. Minderman and Ben Westhoff, "Sing Us a Song," *Riverfront Times*, June 12, 2005.

10 Friedrich Nietzsche, *Twilight of the Idols*, trans. Duncan Large (New York: Oxford University Press, 1998), 9.

11 Matthew Happold, "UK Troops 'Break Law' by Hooding Iraqi Prisoners," *Guardian*, April 11, 2003.

12 "Army Regulation 15–6: Final Report—Investigation into FBI Allegations of Detainee Abuse at Guantanamo Bay, Cuba Detention Facility" (Jones-Fay Report), August 23, 2004, 70.

13 "Composite Statement: Detention in Afghanistan and Guantánamo Bay."

14 "Break Them Down: Systematic Use of Psychological Torture by US Forces" (Cambridge, MA: Physicians for Human Rights, 2005), 10.

15 John Conroy, *Unspeakable Acts, Ordinary People: The Dynamics of Torture* (Berkeley: University of California Press, 2007), 6.

16 Jane Mayer, "The Experiment," *New Yorker*, July 11, 2005.

17 "Who Are the Guantánamo Detainees?," Case Sheet 12 (London: Amnesty International, September 21, 2005).

18 Erik Saar and Viveca Novak, *Inside the Wire: A Military Intelligence Soldier's Eyewitness Account of Life at Guantanamo* (New York: Penguin, 2005), 164.

19 Neil Lewis, "Broad Use of Harsh Tactics Is Described at Cuba Base," *New York Times*, October 17, 2004.

20 Conroy, *Unspeakable Acts*, 131.

21 Donovan Webster, "The Man in the Hood," *Vanity Fair*, February 2005. Questions have since been raised if the man profiled in Webster's article was in the iconic photograph from Abu Ghraib, yet the man interviewed by Webster was certainly at the notorious prison and had endured the same type of treatment. See Kate Zernike, "Cited as Symbol of Abu Ghraib, Man Admits He Is Not in Photo," *New York Times*, March 18, 2006.

22 "The Rock'n'roll Assault on Noriega, US SOUTHCOM Public Affairs After Action Report Supplement, 'Operation Just Cause' Dec. 20, 1989–Jan. 31, 1990," February 6, 1995, http://www2.gwu.edu/~nsarchiv/news/20091022/Panama%20playlist. pdf; Lane DeGregory, "Iraq'n'Roll," *Saint Petersburg Times*, November 21, 2004.

23 Donald Rumsfeld, "Memorandum for the Commander, US Southern Command: Counter-Resistance Techniques in the War on Terror (S)" (April 6, 2003), 6. Ricardo Sanchez, Lieutenant General, US Army, "Memorandum: CJTF-7 Interrogation and Counter-Resistance Policy," September 14, 2003, 5–7.

24 Seymour Hersch, "The Gray Zone: How a Secret Pentagon Program Came to Abu Ghraib," *New Yorker*, May 15, 2004.

25 Montgomery McFate, "The Military Utility of Understanding Adversary Culture," *Joint Forces Quarterly* 38 (3rd Quarter 2005): 46.

26 Adam Piore, "Psyops: Cruel and Unusual," *Newsweek*, May 19, 2003.

27 "Army Regulation 15–6: Final Report—Investigation into FBI Allegations of Detainee Abuse at Guantanamo Bay, Cuba Detention Facility" (Schmidt-Furlow Report), April 1, 2005 and amended June 9, 2005.

28 Aimé Césaire, *Discourse on Colonialism*, trans. Joan Pinkham (New York: Monthly Review Press, 2000), 35.

29 James Hetfield (interview), *Fresh Air*, WHYY (NPR), November 9, 2004.

30 Rosie Swash, "Musicians Tell US to Ban Using Songs as Torture," *Guardian*, December 10, 2008; Tim Reid, "Musicians Demand End to Music Torture on Guantanamo Detainees," *Times*, October 23, 2009.

31 David Peisner, "Music as Torture: War Is Loud," *Spin*, November 30, 2006, http://www.spin.com/articles/music-torture-war-loud/.

32 Glenn BurnSilver, "Skinny Puppy's Music Was Used for Torture, So They Invoiced the Government," *Phoenix New Times* (blog), January 25, 2014, http://blogs.phoenixnewtimes.com/uponsun/2014/01/skinny-puppy-guantanamo-bay-torture.php; Steven Hsieh, "This Band Billed the Pentagon $666,000 for Using Its Music to Torture GITMO Prisoners," *Nation* (blog), February 5, 2014, http://www.thenation.com/blog/178260/band-billed-pentagon-660000-using-its-music-torture-gitmo-prisoners.

33 "Position Statement on Torture" (Society for Ethnomusicology, February 2, 2007), http://www.ethnomusicology.org/?PS_Torture.

34 "Executive Order 13491—Ensuring Lawful Interrogations," January 22, 2009, http://www.whitehouse.gov/the_press_office/EnsuringLawfulInterrogations.

35 Joe Nocera, "Is Force Feeding Torture?," *New York Times*, May 31, 2013.

36 Carol Rosenberg, "Military Imposes Blackout on Guantanamo Hunger-Strike Figures," *Miami Herald*, December 3, 2013.

37 Tom Ramstack, "Accused September 11 Attacker Expelled from Guantanamo Courtroom," Reuters, December 17, 2013.

38 Jeffrey Kaye, "Contrary to Obama's Promises, the US Military Still Permits Torture," *Guardian*, January 25, 2014.

Chapter 14. The Race Is On

1 *The Axis of Evil Comedy Tour*, directed by Michael Simon, performed by Ahmed Ahmed, Aaron Kader, Maz Jobrani, and Dean Obeidallah (Image Entertainment, 2007).

2 Somini Sengupta, "Sept. 11 Attack Narrows the Racial Divide," *New York Times*, October 10, 2001.

3 Ishmael Reed, "Civil Rights: Six Experts Weigh In," *Time*, December 7, 2001.

4 Curt Anderson, "U.S. Justice Department Bans Racial Profiling by Federal Agencies," CBS News/Associated Press, June 18, 2003.

5 See Chapter 3.

6 See UN Committee on the Elimination of Racial Discrimination, "Consideration of Reports of Submitted by States' Parties under Article 9 of the Convention: Conclusion Observations of the Committee" (UN Doc. CERD/C/USA/CO/6, May 8, 2008). See also UN High Commissioner for Human Rights to United States, September 28, 2009, http://www.aclu.org/pdfs/humanrights/uncerdresponse_racialdiscrimination.pdf.

7 Colbert King, "You Can't Fight Terrorism with Racism," *Washington Post*, July 30, 2005.

8 Joanna Kadi, ed., *Food for Our Grandmothers: Writings by Arab-American and Arab-Canadian Feminists* (Cambridge, MA: South End, 1994), xix.

9 Therese Saliba, "Resisting Invisibility: Arab Americans in Academia and Activism," in *Arabs in America: Building a New Future*, ed. Michael Suleiman (Philadelphia: Temple University Press, 1999), 308.

10 Edward W. Said, *Covering Islam* (1981; repr., New York: Vintage, 1997), 6.

11 Orlando Patterson, "The Big Blind," *New York Times*, February 10, 2008.

12 John Updike, *Terrorist* (New York: Knopf, 2006), 302–3.

13 Ibid., 12.

14 Ibid., 112.

15 Ibid., 122.

16 Steven Pinker, "The Moral Instinct," *New York Times Magazine*, January 13, 2008.

17 James Baldwin, *Notes from a Native Son* (1955; repr., Boston: Beacon, 1984), 25.

18 Pew Research Center, *Muslim Americans: Middle Class and Mostly Mainstream* (Washington, DC: Pew Research Center, May 22, 2007).

19 Mahmood Mamdani, *Good Muslim, Bad Muslim* (New York: Knopf, 2004), 15.

20 Melani McAlister, *Epic Encounters: Culture, Media and US Interests in the Middle East since 1945* (Berkeley: University of California Press, 2005), 265.

21 Benjamin DeMott, *The Trouble with Friendship: Why Americans Can't Think Straight about Race* (New York: Atlantic Monthly Press, 1996), 11–12.

22 Frederick Douglass, "The War with Mexico," in *Voices of a People's History of the United States*, ed. Howard Zinn and Anthony Arnove (New York: Seven Stories Press, 2004), 160, 164.

23 William B. Gatewood, Jr., *Black Americans and the White Man's Burden, 1898–1903* (Urbana: University of Illinois Press, 1975), 233–34.

24 Ibid., 187.

25 Ibid., 320.

26 Paul Robeson, "American Negroes in the War," in *Paul Robeson Speaks: Writings, Speeches and Interviews*, ed. Philip Sheldon Foner (New York: Citadel, 1998), 147.

27 Mary Dudziak, *Cold War Civil Rights: Race and the Image of American Democracy* (Princeton: Princeton University Press, 2000), 11.

28 Penny Von Eschen, *Race Against Empire: Black Americans and Anticolonialism, 1937–1957* (Ithaca, NY: Cornell University Press, 1997), 3.

29 W. E. B. Du Bois, "Opposition to the Military Assistance Act of 1949," in *W. E. B. Du Bois: A Reader*, ed. David Levering Lewis (New York: Henry Holt, 1995), 746.

30 St. Clair Drake, "The International Implications of Race and Race Relations," *Journal of Negro Education* 20, no. 3 (Summer 1951): 269, quoted in Nikhil Pal Singh, *Black Is a Country: Race and the Unfinished Struggle for Democracy* (Cambridge, MA: Harvard University Press, 2004), 165.

31 Cedric Robinson, *Black Movements in America* (New York: Routledge, 1997), 138.

32 El Hajj Malik el-Shabazz and Alex Haley, *The Autobiography of Malcolm X* (New York: Ballantine, 1999), 371.

33 James Baldwin, *No Name in the Street* (1972; repr., New York: Vintage, 2007), 178.

34 Edward Wilmot Blyden, *Christianity, Islam and the Negro Race* (1887; repr., Baltimore: Black Classic Press, 1994), 125.

35 Ibid., 44.

36 See C. Eric Lincoln, *The Black Muslims in America* (1961; repr., Grand Rapids, MI: Eerdmans, 1994), 49.

37 William Gardner Smith, *The Stone Face* (New York: Farrar, Straus and Giroux, 1963), 4.

38 Ibid., 55.

39 Sam Greenlee, *Baghdad Blues* (New York: Bantam, 1976), 103–4.

40 Ibid., 160.

41 June Jordan, *Directed by Desire: The Collected Poems of June Jordan* (Port Townsend, WA: Copper Canyon Press, 2007), 288–90.

42 Robinson, *Black Movements*, 123.

43 E. Franklin Frazier, *Black Bourgeoisie* (1957; repr., New York: Free Press, 1997).

44 Michael L. Krenn, *Black Diplomacy: African Americans and the State Department, 1945–1969* (Armonk, NY: M.E. Sharpe, 1998), 16.

45 Von Eschen, *Race Against Empire*, 148.

46 Singh, *Black Is a Country*, 141.

47 Ibid., 140–41.

48 See Charles Henry, ed., *Ralph J. Bunche: Selected Speeches and Writings* (Ann Arbor: University of Michigan Press, 1995), 15.

Chapter 15. Men Behaving Badly

1 Ayaan Hirsi Ali, "Muslim Rage and the Last Gasp of Islamic Hate," *Newsweek*, September 17, 2012.

2 See Matt DeLong, "Newt Gingrich Compares 'Ground Zero Mosque' Backers to Nazis," *Washington Post*, August 16, 2010.

3 David Brock and Ari Rabin-Havt, *The Fox Effect: How Roger Ailes Turned a Network into a Propaganda Machine* (New York: Anchor Books, 2012).

4 David Jackson, "Obama: Egypt Not 'Ally,' nor 'Enemy,'" *USA Today*, September 13, 2012.

5 David Jackson, "Obama: Nations Must Help Protect Diplomats," *USA Today*, September 15, 2012.

6 Jo Becker and Scott Shane, "Secret 'Kill List' Proves a Test of Obama's Principles and Will," *New York Times*, May 29, 2012.

Chapter 16. Chaos and Procedure

1 James Poniewozik, "The Evolution of Jack Bauer," *Time*, January 14, 2007.

2 Jane Mayer, "Whatever It Takes," *New Yorker*, February 19, 2007.

3 "Britons Allege Guantanamo Abuse," *BBC*, August 4, 2004; David Rose, "How We Survived Jail Hell, Part Two," *Guardian*, March 13, 2004.

4 See the Skweyiya Commission Report, October 19, 1992, http://www.sahistory.org.za/archive/skweyiya-commission-report-released-19-october-1992.

5 "Senate Select Committee on Intelligence—Committee Study of the Central Intelligence Agency's Detention and Interrogation Program, Executive Summary" (approved December 13, 2012, updated for release April 3, 2014, declassification revisions December 3, 2014).

6 Ibid., 18.

7 "Testimony of Cofer Black" (Joint investigation into September 11, fifth public hearing, Joint House/Senate Intelligence Committee hearing, September 26, 2002), http://www.fas.org/irp/congress/2002_hr/092602black.html.

8 Quoted in Dan Froomkin, "Cheney's 'Dark Side' Is Showing," *Washington Post*, November 7, 2005, http://www.washingtonpost.com/wp-dyn/content/blog/2005/11/07/BL2005110700793.html.

9 Tim Weiner, *Legacy of Ashes: The History of the CIA* (New York: Anchor Books, 2008).

10 David Frum and Richard Perle, *An End to Evil: How to Win the War on Terror* (New York: Ballantine, 2004), 6–7.

11 Henry A. Crumpton, *The Art of Intelligence: Lessons from a Life in the CIA's Clandestine Service* (New York: Penguin, 2012).

12 For a news report on the actual attack, see Joby Warrick, "Suicide Bomber Attacks CIA Base in Afghanistan, Killing at Least 8 Americans," *Washington Post*, December 31, 2009.

13 Antonio J. Mendez, "A Classic Case of Deception," *Studies in Intelligence* 43, no. 3 (Winter 1999–2000), https://www.cia.gov/library/center-for-the-study-of-intelligence/csi-publications/csi-studies/studies/winter99-00/art1.html.

14 Mahmood Mamdani, *Good Muslim, Bad Muslim* (New York: Knopf, 2004), 15–16.

15 Jessica Yellin, "Drone Program Something You 'Struggle With,' Obama Says," *CNN*, September 10, 2012.

16 Tricia Jenkins, *The CIA in Hollywood: How the Agency Shapes Film and Television* (Austin: University of Texas Press, 2012).

17 Ibid., 47, 54.

18 Frances Stonor Saunders, *The Cultural Cold War: The CIA and the World of Arts and Letters* (New York: New Press, 1999).

19 Hugh Wilford, *The Mighty Wurlitzer: How the CIA Played America* (Cambridge, MA: Harvard University Press, 2008). Andrew Rubin has also very usefully investigated the CIA's role in cultural production during the Cold War years. See Andrew Rubin, *Archives of Authority: Empire, Culture, and the Cold War* (Princeton: Princeton University Press, 2012).

20 Eric Bennett, "How Iowa Flattened Literature," *Chronicle Review*, February 10, 2014.

21 Jenkins, *CIA in Hollywood*, 14.

22 Ibid., 28.

23 https://www.cia.gov/offices-of-cia/public-affairs/entertainment-industry-liaison.

24 https://www.cia.gov/kids-page.

25 https://www.cia.gov/offices-of-cia/public-affairs/entertainment-industry-liaison.

26 Jenkins, *CIA in Hollywood*, 137.

27 Ibid., 32.

28 Ibid., 46.

29 Ibid., 76.

30 Ibid., 37.

31 Ibid., 48.

32 Ibid., 69.

33 Marisa Taylor and Jonathan S. Landay, "'Zero Dark Thirty' Leak Investigators Now Target of Leak Probe," *McLatchy*, December 20, 2013, http://www.mcclatchydc.com/2013/12/20/212378/zero-dark-thirty-leak-investigators.html. In typical fashion for the Obama administration, the government is pursuing charges against those who leaked the names of Panetta and Vickers more vigorously than Panetta and Vickers, the sources of the initial—and illegal—leaks. See John Kiriakou, "I Got 30 Months in Prison: Why Does Leon Panetta Get a Pass?," *Los Angeles Times*, March 9, 2014, http://articles.latimes.com/2014/mar/09/opinion/la-oe-kiriakou-panetta-whistleblower-20140309. Also see Adrian Chen, "Newly Declassified Memo Shows CIA Shaped 'Zero Dark Thirty's' Narrative," *Gawker*, May 6, 2013, http://gawker.com/declassified-memo-shows-how-cia-shaped-zero-dark-thirty-493174407.

34 Jenkins, *CIA in Hollywood*, 99.

35 Ibid., 112.

36 Ibid., 107.

37 Ibid., 109.

38 Gavin Edwards, "'Homeland's' CIA Connection," *Men's Journal*, October 2012, http://www.mensjournal.com/magazine/homelands-cia-connection-20121022.

39 Andrew Bacevich, *Washington Rules: America's Path to Permanent War* (New York: Metropolitan Books, 2010), 27.

40 Ibid., 242.

41 Ibid., 247.

42 Amrit Singh, "Globalizing Torture: CIA Secret Detention and Extraordinary Rendition" (New York: Open Society Justice Initiative, 2013), 6. "Senate Select Committee on Intelligence—Committee Study of the Central Intelligence Agency's Detention and Interrogation Program, Executive Summary."

43 Mark Mazzetti, "A Secret on Drones, Sealed in Blood," *New York Times*, April 6, 2013.

44 Ken Dilanian, "Overall US Intelligence Budget Tops $80 Billion," *Los Angeles Times*, October 28, 2010; Barton Gellman and Greg Miller, "U.S. Spy Network's Successes, Failures and Objectives Detailed in 'Black Budget' Summary," *Washington Post*, August 29, 2013.

45 "Drone Strikes in Pakistan" (London: Bureau of Investigative Journalism, n.d.), http://www.thebureauinvestigates.com/category/projects/drones/drones-pakistan/.

46 "The Civilian Impact of Drones: Unexamined Costs, Unanswered Questions" (New York: Center for Civilians in Conflict, Columbia Law School, 2012), 19.

47 Ibid., 22.

48 Ibrahim Mothana, "How Drones Help Al-Qaeda" (op-ed), *New York Times*, June 13, 2012.

49 C. Wright Mills, *The Causes of World War Three* (New York: Ballantine, 1958), 151.

50 Ibid., 17.

Chapter 17. Coexistence

1 Daniel Blake (Boris Starling), *Thou Shalt Kill* (New York: Gallery Books, 2011), 80.

2 Ibid., 53.

3 Ibid., 53.

4 Ibid., 200.

5 Philip Roth, *Operation Shylock: A Confession* (New York: Vintage, 1994), 200.

6 Black, *Thou Shalt Kill*, 336.

7 Ibid., 337.

8 Ibid., 337.

9 Ibid., 338.

10 Ibid., 340.

Conclusion

1 Franz Kafka, "The Problem of Our Laws," trans. Willa and Edwin Muir, in *The Complete Stories*, ed. Nahum N. Glazer (New York: Schocken, 1971), 437–38.

2 Edward Said, *Covering Islam* (1981; repr., New York: Vintage, 1997), xii.

3 Robert Steinback, "The Anti-Muslim Inner Circle," *Southern Poverty Law Center Intelligence Report* 142 (Summer 2011), http://www.splcenter.org/get-informed/intelligence-report/browse-all-issues/2011/summer/the-anti-muslim-inner-circle.

4 Naz K. Modirzadeh, "Folk International Law: 9/11 Lawyering and the Transformation of the Law of Armed Conflict to Human Rights Policy and Human Rights Law to War Governance," *Harvard National Security Journal* 5, no. 1 (2014): 225.

5 Beth Elise Whitaker, "Exporting the Patriot Act? Democracy and the 'War on Terror' in the Third World," *Third World Quarterly* 28, no. 5 (2007): 1017–32.

6 Gallup, *Muslim Americans: A National Portrait* (Washington, DC: Gallup, 2009); Ihsan Bagby, "The American Mosque in Transition: Assimilation, Acculturation, and Isolation," *Journal of Ethnic and Migration Studies* 35, no. 3 (March 2009): 473–90.

7 Sheerly Avni, "Palestine Vies for Oscar with 'Omar': Director Hany Abu-Assad Discusses Love Story amid Conflict," *Jewish Daily Forward*, March 2, 2014, http://forward.com/articles/193031/palestine-vies-for-oscar-with-omar/?p=all#ixzz2xOvsAmve.

Permissions

"Letter to a G-Man" originally appeared in *After the World Trade Center*, ed. Sharon Zukin and Michael Sorkin (New York: Routledge, 2002), 131–42. Reprinted with permission.

"East of the Sun (West of the Moon): Islam, the Ahmadis, and African America" originally appeared in *Journal of Asian American Studies* 4, no. 3 (October 2001): 251–63. Copyright 2001. The Johns Hopkins University Press.

"Racing Religion" originally appeared in *CR: The New Centennial Review* 6, no. 2 (2006): 267–93. Published by Michigan State University Press.

"Sects and the City" originally appeared in the *New York Times Magazine*, May 23, 2010, 50. Reprinted with permission.

"A Bloody Stupid War" originally appeared in *Middle East Report* 231 (Summer 2004): 36–45. Reprinted with permission.

"The God That Failed: The Neo-Orientalism of Today's Muslim Commentators" originally appeared in *Islamophobia/Islamophilia: Beyond the Politics of Enemy and Friend*, ed. Andrew Shryock (Bloomington: Indiana University Press, 2010), 79–93.

"The Rites and Rights of Citizenship" originally appeared in the *Nation* online, September 9, 2011. Reprinted with permission.

"Between Acceptance and Rejection: Muslim Americans and the Legacies of September 11" originally appeared in *Organization of American Historians Magazine of History* 25, no. 3 (July 2011): 15–19.

"Fear and Loathing of Islam" originally appeared in the *Nation*, July 2–9, 2012, 11–14. Reprinted with permission.

"The Oak Creek Massacre" originally appeared as "Did Islamophobia Fuel the Oak Creek Massacre?" in the *Nation* online, August 10, 2012. Reprinted with permission.

"White with Rage" originally appeared as "Islamophobes" in the *Cairo Review* 7 (Fall 2012): 67–77. Reprinted with permission.

"My Arab Problem" originally appeared in the *Chronicle Review*, October 29, 2010, B13–14.

"Disco Inferno" originally appeared in the *Nation*, December 26, 2005, 32–35. Reprinted with permission

"The Race Is On: Muslims and Arabs in the American Imagination" originally appeared in *Middle East Report* online, March 2010. Reprinted with permission.

"Men Behaving Badly" originally appeared in *Middle East Report* online, September 2012. Reprinted with permission.

Index

Aaronson, Trevor, 11

'Abdallah, Khalid, 213

Abdur Rahman, Ibrahim, 29–30

Abedin, Huma, 150

Absconder Apprehension Initiative, 132

Abu-Assad, Hany, 256

Abu Ghraib, 81, 176, 178, 180, 283n21

"Acknowledgement" (Coltrane), 46–47

Advocacy organizations, 133

African American Muslims: Ahmadiyya, 39–41, 43–44, 47, 265n9; Asiatic identity of, 40–41, 42, 43, 47, 203; Black Muslim identity of, 42, 43; characterization, 250; Coltrane and jazz musicians, 44–47; empowerment of, 40, 203–4, 265n10; introduction of, 35–36; Malcolm X, 41–43, 202, 204; Moorish Science Temple of, 36, 203; NYPD surveillance targeting of, 259n9; pre-9/11 view of, 130; slave, 29–30

African Americans: Arab American friend and leader role of, 192–99; Arab Americans as new, 185–86; Arab identity relation to, 204–6; Christian suppression of, 40, 203, 265n10; citizenship amendment for, 48–49; in Cold War, 201–2, 207; colonialism opposition from, 199–202; etymology of, 203; foreign policy views of, 199–202, 204–7; Islamic roots of, 40; political seats of, 206–9; slavery

redemption of, 107–8, 199; in World War II, 207

Agamben, Giorgio, 90

Aguilera, Christina, 177

Ahmad, Ghulam, 37

Ahmad, Mahmud, 37

Ahmadiyya movement: African American development of, 39–41, 43–44, 47, 265n9; dissension in, 265n9; Indian founding of, 37–38; Nation of Islam compared to, 43, 266n12

Airport security, 186, 261n21

Ajami, Fouad, 102–3

Ali, Haj, 180

Alias, 232

Aliens in America, 134

All-American Muslim, 144

Almontaser, Debbie, 172

American identity: bifurcated cultural views of, 133–36; bifurcated sociological views of, 130–33; characterization, 123–24; citizenship meaning for, 126–27; multicultural crisis of, 161–63; nativist, 136–37; public opinion changes of, 130–31, 160–63

American Mohammedan Society, 29

Ames, Aldrich, 233

Amin, Soheeb, 145–46

Ancient hatreds, 250

Anglo-Saxon ideal, 137

AP. *See* Associated Press

Apuzzo, Matt, 1, 2, 5

About the Author

Moustafa Bayoumi is the author of *How Does It Feel to Be a Problem? Being Young and Arab in America,* which won an American Book Award and the Arab American Book Award for Non-Fiction. He is the editor of *Midnight on the Mavi Marmara* and co-editor of *The Edward Said Reader*. He is Professor of English at Brooklyn College, City University of New York (CUNY).